Singing in Zion

Singing
IN
ZION

MUSIC AND SONG IN THE
LIFE OF AN ARKANSAS FAMILY

Robert Cochran U739360

The University of Arkansas Press 🙰 Fayetteville 1999

03 02 01 00 99   5 4 3 2 1

Designed by Liz Lester

☉   The paper used in this publication meets the minimum requirements of the American National Standard for Permanence of Paper for Printed Library Materials Z39.48-1984.

LIBRARY OF CONGRESS CATALOGING-IN-PUBLICATION DATA

Cochran, Robert, 1943–
    Singing in Zion : music and song in the life of an Arkansas family / Robert Cochran.
        p.   cm.
    Includes bibliographical references and index.
    ISBN 1-55728-547-0 (cloth : alk. paper). — ISBN 1-55728-548-9 (paper : alk. paper)
    1. Folk music—Arkansas—History and criticism.   2. Folk songs, English—Arkansas—History and criticism.   3. Gilbert family.   I. Title.
ML3551.7.A8C63   1999
782.42162'13'00922—dc21
    [B]   99-10087
                                                                     CIP

Sang it sometimes, but I never told a soul.

—Toni Morrison, *Beloved*

—

Acknowledgments

From inception to completion, this project has been the work of a decade, plenty of time for large debts of gratitude to accrue. First thanks must go to the John Simon Guggenheim Memorial Foundation for money and encouragement provided by a 1988 Fellowship that bought a year's time in 1989. That was a wonderful year; by 1990 there was no turning back. The golden spike was a long way off, but track was on the ground, and Promontory Point only ten years ahead.

Phydella Hogan was first my student, then my teacher, long since my good friend. I visit Helen Fultz less often, but from her I have learned almost as much. Thanks also to the following family members and friends who wrote or talked to me, allowed me to read letters and memoirs, or sent photographs: Alma Allen, Walter Allen, Loy Bailey, Mildred Bailey, Bette Curtis, Martha Estes, Kirby Estes, Sophia Estes, Bob Fultz, Buck Gilbert, Leslie Gilbert, Bill Hogan, Jerry Hogan, Joe Hogan, Georgia Guilliams Lamb, Dale Miller, Jeanie Miller, Nathan Miller, Bill Plumlee, Julianne Stewart, George Taylor, Oliva Vaughan, Thurman Vaughan, Lloyd Warren.

For painstaking work transcribing tunes from old tapes, I am grateful to musicologist Alan Spurgeon, his assistants Glen Dale Barney, Chris Barber, and Marc Lau and to Dr. James South, who edited the music typesetting. My work in the University of Arkansas collections was generously aided by Andrea Cantrell, Steve Chism, Mike Dabrishus, John Harrison, Cassandra McCraw, Steve Perry, Ellen Shipley, Ethel Simpson, and Tony Wappel. One wonderful taping session in 1994 was supervised by Scott Lunsford and his assistant Joy Endicott at the University of Arkansas's Division of Continuing Education. Jim Borden helped by taking photographs at a 1994 family reunion in Goshen, Arkansas. My students Elizabeth Foster and Amy Kreitlein conducted helpful interviews with Phydella Hogan, Oliva Vaughan, and Martha Estes. For assistance with the song annotations, I'm grateful to W. K. McNeil, Mary Pearson, and Peggy Rothrock.

Sigrid Laubert, Lori Peterson, and Jeanie Wyant assisted me with typing and proofreading, and Suzanne McCray took time from her own work to provide valuable editorial help. Chuck Adams and Dean Bernard Madison, my supervisors in the English Department and in the J. William Fulbright College of Arts and Sciences' Center for Arkansas and Regional Studies, have provided continuing encouragement and support over the years of this project's accomplishment. My pleasure in the work of scholarship owes much to them, as it also does to four wonderful teachers from long ago: Ruth Dutro, Peter Jacobi, Lyndon Shanley, and Anthony Tovatt. I also owe a scholar's special debt of gratitude to Bill Ferris, Roger Abrahams, and Henry Glassie. When Bill took me along to record a convention of Sacred Harp singers in Mississippi in 1970, I saw for the first time how much fun a folklorist could have. I'd already finished graduate school in English by then, but Roger helped me through the doors into another discipline, and Henry, more than any other, showed me how the folklorist's job should be done—throttle wide open, mind and heart.

At The University of Arkansas Press my manuscript was turned into a book by John Coghlan, Kevin Brock, Brian King, Scot Danforth, Liz Lester, Nancy Saunders, and Beth Motherwell. I also owe thanks to Miller Williams, who first suggested a manageable format for presentation of the song collection.

Good friends tolerated what at times must have seemed boundless enthusiasms over unpromising obsessions. Thanks for patience, company, listening, and questioning to Roger Abrahams, Chuck and Rhonda Adams, László Bákk and Tünde Incze, Dorottya Beczásy, Milton and Mimi Burke, Sidney and Nancy Burris, Joe and Anne Marie Candido, Jack and Tess Clarkson, Alison Cochran, Emily Cochran, Mary Cochran, Ruth Cochran, Sarah Cochran, Stephen Cochran and Barbara Adams, Tom and Debby Cochran, John and Sun Mee Diesel, Bill Ferris, Raymond Garrow, Henry Glassie and Kathy Foster, Jeff Gordon, Peter Guralnick, Marian Heinrichs, Jim Johnson, Frankie Kelly, Zsuzsanna Kiss, Anna Klamer, Sigrid and Gerhard Laubert, Clay Lewis, John and Julie Long, Mike and Debby Luster, Mattie McCray, Bill McNeil, Charles and Pat Mazer, Bob Neralich, John Pickerill, Lynn Pierle, Adrianne Suggs, Ioana Varna, Walter and Hazel Williams. [I remember also Ben Kimpel, Bob Pierle, and especially my father, Robert Cochran.]

Most of all, at last, I've worked with my family. We've gone to gospel sings and bluegrass festivals together, inspected old buildings and cemeteries, heard storytellers talk and fiddlers play, and helped make maple syrup on a Newton County hillside. Your company makes work a pleasure and lifts pleasure to joy. Bob, Shannon, Masie, Jesse, Taylor: my deepest prayer is that your memories may be as warm as your father's. Suzanne: thanks to you everything coheres, adds up to a life. We gather to a center where you are and call it home.

Contents

Prelude

This book is first a portrait of a singing family's musical heritage, second an examination of that family's starring role in the musical life of its rural northwest Arkansas community, and third an account of its own making. The portrait itself is at points painstakingly, even obsessively detailed, driven as it is by a desire to address one fundamental question as fully as possible: How does music serve in the lives of people for whom it is a central feature of their daily activity that they accord it so important a place and preserve it so tenaciously?

Put into the language of scholarship, the same question would be framed by saying that *Singing in Zion* is a study of oral tradition in operation, an analysis of texts within their nourishing context. At a personal level it is a record of a sustained encounter between generous and articulate singers and an outsider of analytic bent whose wish to understand their music was strong enough to fuel years of persistent questioning and listening.

Reading on from this prologue, you will encounter first of all its people, primarily the singers, the Gilbert family, and secondarily the scholar, armed with his queries. The order of making was different. The scholar, in fact, met the songs before the singers—my long study was initiated by the presentation of a notebook crammed with typed and handwritten lyric sheets. Some included brief annotations at the bottom, but most were bare texts, offered with some diffidence in 1988 by Phydella Hogan, a student in a folklore class at the University of Arkansas. "We sing a lot of these songs you've been playing and lecturing about," she said. "I thought you might be interested."

Examining the songs was easy enough, and learning something of their varied origins and histories only marginally more difficult. What was truly challenging was the people who sang and played, who had claimed the songs as their own and had made them an integral part of their experience. They were strangers, and it was an enterprise of long duration to meet them on their own ground, to enter the world they created with the aid of their music. Reversing this order of experience to introduce the people first makes things easier for the reader, since it puts the fruits of our extended collaborative labor more quickly on the table. The Gilbert family singers employ songs in myriad ways, some quite straightforward, some surprisingly complex. Paying close attention, one can witness the ongoing, real-life operation of "oral tradition," that vaunted abstraction. Music, it turns out, functions as much more than entertainment, more even than an agent of social cohesion. The Gilberts use music in all the obvious ways, certainly—to pass the time, fill in hours of otherwise tedious labor, coax a child's sleep, court a sweetheart, or calm an anxious mind. But careful observation will also reveal its presence in less obvious contexts—as fodder for argument and food for thought, as an agent of moral instruction, as a source of utopian images, as an aid to the construction of family history and personal identity.

Singing in Zion, then, highlights not just the songs, or even the singers as knowers and performers of songs, but the lived experience made up of their interaction. The songs by themselves, lifted from the rich matrix of their deployment in singers' lives, may seem to the outsider's cold eye a dismaying mélange of cliches, an impoverished aggregation of crude melodramas. So, too, the lives of the singers, presented merely as straightforward biographical narratives apart from the music so central to their sense of identity, might also seem unimpressive. A better understanding, of both songs and singers, is one that approaches them in tandem, seeking each in the presence of the other. That's the goal of *Singing in Zion*—sustained examination, ending in heightened understanding and appreciation of the richer world and the deeper community a family of singers has created with their songs.

'hear' his voice singing any other words. Is that t
way you remember the ol songs? I 'listen and in
mind I can see Mama or Dad when they sang these son
and I know exactly how they sound. I mean the way t

Singing in Zion

I Know Exactly
How They Sound

THREE SISTERS, grandmothers all, prompted each by the others, their sense of treasure shared, gather their family's songs into a book for their children and grandchildren. Out of their own sense of their music's importance, they produce a huge songbook that seems to them the best thing they possess in the way of family history and is the most tangible, material record of an encompassing musical tradition which guides and sustains their lives. Looking back to grandparents, parents, brothers, and sisters, to places, people, and incidents of the lives they cherish and wish to save for their children and grandchildren, they find their recollections to be at their center a listening, a durable hearing. They find their memories most firmly anchored in song, in singing and playing musical instruments. The past the sisters know carries itself most vividly into the present as a medley of voices, each one precisely etched in memory, as sufficient a signature as any fingerprint's curves and whorls. For them, life is made of words cadenced as music. For them, life is set to song.

In 1959, the sisters began writing down and typing out copies of songs they remembered as their own and sending them to each other as letters. They appended their recollections, exchanged questions and answers about missing verses and alternative versions, even looked in published songbooks for lines and verses that eluded memory. At last they ordered and assembled their collection and distributed copies among themselves. Their work was mostly complete in the 1960s, though occasional alterations continue even in the 1990s.

The collection they assembled reveals itself at last as a long love letter, a birthright tenaciously held and generously given. The result is a lovely, extraordinary achievement, a richly textured realization of its makers' purposes. Their enduring book in their hands, Alma Allen and Helen Fultz and Phydella Hogan had only to turn a page to find memories wakened, cherished moments of their lives revived. For their children, and now even the children of those children, who hear the stories and songs together, another layer is deposited, a richer heritage is transmitted to their care.

Like most large, sweeping accomplishments, the Gilbert family music tradition comprises particulars modest enough in themselves. The unit of building is, in the usual instance, a song or a piece of a song or a remembered singing voice. When Phydella Hogan sees the words of "I Could Not Call Her Mother" written on a page she hears again "how Mother's voice quavered when she sang this."[1] For Alma Allen the distinctive maternal vocal trait was a "sort of 'waver' in her voice," and for her it attached most memorably to "Kitty Wells."[2] Her sister Helen Fultz, making a tape for her daughter Jeanie Miller in 1974, comments after her version of "The Dirty Faced Brat" that "Mother used to sing that just that way. I'm not sure it's right, but it's quite an old-fashioned song."[3] A generation later, the Gilbert tendency to locate memories in sound rather than sight is still evident in the concluding paragraph of a reminiscence written by Phydella's son Joe: "Thanks to Mom and her family, music has always been with me. Even when I'm where I can't hear it I can still 'hear' it."[4]

At times the very text of a song depends upon just this sort of "hearing." Sending "My Horses Ain't Hungry" to her sisters, Phydella Hogan first identifies it as "one of the old songs Dad used to sing," and then goes on to apologize for what may be an incomplete version: "I'm not sure if there is any other verse or not, but I can't 'hear' his voice singing any other words. Is that the way you remember the old songs? I 'listen' and in my mind I can see Mama or Dad when they sang these songs and I know exactly how they sound."[5]

Their songbook, explicitly a gift for their families, a gesture to the future, thus serves its makers as well and aids their memories as effectively as any photograph album. More effectively, for in their "hearing" of their songs the past is not merely recalled; it is made present to them with living force. "I couldn't have been more than three," writes Helen Fultz, "when I used to go to bed real early so Carl, Thelma, Buck, and Alma could sing me to sleep. I was sure then, and still am, that a choir of angels couldn't sing as beautiful as they could."[6] The present they experience is by their efforts greatly enlarged—from the book's pages, safe in the hands of their descendants, the living voices of ancestors speak. At its every opening their songbook returns them to their beginnings, when they were young girls in Arkansas waking to a world of parents and siblings, of relatives, neighbors, and landscapes, of words and music.

For the outsider, things are different. The songbook may seem at once a treasure, a rich mixture of some 225 songs, old and new, traditional and popular, sacred and secular. Songs learned from parents and grandparents are joined to others learned from the Grand Ole Opry or Jimmie Rodgers records. Old ballads are mixed with hymns and temperance numbers, songs found in many collections together with songs unique to this one. In itself the songbook might offer rich insight into the diverse sources of the family's and, by extension, the region's repertoire. But that is all, and it's not enough. The rich heart remains opaque. For Phydella Hogan and Helen Fultz, the tangible book, for all its imposing weight, is only the tip of the iceberg. By virtue of their lifelong experience, the book is for them just the beginning, a mere mnemonic, a magical promptbook which allows them to revive whole worlds out of a single page. But even for their children the songbook by itself holds such magic only to the extent that their parents have read and sung it for them many times and, in so doing, have taught them how to read it deeply for themselves. Lacking such guides, such long experience, it will be to them little more than what it is to the outsider—a sheer surface, imposing in scope but lacking depth. The songbook itself, the outsider soon realizes, is only the explicit fraction of the tradition, not the cake but only the recipe, only the promptbook, not the drama itself.

This study emerged, very slowly, from this realization. It is a book about people who love music, filled with songs and talk of songs but focused always on the people themselves. People talk easily about folksongs, about folk tradition, but these are not such easy things to understand. Very subtle things are going on, despite the apparent melodramas and cliches of the songs themselves and the no less apparent modesty of the singers' world. The result is not a big book, but it took a long time because what's in it was at the beginning understood deeply only by the subjects (and even for them its articulation in a language other than that of singing and playing was a novel and at times difficult endeavor) and not at all by the author, who first encountered it as a large notebook crammed to bursting with songs, notes, and letters, some typed, others on handwritten sheets. The initiating realization, then, was that it wasn't enough just to have the songbook. It had to be read and sung, over and over, with painstaking repetitions and explanations, as to a child.

The central premise of this work, then, is that sustained examination of the musical traditions of a single family will yield, first of all, a series of fine stories, the episodic saga a family elaborates in celebration of itself. But it should also prove of use and interest to a wide variety of folkloristic, historical, anthropological, and musicological investigations far beyond the family's borders. A body of folk music scholarship that for many years has featured a good number of large regional collections and, in more recent years, has produced several excellent studies of individual singers, continues to be frustrated in its analytic aims by a lack of comparable studies focused upon family traditions or those of small communities.[7] The omission is especially glaring in that the whole notion of an oral tradition depends at its core upon a group of people capable of more or less intimate contact with one another and possessing at least some sense of group identity. A region is too big; an individual too small. A folksinger is a folksinger in the first place not because he or she sings certain types of songs or sings them in a certain style or with a certain type of instrumental accompaniment, or even because the songs are learned in a traditional setting, but because he or she is understood to be "our singer" or at least "one of our singers" by a community willing to complete the circuit, connecting itself to the singer by understanding itself as audience. What's requisite, in short, is a conscious bond, mutual ties of obligation on the one hand and appreciation on the other.

The notion is in fact ancient. The very name of Homer's Demodokhos, the *Odyssey*'s singer within the tale, indicates his position within a particular "deme," or locale. If, then, there is one well-known bardic "type" who is itinerant, wandering from place to place earning bread and shelter by his art, there is also a more sedentary practitioner, equally ancient and no less venerated, who is deeply rooted in a particular community, recognized in it as "our poet," or "our singer," or "our historian."[8]

The Gilberts, Aegean traded for Arkansas, fit the bill perfectly. Singing and songs are not only central to their own sense of family identity, but they have long been recognized by their neighbors as "a singing family" and asked by their community to provide music at everything from the most impromptu gatherings to such formalized civic occasions as school and church programs. Even now, seventy years after their debut performances for candy at the Habberton settlement store, they are counted upon (and expect to be counted upon) to provide music for the annual Zion community reunions. These reunions, in fact, offer especially vivid instances of the "traditional referentiality" described by contemporary scholarship as essentially "metonymic" in its power, so that each separate performance, however truncated or fragmentary, will evoke for knowing audiences the "immensely larger canvas of the tradition as a whole."[9]

At recent reunions, for example, the sisters have not always sung together, as in 1993 when Phydella was sick and only Helen and her daughter Jeanie were able to perform. At the 1994 reunion both sisters were present, but they sang only four songs. The entire musical portion of the program was over in perhaps fifteen minutes. But it was central, nevertheless, and it was sufficient, thanks in large part to the intimacy of the group gathered in affirmation of itself, a company by virtue of immense shared experience sustained over long years of close association made fully capable of re-experiencing a vast whole from the representation of a very small part.

What occurs at the level of individual consciousness for Phydella Hogan when she sings or hears or even remembers "I Could Not Call Her Mother" occurs on a much larger scale in the minds of old Zion residents gathered to celebrate their lives and recollections. The songs that were central to those lives then, despite the brevity of their present performance, are even now central agents of remembering and reliving. Their tradition here serves Arkansas hill people as other traditions served archaic Greeks and medieval Anglo-Saxons and contemporary Serbo-Croatians. If "any one performance or text will remain only a partial record" of any traditional work, it is no less true that the same performance is "enriched by an unspoken context" that summons "that which is immanent to become part of the artistic creation in the present time."[10] Each single performance in a traditional milieu thus occupies a rich middle ground. It can never be everything, never be the "work" in its entirety, but it is always more than itself. What occurs most obviously in events like the Zion reunions occurs more quietly every time Helen Fultz sings or Phydella Hogan plays her banjo. A whole world is restored, even as the definitive performance of a particular song remains forever elusive. Traditional poetics, as experienced here by north Arkansas singers and listeners, presents a situation in which denotative, explicit meanings may be "only nominal," less significant than "connotative, inherent meanings . . . summoned to narrative present under an agreement negotiated over generations."[11]

To approach such a tradition seriously, then, is to search for just these "connotative, inherent meanings." For the Gilberts, music is a master key to the whole experience of living. I can learn all the songs, I told myself near the beginning. That will be the easy part. The real task will be to surround Gilbert songs with Gilbert stories, the better to know their songs as they know them. If I can do this, I thought, know not only their songs, but what their songs are for them, I'll know everything important about them. I couldn't, of course, and I don't. I am at last an outsider, no matter how carefully I listen, how persistently I question, how patiently I ponder. But the gift the Gilbert sisters intended for their children and grandchildren expands its range by my study. By my attention and meditation, I catch glimpses of people creating themselves and their lives by means made available to them by their traditions, fashioning order and coping with order's disruption. Such attention is at once my claim to the attention of readers and my thanks to Phydella Hogan and Helen Fultz for admitting so inquisitive a stranger into their company.

I have assumed, somewhat against the grain of current scholarly trends, that such a thing is both possible and worth doing in and for itself, apart from any potential "critical synthesis" it might serve. I even now remember my dismay when I recognized something very much like the disgrace of my own credo in Roger Abrahams' comparison of a study built of "a series of small perceptions, rendered in a manner that does not invite any critical synthesis" to other works of "richer achievement" and more "explanatory power."[12] Despite my admiration for studies of this latter sort, I have always reserved my highest regard for just those efforts founded on "small perceptions" which hold back from "critical synthesis" or "explanatory power" out of respect for the details of the perceptions themselves. James Clifford's "On Ethnographic Allegory" puts the matter succinctly: "The personal does not yield to the general without loss."[13]

I have struggled to minimize such loss, have tried to hold my attention to the particular, to resist what Clifford in the same essay calls "the insistent tug toward the general," to get the Gilbert family singing tradition on the page without undue worry about "the demands of a typifying science."[14] My deepest loyalties, always, are not with would-be scientists, eager for ever more inclusive "laws," but with the Samuel Beckett whose character Moran discovers in the dance of his bees the bottomless joys of endless incertitude: "And in spite of all the pains I had lavished on these problems I was more than ever stupefied by the complexity of this innumerable dance, involving doubtless other determinants of which I had not the slightest idea. And I said, with rapture, here is something I can study all my life, and never understand."[15]

The axis on which all else turns, then, is the fundamental realization of music's potential for cultural centrality. One finds this everywhere —in Navajo creation stories, where a heroic character understands himself as protected by song, in Toni Morrison's *Beloved,* where things too private to be spoken may yet be uttered in song, or in Finnish epics, where shaman bards chant their enemies into ruin and sing blessings on the weddings of their friends. Or, to provide just one more extended example, one finds it among Polish soldiers in the Italian campaign of World War II, as lovingly portrayed by Martha Gellhorn:

> But as they were all young, and as a man cannot worry all the time even for his country and his family and his very hope of a life, we stopped talking about Russia and the future and went over to the repair truck, where two soldiers were playing a violin and an

accordion. We made ourselves comfortable on bundles of hay
around the truck and soldiers drifted together, and the singing
started. It is most lovely music, mournful and gay at once, and
always full of memories. The soldiers have invented songs to com-
memorate every place they have lived and fought these last years.
There are songs of Alamein and Tobruk, and the song of the regi-
ment, and soldier songs that make marching easier. The desert songs
are sadder than the others. They played their own tangos, and *tzi-
gane* music and Brahms and then a sweet, sad love song. . . .

   The moon was clear and new and the music spread over us,
interrupted only by the noise of our own artillery. Suddenly war
was the way you remember it, not the way it is while it is hap-
pening. Just for a moment the present had the strange quality of
already being the past, and one saw this night as it would look five
years from now, and it was beautiful and perfect without needing
five years to gild the memory. Nothing mattered except that these
men should always be young, always brave and gay and fine to
look at, always alive. The violinist and the accordion player grew
tired at last and we walked home through the deep white pow-
der of road dust. All that night our artillery hammered against the
sky so that it seemed the walls of our village would have to crack
and give under this ceaseless pounding in the air.[16]

   The centrality of music, though close to universal, is encountered in
this instance in the Arkansas Ozarks, at the heart of one family's life. That
life has been my first concern; the instance itself, in its own particularity,
wherever possible, so far as possible, has been my goal. The general, the
"critical synthesis," appears only incidentally, as suggested by comparison of the Gilbert tradition with other musics and other families.

   Despite the emphasis on sustained encounter, I have nevertheless
worked to avoid so far as possible the several idealizations and nostal-
gias identified and critiqued in recent discussions of the ethnographer's
art. In particular I have been wary of the "ethnographic pastoral" criticized on political grounds by Renato Rosaldo (for licensing "patronizing attitudes of condescension") and on poetic grounds by James
Clifford (for creating a "structure of retrospection" where the "recorder
and interpreter of fragile custom is custodian of an essence, unim-
peachable witness to an authenticity").[17]

Certainly temptations of just this sort are present. I hope my admiration of Phydella Hogan and Helen Fultz is as evident as my appreciation of their music. The photographer out in the rain happily taking pictures of a ruined house may be reasonably seen as far gone in a pastoral reverie. But it should be stressed that I am not the first to so admire or so appreciate. I am only the most recent and the most distant. The "textualization" of the Gilbert and Scott family experience was undertaken long before I arrived, and was undertaken, what is more, not from without but from within. Phydella Hogan and Helen Fultz have long been for their children and grandchildren what their parents and their Grandmother Scott were for them—embodiments of authenticity, custodians of essence, heroines of saga. When Jerry Hogan, Phydella's youngest son, writes that "I'm too young to have ever seen the entire family play but I have a kind of generalized feeling of warmth and security associated with weekend evening music sessions out at Aunt Helen's," he is celebrating a family pastoral centered on his mother and his aunt.[18] Seventy years earlier, when his children were very young, Jerry's grandfather, Joe Gilbert, already saw it as his responsibility to teach them what it meant to "be a Gilbert" as a complement to maternal lessons in Christian standards. The "pastoral" is, in fact, an integral part of family tradition, a root of family pride. It needed no outsider for its elaboration and was securely in place long before the arrival of the ethnographer.

It should also be stressed that no intrinsic incompatibility stands between personal attachment and professional competence. A family physician who is a personal friend is not therefore less competent in her caring for my children; the electrician who wires my house is not befuddled in his work by the fact that he is my brother. If I have come to care deeply for Phydella Hogan or Helen Fultz, I have not, as a consequence, hesitated to ask whatever questions seemed called for or to draw whatever conclusions seemed warranted. What fuels investigation, after all, is not that cool dispassion often mistakenly associated with "scientific" research and taken as a guarantor of "objectivity." Cool dispassion accomplishes nothing. Cool dispassion is ready to be planted. Only deep interest, borderline obsession, attachment or animus or a mixture thereof, motivates long-term study.

It is also true that I concluded early on, with no better evidence than their own statements, that in the Gilbert sisters I had happened upon a family for whom music was of central, crucial importance. I was new to them then, and a conclusion drawn at the beginning may be justly suspected of foreclosing investigation, of limiting vision, of seeing only that which confirms itself. What actually happens is different and more interesting than confirmation. Every day has its surprise, every surprise is an opportunity to learn, every conclusion is conditional. If I am surprised by the number of popular songs the Gilbert sisters know, I have a chance to learn how avidly they listened to the radio and to records. If I am unprepared for temperance songs, or for nostalgic musical evocations of benevolent slaveowners, I am invited to explore family attitudes toward alcohol and race.

At other times the surprise itself may confirm a conclusion, render it one step less hazardous. Most vivid among these happy surprises was my experience in the Goshen cemetery in May 1993, as my work neared completion. I'd gone to Goshen because Phydella had told me her maternal grandmother, the matriarch whose house at Mayfield had been the central family home, was buried there. Phydella thought her

Goshen, Arkansas, Cemetery Gate, 1993.
Photo by the author.

grave was marked. It is—Phydellia Scott is buried by her husband, and their names are still legible on the stone. Next to it, however, flat on the ground, is a much more humble stone Phydella had not mentioned. Ernest Scott is buried there—and I remembered. He's the cousin in my favorite family picture, the one taken on the hillside at Grandmother Scott's. He's at the end, right on the hillside, left in the picture, wearing bib overalls and holding a fiddle. His gravestone, here at Goshen, is wholly unengraved, but his name and birth and death dates are painted on in bright red. It might be fingernail polish. But there is one additional bit of decoration, also painted. I peer closely, removing my glasses and kneeling on the ground. Finally I make it out: it's a banjo!

It's true! I said when I recognized what it was. Think of anything from Egyptian pharaohs to American Indian chiefs. Grave goods are the central stuff—necessary supplies for the other side. You can't take it with you, says the cautionary bromide, but such harsh assertion may be mediated by your friends, the people who love you. In their sorrow at your passing they do not neglect you. Out of their attachment and their intimate knowledge, they send you off to whatever future faith contemplates equipped with what you most need to be yourself. A tombstone's words and images, understood in this light, might serve as a passport at St. Peter's gate. The grave, all vanity shorn, asserts the essence of the person. A Viking bigshot might need a whole warship, a Mycenaean queen might require her jewels. With Gilberts and Scotts, these Ozark music folks, you get to the red heart in its hour at the bar, what you have left is song. My early conclusion, made five years before at the beginning? It was right. The center is music. Ernest Scott? He was a banjo player.

Considerable attention has been devoted in recent years to searching and at times stringent critiques of various ethnographic strategies. In particular the axioms of traditional "objectivist" researchers have come under fire—claims to impartial detachment in the service of disinterested "scientific" ends have been seen as naive and patronizing, and the results of investigations conducted by such methods have been criticized as at best confused and at worst as serving (consciously or unconsciously) sinister ideological ends. If at times these critiques seem overheated, it should be no less clear that they address themselves to

Grave of Ernest Scott, Goshen, Arkansas, 1993.
Photo by the author.

real shortcomings in both methodology and purpose. It has become obvious that ethnographer/informant relationships are complicated and may be compromised by many factors, not all of them necessarily understood.

The researcher, it turns out, is never absent, despite his or her protestations, despite the fact that the "Absent Editor strategy" is "the oldest and most common" presentational strategy of traditional ethnography. But there are no less dangerous pitfalls in the opposite strategy as well, where the researcher/editor indulges in "heroic extremes of subjectivity" and "self-consciously inserts himself or herself into the entire text."[19] I have tried to profit from these critiques even as I refused to waver from my initial purposes. Those purposes have been my own, though I have tried ever since the beginning to communicate them to Phydella Hogan, Helen Fultz, and the others as fully as I could, even as they shifted and developed over time as the result of our ongoing encounter. I also do not doubt that their reasons for allowing my inquiry have differed in some respects from my own. They, in turn, did not hesitate to communicate with me. We had many opportunities for such exchange in a collaboration that consisted mostly of conversation. Out of his work with the wonderful Pomo teacher Mabel McKay, Greg Sarris came up with a lovely description of "talk itself" which also describes good ethnography as well as any definition I've seen: "It is an art generating respect for the unknown while illuminating the borders of the known."[20]

Gilberts and Scotts

The sisters started as Gilberts—Alma Gilbert Allen, Phydella Gilbert Hogan, and Helen Gilbert Fultz—and they speak again as Gilberts when they undertake the ordered remembering of their lives. Their father, Joseph William Gilbert, married Sophia Scott on November 22, 1901, in her mother, Phydellia Scott's, home near Mayfield, Arkansas. The bride was eighteen; the groom twenty-six. Here, then, are this saga's most immediate founding names: Gilbert and Scott, father and mother. Behind them, on the maternal side, were Stringfields, Culwells, and Millers. Grandmother Scott was a Stringfield, the daughter of Kentucky-born Edward Stringfield and native Arkansan Martha Ann Culwell. She

Scott Family Portrait. About 1900. Sophia Scott is second from left on top row.
Photo courtesy Phydella Hogan and Helen Fultz.

Family Tree

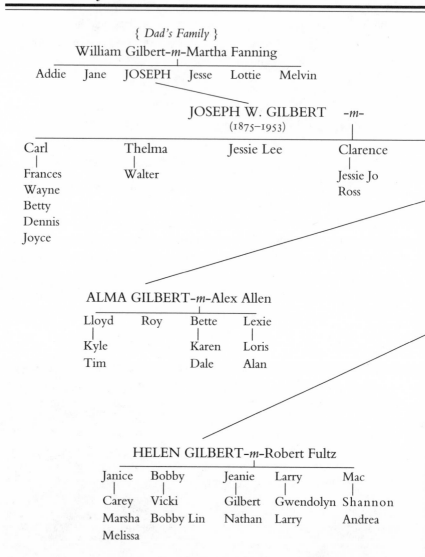

{ *Dad's Family* }

William Gilbert-*m*-Martha Fanning

Addie   Jane   JOSEPH   Jesse   Lottie   Melvin

JOSEPH W. GILBERT   -*m*-
(1875–1953)

Carl	Thelma	Jessie Lee	Clarence
Frances	Walter		Jessie Jo
Wayne			Ross
Betty			
Dennis			
Joyce			

ALMA GILBERT-*m*-Alex Allen

Lloyd	Roy	Bette	Lexie
Kyle		Karen	Loris
Tim		Dale	Alan

HELEN GILBERT-*m*-Robert Fultz

Janice	Bobby	Jeanie	Larry	Mac
Carey	Vicki	Gilbert	Gwendolyn	Shannon
Marsha	Bobby Lin	Nathan	Larry	Andrea
Melissa				

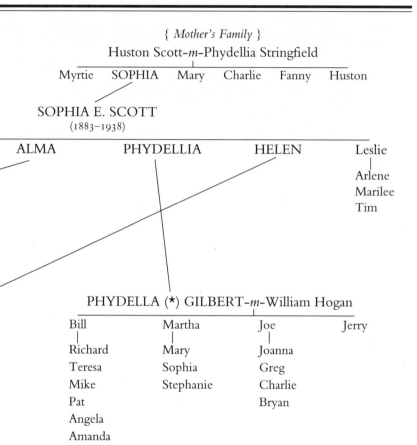

{ *Mother's Family* }

Huston Scott-*m*-Phydellia Stringfield

Myrtie   SOPHIA   Mary   Charlie   Fanny   Huston

SOPHIA E. SCOTT
(1883–1938)

ALMA   PHYDELLIA   HELEN   Leslie
                                                Arlene
                                                Marilee
                                                Tim

PHYDELLA (★) GILBERT-*m*-William Hogan

Bill	Martha	Joe	Jerry
Richard	Mary	Joanna	
Teresa	Sophia	Greg	
Mike	Stephanie	Charlie	
Pat		Bryan	
Angela			
Amanda			

(★) Phydella Hogan dropped the penultimate letter from her given name "back in grade school, sixth or seventh grade," when a teacher insisted, contrary to family practice, on pronouncing it.

was born at Pea Ridge, Arkansas, in 1861, near in both time and place
to the region's biggest Civil War battle. She married Huston Matthew
Scott—the exact year is uncertain, but it must have been about 1880.
The Scotts were also from Kentucky—Huston's father, Peter Scott, was
born in Montgomery County in 1814 and married fellow Kentuckian
Sophia Miller in 1837.

The paternal side of the family, the Gilberts, came to Arkansas later
and from the other direction. Grandmother Gilbert was born Martha
Fanning; she married W. C. Gilbert in Texas and moved to Arkansas
in a covered wagon in 1883. This Grandfather Gilbert, in Alma's vivid
account, crossed the Atlantic to "New Amsterdam" in 1857, a stow-
away orphan of twelve fleeing an unkind uncle.[21] He may not have
been an orphan, he may have come instead with his parents, and New
Amsterdam, of course, did not exist in 1857, having been renamed New
York almost two centuries earlier when the Dutch, who had displaced
the native Canarsie Indians, were themselves supplanted by the English
in 1664. But these are matters of bare fact, of secondary importance in
this context. Family histories, like national epics, have ends beyond
mere accuracy in view. In family stories ancestors are at least lifted to
legend and at most simply concocted from thin air, just as national
heroes like George Washington or Brutus the Trojan are burnished like
saints by Parson Weems and Geoffrey of Monmouth.

More significant than historical detail is the musical mnemonic specific to the story, "Fair Nottingham Town." "Our Grandfather Gilbert's
family came from England to Texas when he was just a boy," according to Phydella's less flamboyant recollection. "This is an old song they
brought with them. Grandpa taught it to Dad, and he taught it to us."[22]
"Fair Nottingham Town," then, is treasured in the Gilbert family both
as a song and as a piece of family history. The history, for them, is sustained in the song. Grandfather Gilbert has been dead for a century, but
he lives in the memory of his family every time they sing the song they
know as his.

Brought together in northwest Arkansas by the meeting of these varied adventurings, Joe Gilbert and Sophia Scott made the accident of their
meeting significant and enduring by a willed and welcomed courtship.
Their marriage produced eight children, five daughters and three sons.
Carl, the oldest, was born in 1903, followed by Thelma, and then Jessie

Lee, who died as a days-old infant. Next was Clarence (called Buck), and then Alma, the eldest of this volume's makers, born February 13, 1912. Her father called her Billie, and the nickname stuck. Phydella was next, born six years later, on March 12, 1918. Helen came three years later, on April 9, 1921, followed by Leslie, the youngest, in 1924.

Joe Gilbert was a blacksmith who lived with his wife and growing family in various rural Washington and Benton County communities in northwest Arkansas—Healing Springs, Osage Mills, Whitener, Spring Valley, Habberton, Cave Springs, War Eagle, Mayfield, Zion, Goshen. "We moved a lot, but never very far," says Phydella.[23] The life the sisters remember was often difficult—the frequent moves were at least in part determined by economic hard times, and both women remember even today times when their father couldn't spare five cents for crepe paper for a school pageant or was forced to turn away a hungry hobo with a bitter admission of penury. "'I've got nothing to give you,' Dad told him," recalls Phydella. "'I don't even have enough to feed my own.'"[24]

Even now, nearly seventy years after the fact, Phydella Hogan's memories of back-breaking and unending work remain vivid:

Joe Gilbert and Sophia Scott Gilbert, Wedding Photo, 1901.

Photo courtesy Phydella Hogan and Helen Fultz.

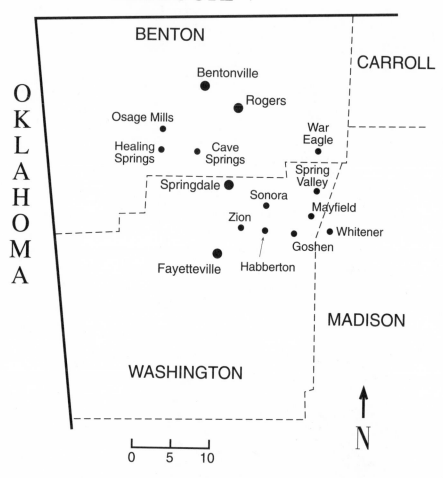

MISSOURI

BENTON

CARROLL

OKLAHOMA

Bentonville

Rogers

Osage Mills

War
Eagle

Healing
Springs

Cave
Springs

Spring
Valley

Springdale

Sonora

Mayfield

Zion

Whitener

Goshen

Fayetteville

Habberton

MADISON

WASHINGTON

N

0   5   10

Northwest Arkansas

I remember Dad always got up early the morning of the wash day, which was usually Monday, if it wasn't raining, and filled every tub and wash kettle on the place. And then you'd still have to draw some more before you got through because you had to wash them through one suds, and then—in the case of the white clothes you'd put them in a kettle and boil 'em with some more suds.

And then you washed the load of the colored clothes, and by then the white clothes should be boiled, so you wrung out these colored clothes and dumped that water and dipped out the hot clothes with a long stick, a broom handle or something, into the tub. And then you added cold water to that, until you could put your hands in it. You rinsed them out of that water, put 'em in a clear water and then in a bluing water. And wring 'em each time, by hand, and then they were ready to hang on the line, unless you had to starch. . . .

Then you put the colored clothes back through the warm suds, rinsed them and blued them—it didn't matter, I guess, if they went through the bluing, but Mother always said it made 'em brighter. . . . But everything had to go through at least three waters, and some of it four. By the end of the day you were just ready to cave in.[25]

Joe Gilbert, in the memories of his children, emerges as an exceptionally supportive husband to his physically fragile wife: "I can remember after Mother got not too well and Dad wasn't working full time, in the winter time he stayed and helped her with the washing. . . . Most men did not do that. Our Dad was ahead of his time about helping the family in the house. Because most men did not. Dad always got up and built the fire—I think every other woman in the neighborhood got up and built the fire in the morning."[26]

The most durable address throughout the time of their growing up, the true "homeplace" in the sisters' memories, was their maternal grandmother's home near Mayfield, where their parents had married. They visited every year in October, making a slow journey by wagon through the rural countryside from wherever in the area they were then living, and staying for several days of visiting with grandparents and various uncles and aunts, playing with cousins, and making music. What began as the family matriarch's birthday celebrations eventually took shape as

Joe Gilbert and Sophia
Scott Gilbert. Zion,
Arkansas, early 1930s.
Photo courtesy Phydella
Hogan and Helen Fultz.

a family reunion, still held even now, though the date has been moved
from October to June to accommodate school schedules.

From the very beginning, in the sisters' earliest memories, music
held the center. Neither parent played an instrument, but both "liked
to sing," according to Alma's written account, "so they attended most
of the singing conventions and the local church services" (*A Way of
Life,* 2). Phydella's recollections are similar: "Singing and playing are
the earliest memories I have. . . . My mother was real small . . . not in
good health. My father was tall. Neither played instruments, but both
sang. Mother had a beautiful voice. You couldn't go into the house—
I remember coming in from school, you never had to wonder where
Mother was, you could hear her singing or humming, might be an old
folk song, might be a gospel tune. I remember the smell of the house,
like something good."[27]

Phydella's daughter, Martha Hogan Estes, exactly one generation later, has strikingly similar memories about her mother: "Mother's banjo is one of my earliest memories. I can never remember when we didn't have Mother's banjo. . . . Anytime anybody came to see us she played—like other mothers read bedtime stories she sang songs to the kids." Martha Estes's favorite song was a banjo piece called "Blue Bells":

> I have no idea where she learned it or where it came from, but "Blue Bells" required special tuning of the banjo—most beautiful song I'd ever heard, still is.
>
> I'd start in when Mama started playing. She'd go through "Turkey in the Straw" and all the stuff we heard all the time. And I'd start whining, "Please play 'Blue Bells' for me. Please play 'Blue Bells' for me." And she'd postpone it and postpone it and postpone it, and I'd whine around and pout, like I said, and then finally she'd tune it. And to me, when she tuned that banjo, that was love. Mama loves you when she would stop and retune the banjo to play that special song. . . . I just get teary-eyed when she plays that thing.[28]

The Best Banjo in the World

Musical instruments are prominent in the memories of the previous generation, too, as far back as the sisters can recall. "Carl, Thelma and Buck played guitar, banjo and auto harp," wrote Alma. "Being smaller I sang, but in later years played guitar and auto harp also. Sometimes some other cousin or neighbor joined in with a harmonica or even a jews-harp. We had duets, quartets, solos and group singing."(*A Way of Life,* 30) Gilbert family memories have fewer tales more fully elaborated than those celebrating the acquisition of musical instruments. In Alma's account the first such purchase, in 1918, is vividly dramatized, with various family members given speaking parts in the campaign for paternal approval, and even the postman, Mr. Phinney, appears briefly to deliver the Sears and Roebuck catalog. The climax comes after dinner, with sister Thelma—"he won't turn *you* down on anything," says Carl—selected to speak: "Then Thelma couldn't be calm and serious any longer but burst out, 'Oh, we've found the *very* right banjo for us in the catalog and it only costs $4.95 and we want it more than we've ever wanted anything, and *will* you buy it, please, Dad?'" Dad, of course, soon grants his approval, and a banjo of rare merit soon arrives. "I have never since seen a banjo that looked or sounded so wonderful," wrote Alma Allen.[29]

Thelma and Carl, being the oldest, had first access to the new instrument, but it was their younger brother, Buck, then just nine, who became its master. "Almost before the others really noticed," remembered Alma, "he could pick that banjo until the Buffalo Girls danced right out onto the floor and Old Dan Tucker combed his head on a wagon-wheel. The strings fairly popped when he discovered Green Corn and Cripple Creek."[30]

"After that," says Phydella, "any of us that wanted an instrument Dad would figure out a way to get it. The next instrument I think he got was the—they called it a mandolin-guitar-harp but I guess you'd call it a zither. It also came from Sears. I believe he had to give ten dollars for it. We laid it on a table and used two picks, but oh that was so pretty, with folk songs and gospel songs. That was for my oldest sister Thelma."[31]

Phydella was six years younger, and her account of the initial banjo purchase is briefer, different in its choice of detail. A conspicuously small child herself, she makes her story a tale of the small brother's struggle: "About the year I was born Buck decided he wanted a banjo. Dad sent off to Sears, paid five dollars for a banjo. He [Buck] was small enough that that banjo neck, he had to be sitting on the couch so he could rest the banjo head on it." Phydella also praises Buck's skill on the instrument, adding that he also played the fiddle for a time, and switched to the mandolin as an adult. His joking explanation was that some people back then thought the banjo "too hillbilly." Buck, she concludes, "actually was the best musician in the group."[32]

As it happens Buck Gilbert's own memory of this banjo purchase has been preserved. In his account the inspiration came from Mayfield: "Our cousin Ernest who lived with our Grandma Scott at Mayfield had a real good 5-string banjo and could pick it pretty good, so us kids persuaded Dad to buy us a banjo. He ordered it from Sears Roebuck and paid $4.50 for it. I was too little to hold the banjo while sitting in a chair so I would sit on the floor, cross my legs and put the banjo between them. That is how I learned to play it, and it was a long time later before I could sit in a chair and play it. We picked that old banjo until we wore a hole in the calfskin head."[33]

Later instrument purchases were the result of carefully planned finance campaigns among the children. "I remember the first guitar Buck and I bought," wrote Alma. "We had raised capons—I can't remember how many, or if we'd raised them on 'shares,' or if Buck bought the baby chicks and I fed and watered them. But I do know when they were sold I went to Fayetteville and bought us a guitar, and I think the price was $15.00."[34]

But the first banjo purchase, back in 1918, was pivotal. Joe Gilbert is quoted by his daughter Alma as saying many times that the "money spent on that banjo was the best investment I ever made. It kept our kids at home and their friends came, as our house was full of songs and laughter."[35] Speaking half a century later in praise of her own parents, Jeanie Fultz Miller paid tribute to another "house full of songs and laughter," a result of her parents' willingness to host Sunday afternoon square dances in their home. "When we were growing up," she remembered,

Helen Fultz, Buck Gilbert, Phydella Hogan. Family Reunion, Mayfield, Arkansas, about 1978.
Photo courtesy Phydella Hogan and Helen Fultz.

"the kids could always come to our house. But there were parents that didn't want their own children's friends to come to their houses just because of trouble."

The square dances began later, when she was a teenager:

> We started watching *Ozark Jubilee*—'course we knew about square dancing, but that's when it became a big deal in our life. They had the Promenaders on *Ozark Jubilee,* over [in Springfield, Missouri]. The girls had gingham dresses and the boys had gingham shirts. This was real glamorous for us. But anyway, we managed to get some fiddle records. We would've loved to have a live fiddler, but we didn't have one so we had the records.
>
> We had dances on, usually, Sunday afternoon at our house. Mom and Daddy lot of times went to a ball game. There were always community ball games you know, back then. There were just enough kids, just about, to make one set. Daddy taught me the calls—I was the caller, first. I would call and dance, lots of times. Sometimes, if there were enough kids, I didn't.

Jeanie then ends the story as she opened it, creating out of her music-based memories a lovely narration framed at both ends by appreciation of wisdom of her parents: "I remember when we always could just buy these old cheap linoleums, nine by twelve, and they never lasted very long anyway. They'd wear out real quick, but it was a big deal for Mom when she got a new linoleum. Made the house look so clean and bright and new. I think in a matter of weeks we danced the pattern off that new linoleum. But she never complained."[36]

Better than the Carter Family

Joining all these instruments to their own voices and the songs they learned from every available source, the Gilberts built their lives around music, playing and singing at church and school programs, at neighborhood parties and family reunions, in medicine show contests, and even, much later, in academic folk festivals. Helen and Phydella, as very young girls living in the Habberton community, sang at the neighborhood store for payments in candy until their mother noticed a lack of appetite at regular meals and put a stop to their budding careers.

"People would ask us to sing," Phydella remembers, "but Helen would say, 'No, they'll look at me.' I'd say, 'Hide your eyes.' We'd sing 'I'm a little wildwood flower, / growing wilder every hour. / Nobody cares to cultivate me / 'cause I'm as wild as I can be.' I wasn't over five then; Helen was just two."[37]

Helen's daughter, Jeanie Fultz Miller, was older when she made her debut, but evidently exhibited a similar shyness. "Probably when I was about eleven or twelve. . . . But oh, I was so bashful. Mom couldn't hardly get me up there. First I remember singing was at a revival, just me and Mom. And we sang 'Jesus at the Well' and 'Summer Land of Love.' And I just nearly panicked and ran out of there, when we were supposed to sing. But we sang, and then we got a lot more praise than any of the other singers, I remember that. And that encouraged me."[38]

The medicine show contests were less frequent, and also less rewarding, though at least one offered a five-dollar prize to the winner. The sisters were green at the time—only later did they realize that the fix was in. Phydella remembers:

Habberton Church of Christ Sign.
Photo by the author.

We went to Springdale and got in a contest. . . . Alma was with us that time; she was married but she went with us. We got up on the stage—they were having some kind of talent contest, everything from singing to magic tricks. Oh man, we were really getting applause. I think we had to do two numbers. I don't remember what we did, some popular song at that time, maybe Jimmie Rodgers, we did them as fast as they came out. . . .

We got a big hand—they called us back. We thought we had it made. The crowd was going nuts. Then the show brings out this magician. He ate some fire. Of course all the kids, the crowd went wild. They were supposed to be measuring the applause, and that's who got the prize. We finally figured he was a member of the medicine show troupe. Their own person got the five dollars. But we had fun.[39]

On at least one occasion the girls were also invited to sing over the newly established radio station in Fayetteville, but their father refused permission, alarmed, or so he said, at the prospect of a career in show business that would lure them from their home and expose them at a too tender age to worldly temptations. Phydella remembers the time well: "Sam Woods came up one night—we were at Zion then. He lived down below the schoolhouse there, worked for Kelly Lumber Company in Fayetteville. He said his company wanted to sponsor some local talent. . . . [said] 'They're better than the Carter Family.' Dad said, 'That's what I'm afraid of.' Oh I was so mad over that for so long!"[40]

Such anecdotes as these make clear that the Gilbert girls were valued as singers and musicians not only by each other and by their parents and relatives, but also by their friends, teachers and schoolmates, and neighbors. Early on, in the several very small rural communities in northwest Arkansas where they lived at various times, but most especially in Zion, where they lived for a longer period and where Phydella Hogan and Helen Fultz attended school together, their music was regarded as in some sense a prized possession of the community at large. The Gilberts, even as young girls, were appreciated as "our singers" by their fellow citizens.

Fifty Years Later

In 1989, after this understanding had been operating for more than half a century, Phydella Hogan enrolled in a folklore class at the University of Arkansas in Fayetteville. Halfway through it she approached its teacher and asked with some diffidence if her family's songbook would be of interest. It was. In hand was a large, diverse collection of songs, assembled not by a collector from outside the tradition but by a family centrally within it. And there was more. Thirty years earlier a previous folklore teacher had interested herself in their singing. She had made tapes; they were in the library. Phydella's 1989 teacher heard opportunity knock—here was a chance to explore family music traditions at a level where they actually operate. Music is at the center of these folks' lives; they have long understood themselves as musicians and they understand themselves as musicians now; by knowing their music intimately, the observer will be able to watch that music serve its function, see it earn its cherished place in their lives.

Long-time friends and neighbors were also available. The old community renewed itself every year at its reunions. Local churches had managed to survive the deaths of schools and post offices; the old hymns were still being sung by tiny, elderly congregations. Here then was opportunity again. Given sufficient patience and close attention, the outsider could study a local music tradition up close, could witness in the routines of daily life in a particular place the subtle interactions between cultural inheritance and individual need.

In my efforts to better understand this treasure—for I soon came to recognize Phydella Hogan's offer as both an intellectual challenge and a personal demonstration of trust—I gradually worked out a two-pronged method of proceeding. I wished in the first place to understand as deeply as I could the place of music in the life of a family for whom music was of central importance. And in the second place I wanted to examine the role of the Gilbert family in the local communities where their talents were appreciated and appropriated to communal interests. What, I asked at the beginning, reducing my huge task to a one-line query, does the music they claim as their own give to this family, and to the family's home communities, that all involved insist so tenaciously on its preservation, its handing on from generation to generation? To this end, I needed to know as much as I could about the family and its communities and as much as I could about the music. This was a big order on both accounts, since of the communities I knew nothing and of the family I knew only Phydella Hogan, and I knew her only as a teacher knows one student in a class of thirty. I was an outsider, not even a southerner.

Of the music I also knew little. I was a fan; only my children at bedtime know me as a performer. Folk music research was mostly new to me. It was a huge field, but this was in itself no insuperable problem. I'd gone to Romania as a Fulbright lecturer in 1985 knowing nothing of joke scholarship either. But when I found there a nation of the most sophisticated jokers imaginable, I simply collected the jokes, knowing that the scholarship would be there waiting when I returned. The situation here was similar—a scholar's paradise. Adventures of learning were ahead. The only thing to fear was hurry.

I began by conducting intensive interviews with Phydella Hogan—our initial sessions took place on October 3, 5, and 12, 1989—and built on these by reaching out to contact other family members. Helen Fultz was by far the most important, but there were many others: brothers and sisters, children and grandchildren. I never met Alma Allen, but before long I was given a copy of *A Way of Life,* the autobiographical account she'd prepared in 1952 to prevent "our grandchildren having no background." Before I was done, I'd also read Buck Gilbert's more laconic handwritten account of the same period.

In my researches on the Gilbert family, I went far beyond the subject of music narrowly conceived. I encouraged every story and taped and wrote down every anecdote. I attended family and community reunions and church services, visited and photographed old houses, cemeteries, schools, and churches. I pored over family photographs, read memoirs and poems and even recipe books. I wanted, as best I could, to know the family history, the family stories and jokes, the family songs, as a member of the family would know them. Before I finished at the end of 1995, I had interviewed scores of family members and friends, some of them many times.

At their best these times were exhilarating. They made me feel like an honorary Gilbert, a man with two families. At other times I felt fool-

Scott Family Homeplace, Mayfield, Arkansas, May 1994.
Photo by the author.

ish. And sometimes I felt both exhilarated and foolish at once. In the spring of 1994, to cite an especially prominent example, I learned that the old family homeplace in Mayfield, home to the earliest reunions the sisters remembered, was not in fact gone, bulldozed to make way for chicken houses as I'd been told. No, said Mr. Thurman Vaughan, who now owned the land. The house was empty, long derelict, but it was still there. Mr. Vaughan had lived in it himself, he said, but that was long ago, a quarter century at least.

Two days later and I'm there, hiking half a mile through fields and climbing over cattle gates and fences while Phydella waits in the car. The first thing I notice, over the shoulder of a hill, is the vine-covered stone chimney. It's much smaller than I'd imagined from Helen's and Phydella's stories, a humble place, even at its best. From halfway up the steep hill to the front, a fine view of fields and wooded hills drops away to the east, a small blacksnake curves away through the grass near the porch, and the outlines of the garden plot are still distinct down the hill to the rear.

Everything is so still, so silent. I've been busy with this study for five years, and at last I've come here, to the place Phydella and Helen remember as the taproot of the family tree, their deepest native ground.

Scott Family Homeplace, Mayfield, Arkansas, May 1994.
Photo by the author.

I have to smile—only a Schliemann hopelessly gone in idiosyncratic obsessions could be moved by such an unlikely Troy. Nobody outside this community, I remind myself, cares at all about these people or the lives they made. But I do, and I am moved, a man of fifty with a boy's pleasure, lost in a work that is play at its best. "The history of the poor," wrote Eduardo Galeano, "is either sung or lost."[41] The Gilberts weren't rich—they still aren't rich—but they sang their lives, and it's not lost. I see the rain coming, sheets of water falling out of clouds just a mile or two away. But still I stay, shooting picture after picture; Helen and Phydella and Martha and Jeanie will be interested if nobody else is that I am standing on the porch to take a photo from the same place that someone else took one sixty years ago—my favorite, of Helen and Phydella and Alma standing with instruments on the hillside with two cousins. The rains hit just as I sprint back down the hill's curve. I'm soaked and laughing by the time I reach Phydella and the car.

The second area of investigation proceeded somewhat differently. I organized the study of specific musical traditions geographically, arranging the available collections and studies in a series of concentric circles.

Working outward from the family center, I found an innermost circle, closest to the family, in figures from the immediate neighborhood, people who knew the Gilberts personally. Here, for example, were friends, neighbors, and in one long-lived instance, a former teacher who remembered the Gilberts as a singing family, always ready to supply the entertainment at parties or school programs. In Elkins, Arkansas, I was able to meet and interview Mrs. Julianne Stewart, who was Julianne Woods when she attended second grade with Phydella Gilbert at the Zion school. "Some families are like that," Mrs. Stewart said, "just musical. The Gilberts were just blessed that way. They could sing and play instruments. They all sang and played, but I was Phydella's age, so I thought she was the best. But I remember Helen was wonderful too."

Mrs. Stewart also had vivid memories of the time her father tried to talk Joe Gilbert into letting him take Phydella and Helen into Fayetteville to sing on the radio. "Kelly Brothers Lumber Company had a fifteen-minute show—my father worked for them. He wanted them—Phydella and Helen—to go to Fayetteville to play on the radio station. He'd say, 'No, Sam, they can't go. You know how people are out there.' 'Now Joe,' he said. 'I'll stay with 'em every minute and bring 'em right back home. They don't have to sing but fifteen minutes.' But you know he never would let them go. Phydella really wanted to. Helen was shy but Phydella was all ready for Nashville. That was about 1927, maybe 1928."[42]

In Farmington, Arkansas, Mrs. Mildred Bailey and her husband, Loy, had similar stories to tell. She was Mildred Ragsdale before her marriage, and like Julianne Stewart she went to school with Phydella and Helen at Zion. "The Gilberts were recognized as the musical people," Mrs. Bailey said. "The girls all sang at church, did the music for school programs. Mary Cardwell—on Sunday afternoons we would go to her house. She gave us thick cookies. Not only church songs— 'Dirty Faced Brat,' others like that. Alma came to our house—my father played violin."

Mrs. Bailey also remembered the importance of informal "play parties" in the community: "We had lots of play parties—'Sally Goodin,' 'Dusty Miller,' 'Four in the Middle.' So music was one of the entertainments we had. About the main entertainment. . . . The Gilberts weren't the only musical people—Bob Fultz, Helen's husband, he played guitar—but they were the best."⁴³ These high assessments (and also the memory of Phydella Gilbert's ambition) are echoed in comments by Mrs. Georgia Guilliams Lamb, who taught both Phydella and Helen at the Zion School in the 1920s. The Gilberts, she wrote, were "a well thought of family, very musical—played stringed instruments and sang—always ready to help with their singing and playing."

Nearly seventy years after the event, Mrs. Lamb remembered a Christmas program in which Phydella and Helen sang all the parts from behind the curtain. "They could harmonize well—best in the school. Phydella wanted out on stage to be seen. I explained that they had the most important parts. Phydella realized when the program was over from all the compliments to me and her mother." That Mrs. Lamb understood the music of the Gilberts as a form of civic service is clear from the close of her recollections: "The Gilbert family [was] always ready to

Zion School Photo, 1931–32. Phydella Gilbert is third from right, fifth row (second row from top). Helen Gilbert is just to her left, second from right. Leslie Gilbert is seated, fifth from left, front row.

Photo courtesy Phydella Hogan and Helen Fultz.

help with anything that meant something to the community. Sometimes they had their own programs at home."[44]

The memories of these neighbors offer insight into the position accorded the Gilberts by friends and neighbors in their own communities at the time when Alma, Phydella, and Helen were growing up. In Osage Mills, Sonora, Habberton, and especially at Zion, the Gilberts were recognized as "blessed that way," as always ready to provide music in support of local social life at everything from private house parties to the major school and church festivals which highlighted the community's year.

Even now, more than sixty years after these remembered days, with the Zion School closed for half a century, their former neighbors continue to rely upon the Gilberts for music at the annual Zion reunions. "We've been playing there the last three or four years," says Phydella. "Lloyd Warren arranges everything. Every year he just calls up and says, 'I hope y'all can bring the music again this year.' Last year we had a hard time. Helen couldn't come, so it was mostly me and Jeanie and Leslie. I don't sing at all, and Leslie woke up with a sore throat, so Jeanie had to carry all the singing. I hope Lloyd doesn't just leave it all to us again this year. It's getting harder and harder to get enough of us there."

"I think maybe the first one was in 1986," says Helen, joining the conversation, "in the Park [Wilson Park] in Fayetteville. We went—you remember we didn't recognize Morvin Plumlee! Otis Cardwell was running it then."

Phydella laughs in agreement, then tells a wonderful story about Otis Cardwell. "He was one of the big shots in the Zion community—school director. His wife was treasurer of the cemetery association. One year when Dad was sick he paid us to clean the cemetery grounds. Mow the grass, you know, and clip around all the headstones. When we got it done he didn't want to pay us what he paid Dad.

'I can't pay kids that much,' he says. I said, 'Why not? It took us longer but we did the same job.' He finally paid us. Then he got us to clean the schoolhouse. Paid us for that too."

Helen then comes back in, returning to Otis Cardwell's role in the first Zion reunions: "He brought in The Merits. They did a whole concert of gospel music. Nobody could talk. Lots of 'em didn't like it. We

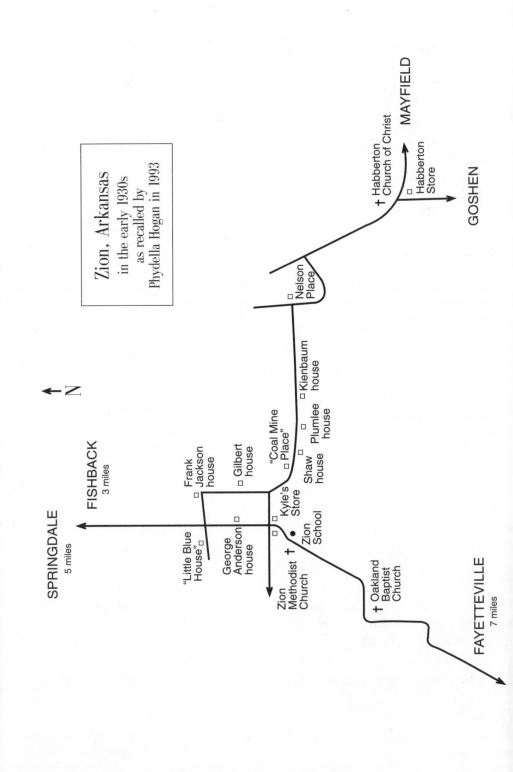

Zion, Arkansas
in the early 1930s
as recalled by
Phydella Hogan in 1993

N

SPRINGDALE
5 miles

FISHBACK
3 miles

MAYFIELD

GOSHEN

FAYETTEVILLE
7 miles

"Little Blue House"

George Anderson house

Frank Jackson house

Gilbert house

"Coal Mine Place"

Kienbaum house

Shaw house

Plumlee house

Kyle's Store

Zion Methodist Church

Zion School

Oakland Baptist Church

Nelson Place

Habberton Church of Christ

Habberton Store

like them a lot, but people came to the reunion to visit. Everybody asked Otis why he had 'em sing so long. 'I gave 'em $300,' he said. Like he had to get his money's worth. Year or two after that they put Otis in a nursing home."[45]

Here again, as on so many other occasions, a reminiscence begins and ends in music, but reaches out in the middle to fill in with other anecdotes the life that music shaped.

At Zion, too, there was another family, Mr. and Mrs. T. M. Davis and their children, whose interest in music was at least as strong as the Gilberts'. "They moved into what we called the 'Little Blue House,' a quarter mile north of the Zion store," Phydella recalls. "Same house that Mildred Bailey lived in earlier. Oliva [Davis] was about five or six then, and she wanted me to go play with her. I was about six or seven years older. They were poorer than we were, if that's possible. Oliva's father didn't work, was always taking aspirin. . . . Mrs. Davis was always working. I remember once she said she liked my hairdo."[46]

Both Mr. and Mrs. Davis appear in several of the early folksong collections from the region, and their daughter Mary Jo, the musical pride of the family, was even featured in a CBS television show devoted to Ozark folksongs in 1954. The folksong collections at the University of Arkansas include many songs from the Davis family. Oliva Davis Vaughan and Phydella Hogan have known each other for more than sixty years: "We knew the Gilberts when I was six, the first time," says Mrs. Vaughan. "Then we moved away to Fishback. We came back when I was about ten years old; we got even better acquainted with them then." Mrs. Vaughan has vivid childhood memories of hearing the Gilbert sisters sing: "When the Gilberts came over with those zithers—lay them on the table and picked them with those sticks, little match sticks, and made music that just was out of this world. It was like going into another world altogether. It was fantastic."[47]

Comparing the Davis family with the Gilbert family, one reaches a distinction based not on musicianship, and certainly not on size or alleged traditionality of repertoire, but on community standing. Mr. and Mrs. Davis, and especially Mary Jo Davis, were recorded again and again by students and collectors of folksong, but unlike the Gilberts they did not sing actively in their local neighborhood or in local churches and schools. "They didn't sing out in the community like we did," says Phydella. "But it was like once we knew a song was theirs we maybe wouldn't be so likely to sing it. I don't remember ever copying a song they did. I really don't know why. We'd play for them to sing, but if they ever had an instrument I never saw it. I liked to hear the mother sing—Lula. She was a really good singer."[48]

There is something of this distinction in Roger Abrahams' description of Almeda Riddle. Mrs. Riddle was for many years a very well known Ozark folksinger who appeared at folk festivals all over the country, sat on panel discussions with folk music scholars, and recorded several widely distributed albums of traditional music. She was also, says Abrahams, "a lifelong collector of ballads," who, if she lacked "the scholar's objectivity," had "a full measure of his fervor for authenticity." Like the Gilbert sisters, she was "a person who has virtually lived her life in songs and whose values are reflected in the choice of the songs she will sing."

At the same time, however, Mrs. Riddle described herself as regarded in her own community as "something of a 'kook.'" Abrahams reports that "many neighbors seem to think that her search for ballads is a mild nuisance, seeming to say that 'the old girl never grew up.'"[49] Almeda Riddle, then, like the Davises farther west, was a great favorite of folk music enthusiasts and scholars, but was less acclaimed at home. The Gilbert sisters were in no sense serious collectors of folksongs, and they had none of Mrs. Riddle's concern for authenticity, but they saw themselves and were seen by their neighbors as the community's singers.[50]

We All Liked All Kinds of Music

The sisters' comments on their songs make clear the varied tastes of both their teachers and their auditors. From their mother they learned sentimental ballads, grandly pathetic tales of orphaned children, perishing mothers, and betrayed, abandoned lovers, unabashed tear-jerkers their father called "Oh my God" songs. They were great hits with the girls. "The Frozen Girl," for example, is the heartrending tale of an orphan girl who freezes to death on the "marble steps" of a "rich man's hall" after the owner's brutal rejection of her plea for bread and shelter. She's his niece, as he recognizes with "eye so wild" in the morning. The girls loved it, and pestered their mother for repeated performances: "We would ask her to sing it," writes Phydella Hogan, "and then sit and bawl!" "Poor Bennie," the sad tale of a child's unsuccessful attempts to summon a drunkard father home in time for a sibling's death, was another favorite, according to Phydella: "Mother used to sing this and all us kids would cry and then beg her to sing it again." Identical tastes surfaced in the next generation, with "The Blind Child" being the great favorite of Joe Hogan, Phydella's second son: "Joe, he liked the one about the little blind girl. He couldn't have been over three or four. He'd say, 'Mommy, sing the one about the girl with the bandage on her eyes.' That's all he could think of for being blind."[51]

Such tastes were apparently not unusual. Almeda Riddle, recalling "Don't Go Out Tonight, My Darling" as the song most requested by her granddaughter Erma Dene, reported a very similar scene: "She was four years old. She'd come down there and immediately she'd ask me just as quick as she came. And she'd just sit there and the tears would just pour down her cheeks." Troubled by this response, the grandmother once refused to sing the song:

> "And I said, 'Erma Dene, I can't do that.'"
> "Why?"
> "Well, you just sit there and weep and cry. Honey I don't want to do it." She said, "Granny, I just love to feel that way." She said, "I'd rather feel that way than any way I know."[52]

Joe Gilbert's tastes were markedly different; he liked nonsense and comic songs, and he especially enjoyed pieces like "Old Grey Beard and His Leggins," which allowed his children to dramatize its actions. From their older brother Carl they learned "badman" ballads, tales of swaggering ramblers and gamblers who came mostly to grievous ends. "But Carl just loved the sentimental ballads too," adds Phydella. "We got our tune for 'My Mother Was a Lady' from him. And Thelma had a good sense of humor. She made up a lot of those little skits we did." "We all liked all kinds of music," concludes Helen.[53]

As they developed their individual leanings toward a particular instrument or type of song, all the Gilberts picked up new songs every-where, in the beginning at home and in church, a little later from teach-ers and migrant fruit pickers, relatives and neighbors, later still from records and the radio and in-laws. As the sisters grew older, then, and as they eventually married and left Arkansas for longer periods (as Alma did) or shorter periods (as Helen and Phydella did), they gained access to new songs from ever more far-flung sources. But they began at home, acquiring a local musical culture that was theirs by virtue of the time and place of their birth. Helen Fultz, for example, still associates "Empty Cot in the Bunkhouse" with a grape harvester and "guitar picker named Harold" who played a seventh chord in his accompani-ment to it. It was a C7, she wrote, once again anchoring her memory in sound, the "first time I ever knew there was such a thing."[54] "We had campers every spring and fall for the strawberries and the grape har-vest," Phydella remembers. "There was a camp house, but one couple came in the first house trailer I ever saw. Some of 'em had guitars and harmonicas. One year there was a German boy—Herman Klein, every-body called him 'Red.' Didn't speak English good, but he sang one song. All I remember is 'stein, stein, stein.'"[55]

The airwaves over northwest Arkansas were filled with music in the years when the Gilbert children were growing up, and they tuned in to new stations at every chance. "There was no REA at the time," writes Helen, "but Alex bought a wind charger and kept batteries charged up for the radio and a light or two."[56] They learned a great portion of the repertoire they regard as theirs from radio programs and popular records, and their experience offers a wealth of information to researchers interested in what has been described as "the crucial inter-action of folk tradition and electronic media in the southern United States . . . since the turn of this century." Radio stations and commer-cial recordings, initially stigmatized as destroyers of oral tradition, have in fact "merely replicated the earlier function of popular print in pre-serving and transmitting existing folksongs or in generating and dis-seminating new compositions on the folksong model."[57]

In 1924 the University of Arkansas station KFMQ began regularly scheduled broadcasts which mixed performances of popular and tradi-tional music with play-by-play coverage of football and basketball games and lectures by faculty members on such topics as "The Origin of Halloween" and "Increasing Farm Income." In September of that year, in a program broadcast specifically to test new equipment, listeners were treated to music by the Black Diamonds, a local African American string band, and in January 1925, the station carried the first of several old-time fiddlers' contests.[58]

Phydella Hogan recalls that Sam Woods had the first radio she remembers, a big, battery-operated affair that he hooked up to his truck. "Sam Woods had the first radio we heard," she says. "Mother went down with us. There was a lot of static, and on the way back she complained she couldn't understand a word they said. Said she'd a whole lot just rather listen to the girls sing."[59]

In addition to the local stations where they just missed stardom, the Gilberts listened to country music and gospel shows from such powerful stations as KWTO in Springfield, Missouri, KWKH in Shreveport, Louisiana, WSM in Nashville, Tennessee, and KVOO in Tulsa, Oklahoma. KWTO in its heyday was producing up to 156 hours of live programs each week, mostly in fifteen-minute segments staffed with everything from local talent to nationally syndicated shows. After 1948, KWKH was home to the famous *Louisiana Hayride,* while KVOO for its part was featuring Gene Autry as "the Oklahoma Yodeling Cowboy" in 1927 and by 1934 had daily shows featuring Bob Wills and the Texas Playboys.[60]

Phonograph records were a no less prized new form of entertainment in the 1920s and 1930s, and popular records were loaned among neighbors and played continually on windup Victrolas. "Billie and Alex had one after they got married, even before they got a radio," says Phydella. "You had to wind it up after every record. If you didn't it would slow down before it got to the end and sound real whiney. It didn't have a horn—those were older. The turntable was on top, and it had a cabinet down below with slots to hold the records. Old 78 rpm records, that's what it played."[61]

Similar stories can be found again and again in the biographies and early memories of hundreds of southerners (and not only southerners, remember Hank Snow) who later made careers for themselves in the fledgling music industry. The radio and phonograph records came to thousands of isolated hamlets as audible echoes of the visible highways and railroad tracks that stretched away over the horizon. Sophia Scott was not impressed, and her husband was fearful, but their children listened spellbound.

Still other songs came into the family later and from further afield. Phydella learned "The Derby Ram" and "When I Was a Little Boy" from her father-in-law. The latter song she identifies as "an old Irish ballad," and here her memory once again anchors itself in recollected sound: "when he was 'mad' or drunk his brogue became so pronounced that you could hardly understand him." "The Green Willow Tree," the Gilbert version of the traditional ballad known also as "The Sweet Trinity" or "The Golden Vanity" (Child 286), is credited to Margaret Hogan, Phydella's mother-in-law.

The Gilbert repertoire also features several songs taken from the popular magazines that circulated in their home and community. "Several of the magazines that Mother took—one called *Comfort Magazine,* it always had a page of poetry and some songs," recalls Phydella. "Dad took *Progressive Farmer* and *Grit,* and they always had a few poems and songs. And Dad also took the weekly *Kansas City Star.* . . . Then we bought all of kinds of little western stories—once in a while they'd have one in the back." Tunes were rarely printed, but their absence provoked little worry in the Gilbert family: "But anyway, there were . . . regular poetry columns and then they'd have songs, and they'd say, 'to the tune of so and so.' If it didn't have any tune, well you just made one."[62]

If it is true, then, that songs in a family tradition characteristically achieve their place in association with the persons and places of their initial learning and memorable performance, it will also be true that the tradition as a whole will be coherently legible in the other direction. Not only will the songs serve as mnemonics for an encompassing family history, but the prominence of certain types of songs will also suggest their thematic or formal importance to the family or to certain of its members. A family tradition dominated by hymns, for example, could indicate participation in church activities as a significant part of that family's life. Within such a tradition a particular liking for songs of apocalyptic content might be taken as suggesting a high family interest in the hereafter, or a theology rooted in eschatological concerns. Another family tradition especially rich in banjo or fiddle instrumentals, breakdowns, reels, hornpipes, and other dance tunes might be understood as indicating very different interests, another lifestyle altogether, a radically opposite view of the world.

The Gilbert tradition exhibits no such domination by one or even several genres; it stands out more for its breadth than for its depth. Though especially rich in comic songs and in sentimental ballads, the favorite types of the family's father and mother, the collection also contains a good representation of hymns, cowboy and western songs, and "minstrel" pieces and banjo tunes from the blackface vaudeville and medicine show repertoire. There are also railroad and other disaster songs, temperance ballads, patriotic and wartime numbers, badman and outlaw ballads, even an "Indian" version of "Way Over in the Promised Land." The inclusion of cowboy songs and railroad ballads may in large part reflect their general popularity—Almeda Riddle, born in 1898 and raised two hundred miles east of the Gilberts in Cleburne County, recalled that from "nineteen-and-four until about 1914 or '15 or even later, there were quite a few songs about the railroad. . . . You see the railroads were building and there were just lots of railroad songs. . . . Before that it must have been horses, and that's maybe why cowboy songs were popular, from the 1870's on. To be a cowboy or an engineer was a sort of a hero."[63]

But most often the family has motives in addition to such general popularity when it makes a song one of its own. The so-called "Indian" version of "Way Over in the Promised Land," for example, is attributed to Joe Gilbert, who apparently learned it from Cherokees "while he lived in what is now the state of Oklahoma but was then called Indian Territory."[64] As Jean Ritchie points out in her autobiographical memoir, *Singing Family of the Cumberlands,* the connection of song to family history may be arbitrary or even accidental, and therefore opaque to outsiders. The lovely hymn "Twilight A-Stealing," for example, always reminds her of her own sore toe, because her father once sang it while holding the injured girl in his lap. Her sister May's marriage is forever associated with the entirely inappropriate "There Was an Old Woman and She Had a Little Pig" because her sisters Jewel and Pauline, the youngest ones present, had volunteered to sing it when music was called for. "It's curious," Ritchie concludes, "how songs will take on meanings that don't really belong to them like that."[65]

Each family member, inheriting the enormous and varied family and local tradition, thus takes possession of greater or lesser parts of it in uniquely individual ways. Buck Gilbert shared his father's taste for comic songs—with his banjo talents he seems to have started as a "banjo comic" in the Uncle Dave Macon mold. Helen Fultz now describes bluegrass as her favorite music, and both Helen and Phydella remember their older sister Thelma as liking "the church songs" best. Alma shared her mother's love for the "Oh my God" ballads, though in her own later compositions she would concentrate on religious songs.

Martha Hogan Estes, Phydella's second child and only daughter, possessesing a clear memory of many songs and so proud of the family tradition that she's struggling in the 1990s to learn the banjo from her mother's teaching, nevertheless centers her own recollections upon the comic songs, associated for her with her mother and her Aunt Helen. "Our mothers were silly," she says of Phydella and Helen. "Other peoples' mothers were sedate, proper mothers. And our mothers were just clownin' around all the time. They'd put on these stupid little skits for us kids, and they sang songs to us and they'd dance with us. Crazy stuff. . . . They were just babies really—neither one of them even thirty—and all those kids to take care of. Seven kids between the two of 'em. It was pretty wild."[66]

Almeda Riddle, just after noting that "nearly all" her songs "have stories to them," qualifies the claim by remembering that "How Tedious and Tasteless the Hours," a storyless song, "has been such a comfort to me through the years. It tells no story, yet I love the song. It runs along with my experience."[67]

It runs along with my experience—this is precisely the point. From an available repertoire huge beyond the capacity of any individual each person chooses as his or her own those songs most appealing on a unique mix of aesthetic and personal grounds. From Joe Gilbert and Sophia Scott in the parental generation to Phydella, Helen, Buck, and Alma Gilbert in the second, to Martha Hogan Estes and Jeanie Fultz Miller in the third, they lay proud claim to their family heritage as one, but each then chooses individual treasures out of deeply personal experience and motive.[68]

Something of this variation in individual tastes and experience is apparent in the comments appended to the various songs in the collection, as well as in other remarks elicited in interview situations. "Jerry, Go and Ile That Car," for example, would appear to have only the most tenuous niche in the collection. Alma sends a two-verse fragment to Phydella, who adds four stanzas of her own, almost certainly located in a printed version during the period when Phydella was actively looking for fuller versions of family songs in the public library in Lincoln, Nebraska. She also adds a note, clearly addressed to Alma, that alludes to no family memories. For Helen Fultz, looking over the whole collection thirty years later, the whole exchange, song included, is simply not a part of her experience. "Never heard of it," she writes. "Washed My Hands in Muddy Water" is likewise Phydella's song, learned later than most others in the collection and learned not in Arkansas from her family or neighbors but in Nebraska from other musicians. "Old John Bull" has even less claim—it is remembered by neither Phydella nor Helen. Phydella's note surmises that "the older kids must have sung it since Billie remembered it so well." "Nighttime in Nevada," on the other hand, is not included in the family book, but it is nevertheless a great favorite of Helen's, cherished in her memory as a song associated with her courting days with her husband, Bob Fultz.

The family tradition, then, as it is recognized by its bearers, is in no sense a simple aggregate of songs known by one or another family member. Each individual knows many songs not included in the collection, and the collection includes several songs known by only one or two family members. This is especially true of religious songs, but it holds across the whole spectrum of song types. "We know it, but it's not one of ours," they respond, again and again, when asked about well-known absent pieces. The fit between individual and group is imperfect, and no stable criterion exists to determine the degree of general acceptance requisite for inclusion in the collection, but the family as a group operates within the available repertoire much as its individual members do, out of a nearly infinite variety of motives taking possession of some songs while ignoring others. They give their tradition stability over time by making an ancestor's previous love of a song a primary motive for their own claim upon it. The tradition, at last, must be recognized as chosen, as held dear, the equivalent in spirit of the homeplace or the family Bible. These are not just songs. These are our songs.

Carl's Songs

If in Martha Estes's memories the Gilbert tradition is seen operating forward from Phydella and Helen, just as in theirs it operates forward from Joe Gilbert and Sophia Scott, it can just as well be examined with retrospective interests in mind. Bringing together all the songs associated with a given family member, for example, may not merely exhibit that person's taste in songs, but also offer a glimpse into deeper waters. Examining the Gilbert collection in this manner one might note, for example, that three songs are specifically noted as learned from Carl, eldest son of Joe and Sophia, older brother to the sisters. "Bad Companions" and "Rovin' Gambler" suggest their generic associations clearly enough by their titles alone, but "Home Sweet Home" requires a closer look. The "sweet home," it turns out, is yearned after from exile by a cowboy who, speaking to his mates around a campfire "On Franklin's range one night," tells the sad story of two friends whose fight over a "pretty little girl" ends when "I struck him with my knife." The song ends in grim summary: "So now you know the reason / Why I'm compelled to roam. A murderer of the deepest / Is far from home, sweet home."

In "Bad Companions" the basic scenario is similar, featuring a narrator whose happy home in Pennsylvania, complete with "beautiful hills" and "kind old mother," is destroyed by dislike for the father and a restless yearning for "far rambling." But time here is later than in "Home Sweet Home." Roaming days are over, having come to their unsurprising end on the gallows after an interval of drinking and sinning "both day and night" leads to another fatal stabbing, in this event not of a rival but of the "fair young maiden" herself. The "Rovin' Gambler" is a much more pleasant fellow, having only his wide travels in common with the other protagonists. He's "gambled out in Washington" as well as "down in Spain," but now he's evidently planning to "gamble my last game" by "going back to Georgia" to settle down with a "pretty little girl."

An older brother, then, is remembered by his sisters in connection with three songs. All have roving and roaming at their center, all involve the narrator with a beloved woman who is left behind in one instance and killed in another, all remember a happy homeland either with yearning or plans to return.

With such music in mind, one turns to what is known of biography. Carl Gilbert was always by virtue of age alone a vague and distant figure in the childhood memories of Phydella and Helen. By 1923, when the latter was two and the former five, Carl was twenty, married, and gone. But Alma was only nine years his junior, and she worshipped

Carl Gilbert, Montana, late 1920s.
Photo courtesy Bette Allen Curtis.

him. "Carl was my 'big' brother and I adored him," she wrote, remembering the thrilling adventures they shared at Osage Mills in 1918. "Each Saturday morning he rode his bike a mile up the road to Piercy's for milk. He not only carried a gallon of milk, but allowed me to ride on the handlebars as well" (*A Way of Life,* 16).

But these shared childhood memories of Carl were ended soon enough. In the summer of 1922, at nineteen, he worked the Kansas wheat harvest, sending money home to the family, and early in 1923 he married a local girl named Edith Lemming. By the end of the year they had a daughter. Six months later, without warning, while his wife was visiting her parents, Carl disappeared, simply vanished without a trace. Nobody knew he was going, nobody knew where he'd gone.

Nearly a decade later, with Edith dead of pneumonia and the country deep in the Great Depression, a neighbor noticed a magazine advertisement placed by a woman named Cora in Conrad, Montana, seeking the "whereabouts of Carl W. Gilbert." Alma answered the ad, and the reply made it clear that Carl had struck again, marrying, fathering a child, and disappearing almost immediately after the birth. "I knew, before I had read the first paragraph," wrote Alma, "that Cora had been married to my brother Carl. But he had left her, too; left her with a three-week-old baby, who was now past three years! My hopes went plunging down and my heart ached for the misery he was causing, and for the turmoil his mind must be in to do these things" (*A Way of Life,* 139).

Cora soon came to Arkansas for a visit, bringing her young son, Wayne, recognized by all as "the spitting image of Carl" (*A Way of Life,* 140). The women and their children developed friendships, but still there was no trace of Carl. That would wait almost another decade, until the early 1940s, during the Second World War. Sophia Scott Gilbert, long in poor health, died in 1938 without ever seeing her oldest child again. Alma and Helen, joining the great Depression-era tide of Arkie and Okie migrations, had moved west with their husbands and children to Calipatria, California, in the Imperial Valley. Then, one day, a postcard arrived from Carl. He was living to the north in Paso Robles, near San Francisco, and had married yet again. Alma and Alex Allen managed a visit, coping with wartime gasoline rationing by signing up to pick fruit, but the reunion was a disappointment. They stayed only one night. "We had drifted too far apart to ever be close again," Alma wrote. "My throat ached and my eyes filmed with tears as we drove away, for I had been disillusioned. My idol had feet of clay. For once, I was glad that Mama couldn't hear him talk. His excuses were too thin" (*A Way of Life*, 158).

In 1950, Carl did return to Arkansas with his wife and new family. He "stayed with me for awhile," writes Phydella, "helping me when Dad had a bad illness and almost died." He stayed about a year, living mostly in nearby Bentonville. "Carl tried to make peace with Dad," Phydella continues, "and waited on him very patiently while he was ill. But Dad didn't really forgive him for leaving—especially for the grief he had caused Mother."[69]

Carl died in 1953 in New Mexico, and Alma, loyal sister even to the last, made the trip to his funeral. Her brother may have disappointed her, but he retained his central importance. Alma's autobiographical memoir closes upon her thoughts at Carl's funeral. The other sisters, Helen and Phydella, who knew him less well, are generally more forgiving in their recollections. Some blame is displaced to his first mother-in-law, who evidently judged him harshly for his inability to gain steady employment.

Alma Allen with daughter Bette, 1948–49.
Photo courtesy Bette Allen Curtis.

A letter written by her, telling Carl not to return for Edith after her summer visit, is cited by the younger sisters as the immediate cause of his initial departure. "Mama saw the letter," says Helen. Even his second disappearance is mitigated in Helen's and Phydella's retellings by Carl's apparent fears of illegal attachments. "He didn't know Edith had divorced him and then died," says Phydella. "He was afraid he was a bigamist." Joe Gilbert, in his daughters' memories, also gets some responsibility for Carl's troubles. His son evidently had a talent for drawing, but the father would not hear of art school or lessons. The two fought bitterly, and the father apparently predicted with some heat that the son would never amount to anything, that he would never "stay with anything" long enough to make a success.

It's clear enough that bad things happened to Carl—terrible and troubling things. He violated more than once the most deeply held values. He abandoned mothers and children. But his sisters, even Alma, the most grieved and the most inclined to judge Carl harshly, struggle to understand and forgive. They seek, with generosity of spirit, to understand "the turmoil his mind must be in to do these things" (*A Way of Life,* 139).

Buck Gilbert's handwritten memoir mentions Carl at several points, usually in unflattering terms. One of Carl's brief visits home is described at some length: "Carl stayed most of the winter, and Mr. Welch gave us a job cleaning the brush from a small patch of land that he wanted to farm. We were supposed to cut all the brush, put it in piles, and burn it. While burning the brush we became careless I guess, for the fire got out of control and set the woods on fire. It burned up about a quarter mile of a rail fence. I think my brother's motto was, 'Never hang around when you can see trouble comin', so he took off again. My Dad and I had to split several hundred rails and re-build that fence."[70]

Knowing this much of Carl's life, and knowing too these variations in family interpretation, one senses again the vital role played by the songs. "Home Sweet Home" and "Bad Companions" confront the sins of their protagonists squarely enough. Both speakers sing of wasted or hollowed lives. But both are also finally presented as innocent at the core, if only in their recognition of error and their acceptance of their fate. The restlessness basic to "Bad Companions," the itch to ramble, is understood as a fundamental flaw, removing the innocent from the protecting influence of his virtuous home and throwing him into the fallen world with its tempting depravities and vicious associates. It is comforting, even now, for his sisters to sing these songs, and especially to associate them with Carl. They explain a brother's fall, deflecting guilt, supplying that traditional Christian redemption which finds its origins in remorse. "Rovin' Gambler" even adds a plan for eventual return.

But what about Carl himself? After all, the sisters did not simply attach these songs to his name themselves in a retrospective effort to comprehend his behavior by applying familiar models. That would make sense, but according to Helen's and Phydella's recollections Carl taught them these songs. They were introduced into the family repertoire by Carl; he sang them, made them a part of his self-presentation on his return visits. These are more than new songs, they say. They assert a newfound, chosen identity: "This is who I have become."

The family songs, then, not only aided the sisters in their continuing attempts first to understand their brother, and later to forgive him, but also contributed, in this instance disastrously, to Carl's attempt to create and project himself. Singing "Bad Companions" or "Home Sweet Home" to his admiring younger sisters, the young man could experience vicariously the heady feeling of being a rambling man, a wanderer, an outlaw. He was already, by virtue of age and wide experience, a figure of impressive weight. He'd been to Kansas, after all, had worked in the wheat harvest. By the standards his sisters applied, he'd seen the world. Back home, strumming his guitar and singing these songs, he could summon to himself the appealing and appalling trappings of the dashing young man marked by doom, the enormous, mythic aura of every uprooted wanderer from Cain to Jesse James. Singing a song, he could try on a life. Subsequent events suggest he must have liked the fit.

Dear Charlie

Even a single song, then, may be understood differently and turned to different private purposes by different singers and listeners, each with his or her own yearnings, his or her own perplexities. The same songs that once added swagger to Carl's life now bring comfort to his sisters. Comprehended in this way as a repertoire with various parts played in comparative and contrastive tension one against the other, the songs of family and regional tradition emerge as something much deeper and more fundamental than agents of entertainment. They become guides for living, teachers, their characters and situations seen as offering lessons to contemporary experience, their resolutions understood as offering advice for contemporary action.

Jeanie Fultz Miller, talking one afternoon in her mother's kitchen, provided an especially articulate description of how the music could be understood as providing moral guidance, as offering a model of life as it should be lived: "That old country music, before it started to be the style to sing about illicit love affairs all the time, that was the way people out here in the country lived, most people anyway. Or tried to live. You maybe couldn't live up to them. The mothers in the songs were so perfect, you know. But you could try. It was kind of like an ideal. 'Little Green Valley,' 'Blue Ridge Mountain Home'—those were my favorites. 'The Girl I Loved in Sunny Tennessee.' That's why I loved those songs so much. I was living in that world. It's still precious to me, like a square of sunlight on the kitchen floor."[71]

No more perfect illustration could be found, despite the casual circumstances, of what has been characterized as the "metonymic referentiality" of oral performance, even at its most humble. Jeanie Miller, attempting in casual conversation to communicate uncasual values, first names the songs she loves as precious and then says they function "like a square of sunlight on the kitchen floor" to summon the cherished "world" she experienced as a child and still holds today as "kind of like an ideal." Her auditor, she can only hope, shares enough of her tradition to understand her image as iconic, as bearing more than purely denotative sense. The "square of sunlight" is more than geometry, more than weather. It is illumination, epiphany. It summons an integral world. For Jeanie Miller, and for those who share her tradition, the smallest phrase from a song she loves has the power to restore not only a remembered living person and singing voice but also the roomful of listeners, the house of their gathering, the weather of a long-ago day. The "square of sunlight" restores the whole kitchen.

Bob Fultz and Jeanie
Miller, Mayfield
Church, May 1994.
Photo by the author.

Communication is another matter. That world is communicated if and only if "the artist and the perceiver know how to interpret the simple forms as the complex reality they stand for."[72] Without such knowledge, the immense whole of shared experience too casually called tradition, the songs she loves are only noise, their music a monotonous shrillness grating to the ear, their lyrics a melodramatic surge of cliches. From the most casual conversations to the most formal performances, oral art depends at last upon intimacy.

The language of recent historicist scholarship, understanding the family's musical heritage as Jeanie Miller understands it, would also recognize the Gilbert songs as "ideological" in the sense that they are involved in the very production of meaning, the elaboration of a structure of interpretive categories for the articulation of specific ideas and attitudes. The Gilberts employ their songs as English Renaissance thinkers employed "religious discourse" for the discussion of issues far beyond specifically theological matters. As Debora K. Shuger, in her rich study *Habits of Thought in the English Renaissance,* observes: "Religion during this period supplies the primary language of analysis. It is the cultural matrix for explorations of virtually every topic: kingship, selfhood, rationality, language, marriage, ethics, and so forth. . . . That is what it means to say that the English Renaissance was a religious culture."[73]

Their songs provide the Gilberts with just such a culture, just such an ideology or discourse. They are more than food for thought; they are the very atoms of thinking. Manipulated and combined in infinitely varied ways with the overlapping but differently codified lessons of church, school, and home, they serve at last as aids in the organization of lives, the development and articulation of personalities, the shaping and direction of perception and judgment. If young Carl Gilbert found a career of glamour and disaster by identifying with the homeless wanderers of his favorite badman songs, his niece Jeanie Miller, making her own very different choices from the music that was her birthright, shaped a deeply rooted life centered in pastoral and familial values. The songs are for the Gilberts and their neighbors a vehicle for the articulation of subjects far outside strictly musical concerns. This, at least in part, is what it means to say that theirs is a folk musical culture.

A straightforward example may help clarify the point. The sisters' collection includes a spurned girl ballad they call "Dear Charlie," and attributed somewhat hesitantly to "Aunt Myrtie," their mother's sister. The speaker is the spurned girl herself, recently jilted by mail. Charlie's letter reports his new love for a certain Miss Gray, returns his old love's letters, and evidently seeks the return of a ring, a picture, and his own love notes. "Dear Charlie" is the girl's proud, wounded, finally obliging answer. "Here is your picture, dear Charlie," says one verse, adding that its faded condition is the result of frequent kissing. "Here is your ring, dear Charlie," opens another, which goes on to ask that Miss Gray receive a new band or at least be told the returned one's prior history. But earlier than these verses is the second, dealing with the letters: "Here are your letters, dear Charlie / I burned mine as they came. / And I hope without reading them over / You'll submit them at once to the flame."

"Dear Charlie" is a silly enough song, certainly, thoroughly predictable both in its contents and their overwrought expression. But that would seem to be a point very much in its favor, given another young lady in a similar situation—like Alma Gilbert in the summer of 1925, in Zion, Arkansas. Her future husband, Alex Allen, is a new boy just arrived in town, he and his older brother Burl have access to the family "Model T Ford touring car," and Alma needs to provoke a rupture with a current beau, suddenly understood as awkwardly in the way. "I had seen John with another girl," she wrote fifty years later, "and he had seen me in the car with Thelma, Burl and Alex; that was enough to start on. John sent word to me by a mutual friend to return his gifts— a bracelet, several strings of beads, and his letters." Alma's account does not specify what she did with the beads and the bracelet, but it does say what she did to the letters. "But it hurt my pride," she continues, "to be asked to return his letters, so I burned them, one at a time, under the wash kettle" (*A Way of Life*, 92–93).

They burn different letters, of course, and Alma's deliberate sabotage of her relationship with John bears only limited comparison with the situation in "Dear Charlie." But a basic consonance seems nonetheless clear. "Dear Charlie" provided Alma with a model for the last acts of a courtship gone bad. No doubt there were other models, other guides to the actions and attitudes proper and appropriate to a young woman living through such a moment and required to act the part. But the image in the mind's eye of love letters curling in flame, of once-cherished pages flaring and then turning black and cold—these must have seemed powerful tokens of irreversibility and finality, a suitably dramatic and flamboyant gesture. Confronted by new experience, called upon to act an unfamiliar role, Alma found guidance in the songs of her family tradition.

Similar instances from other sources suggest that this use of song is by no means unusual. Jean Ritchie's account of her youth in the mountains of southeastern Kentucky describes a fiddler boyfriend who announces his arrival at a festive molasses-skimming party by playing "Goin' to See My Truelove" as he approaches. The song meshes perfectly with the event—on a cold night a young man is on his way to a party where his sweetheart waits; as he plays the tune other people sing. "The days are long and lonesome, / The nights are a-gettin' cold; / I'm goin' to see my truelove / 'Fore I get too old." As Ritchie tells the story, the fact that the song precedes the boyfriend gives her time to prepare herself for his appearance. "Well, when I heard Cleve's fiddle playing that tune, I began to brighten up. I must have looked better because Jim Hall came over right then and asked me to dance with him. It made me proud to be dancing when Cleve came into the firelight. I was glad I wasn't standing with the little children, looking on."[74]

Conversations in Song

All I've got is a red guitar,
three chords, and the truth.
    —Bob Dylan/U2

Remembering, in the winter of 1990, the songs they sang as girls for their neighbors at Zion, Phydella and Helen make vividly clear the important role of music in local discourse on the battle of the sexes, that most enduring of subjects. The account belongs mostly to Helen, with Phydella providing corroboration and detail:

> HF: These people were mostly Andersons and Jacksons—Jewel and Frank Jackson, Raymond and Nola Anderson, Fern Anderson, Bill Anderson. . . . On the weekend they'd get us to come down like on Saturday night, you know, and sing for 'em.

> PH: If they had company they always had us down. Now at that time we just had the banjo. We played and we sang.

> HF: Their husbands would, they liked to have you to sing these songs, you know, that made women sound like they were hard to put up with. So they'd have us sing about the song "Twenty-One Years"—that was new then—where the man went to jail because of something the woman did. Well, then the women turn around and have us sing "Frankie and Johnny" because that put the men in a bad light.

> PH: They liked "Seven Years with the Wrong Woman." And then we finally learned that "Seven Years with the Wrong Man," remember that?[75]

Here the singers are young girls, singing for older couples who include the songs in a jocular, ongoing banter. But within this harmonious context a discussion is conducted, a finally abstract consideration of the nature of men and the essence of women is achieved. Varied perspectives are deployed, competing arguments put forward, and the whole exchange is accomplished in large part by means of songs.[76] The young singers in this instance serve their community as spokespersons for *both* points of view on a current issue. Their own positions count for little or nothing in the moment of their performance, however much they may be inclined to later, more private considerations of the issue. They are for their neighbors a living, portable jukebox, playing favorite tunes upon request.

The Gilbert family singing tradition, rich in songs offering differing and even opposing viewpoints on a variety of subjects, thus presents a repertoire fundamentally different from the "distinctive personality" William McCarthy's careful study finds revealed in the "bitterly subversive songs" of Agnes Lyle, the great Scottish singer who was William Motherwell's most prolific informant. In place of the "axiological unity" apparent in Agnes Lyle's repertoire, the Gilbert tradition exhibits a variety better suited to dialogue.[77]

Such differences are hardly surprising. The repertoire of a single individual, after all, is likely to reflect "the life experiences, preferences, prejudices, and tastes involved in the formation of the personality, and the entire cultural context as assimilated by the personality."[78] Though greatly removed both in space and time from Agnes Lyle's early-nineteenth-century Renfrewshire, the repertoires of individual Ozark singers would seem to reveal no less intimate interactions of milieu, tradition, and personality. Roger Abrahams, for example, after his own intensive work with Almeda Riddle, noted that "if a theme or situation conforms to her standards of interest and beauty she will learn every song she encounters which explores the subject. This is why she sings so many dying soldier, cowboy, graveyard, railroad, and parted-lover ballads, shape-note and brush arbor songs. Her repertoire is all of a piece."[79]

Lucille Burdine and William B. McCarthy, in their study of Newton County sisters Susie Campbell and Julie Hefley, noted that Julie, "the romantic one," remembered children's songs and nonsense pieces, while

Susie, "the more conservative of the two, and Pentecostal," recalled disaster songs like "The Miner's Child" and "The Great Titanic." "How much like each one of them!" conclude Burdine and McCarthy.[80] Their study, brief as it is, is an excellent investigation of an Ozark family song tradition in many ways comparable to that of the Gilberts, though Burdine and McCarthy are interested primarily in "the way that the sisters divided their common inheritance," with each one making "distinctive and selective" choices in forming a personal repertoire out of a family tradition.[81]

The family tradition itself, on the other hand, reflecting the individual tastes of various members, will characteristically exhibit a greater variety. And when the family is recognized in its home community as "a singing family" and called upon for entertainment at various formal and informal community events, its repertoire will show still greater diversity, will come to reflect the tastes of the wider community. This, for the Gilberts, is very much a matter of conscious responsibility. Some songs you sing because you like them; other songs you sing because your neighbors like them and ask you to sing them. Phydella Hogan, for example, still remembers "Utah Carrol" in particular as a song in this category. "We hated to sing 'Utah Carrol' because it was so long, and the tune was so monotonous. But everybody wanted it! 'Oh, sing "Utah Carrol,"' they'd say. Because it was a complete song, probably. So we sang it a lot, mostly when we had company."[82]

One other song, "Jealous Lover," is especially interesting in this regard. The sisters loved to sing it; they found the tune lovely. But their sense of the song's overheated pathos was embarrassing. "We got to thinking how silly it was for that girl to just get down on her knees and beg instead of fighting him or trying to run away," says Phydella. "But we liked the tune of it—it was beautiful. But those old tragic songs were much in demand, especially by the older people."[83] Embarrassing lyrics, a beautiful tune, great local demand—"Jealous Lover" poses a problem for Zion's youthful singers. They solve it by singing the song in two ways—in the community, for the older people who loved it for its pathos, they sing it straight; at home, for themselves, they make fun of it, make it in fact a parody of the whole class of "Oh my God" songs derided by their father.

In all these varied instances one sees music consciously employed to guide experience, communicate feelings, carry on conversations. Knowing as much as possible of such instances may help the songs themselves appear less preposterous than they must seem when they appear one after another in collections, stripped of their context and printed baldly on a page. The songs treasured by the Gilberts and other families are indeed well stocked with dying and orphaned children and mothers, suicidal and broken-hearted lovers, slain soldiers, penitent drunks, and mangled engineers. But children and mothers really do die. Jessie Lee died. Thelma died after a miscarriage. Lovers really do sometimes meet terrible ends. Carl's first wife, Edith, died. Soldiers really do die. Alma's son Roy Lee died in Korea. Workers really are injured and killed. Joe Gilbert's brother Jess was killed in an Oklahoma oilfield accident.

Edith Lemming, according to Alma's report, "had never taken care ·of her health since Carl left. She would walk out in the snow and sleet with her head bare, as if unfeeling, uncaring" (*A Way of Life,* 121). Even the language here suggests the stark, vivid world of story and ballad. Edith Lemming wanders astray, distracted, an Ozark Ophelia, a character out of "A Little Rosewood Casket." It's not farfetched to imagine her local and regional traditions as showing Edith Lemming how to be heartbroken, how to die, and showing her neighbors at the same time how to understand and interpret her death.

Worst of all, perhaps, in the list of tragedies so prominent in popular song, is the fact that people really do kill themselves. Joe Gilbert took his own life. An ailing man of seventy-seven, fearing himself a burden on his already hard pressed daughter, he shot himself in 1953 in Phydella's Fayetteville home. Grieving and devastated, his children gathered and buried him beside his wife in Zion cemetery, sang him away with "Church in the Wildwood." It was a lovely song, their father's favorite, but it wasn't what he'd wanted.

Years before, as several of his children later remembered, Joe Gilbert had expressed his delight in his son Buck Gilbert's banjo version of "Blue Bells of Scotland" by saying he'd rather have it played at his funeral than any other song he knew. "He said it several times," says Phydella. "'All the music I want at my funeral is for Buck to play "Blue Bells" as they put me in the grave.'"[84] Helen Fultz's written reminiscence is almost

Grave of Joe and Sophia Gilbert, Zion, Arkansas.
Photo by the author.

identical on this point, even to the phrasing, except she remembers the desired song as "Cripple Creek": "Dad would say, 'I'd rather have Buck play "Cripple Creek" at my funeral than any other music I know.'"

Both sisters go on to comment on the fact that their father's wishes went unremembered in the grief of the day. "He [Buck] didn't, of course," writes Helen. "Things like that just aren't done. What a shame."[85] "I don't think Buck could have done it anyway," says Phydella. "He was grieving too hard. I was so out of it then I didn't even think of it. Nobody did."[86] Here, for the only time in all the Gilbert stories, was shock so great, sorrow so deep, that for the moment not even music could heal or even help.

But the central point here remains the obvious one: a more intimate knowledge of the lives of people who sing and cherish a body of songs enables a better appreciation not only of the songs themselves, but also of their creative deployment and utilization by the singers. People act their lives as players, and build the play from every drama that they know. The Gilberts know songs, and they live their lives in a world made articulate in their music.

We Would Laugh at Them

In several instances the idiosyncratic manipulation of texts by performers is strikingly obvious. "Jealous Lover," already discussed as a song sung by the Gilbert sisters in response to requests, is an especially lurid murdered-girl ballad singled out by Vance Randolph as a good example of the ability of Ozark singers to take the melodrama of their songs with total seriousness. In the introduction to his huge *Ozark Folksongs* collection, Randolph recalls a memorable performance of the song by a "very old fellow" who interrupts his rendition just after the maddened lover plunges his knife into the "snow white bosom" of his beloved:

> "Oh Gawd!" he shrilled, "the son-of-a-bitch! Dod *rot* such a critter, anyway!" Our host, a hard-faced moonshiner with at least one killing to his credit, muttered some similar sentiment, and there were grunts of sympathetic approval from several other listeners. It would have been a hardy "furriner" indeed who showed the slightest flicker of amusement at that moment.[87]

Well, the Gilbert sisters are in no sense "furriners" to Ozark song tradition, and no doubt they would have known the appropriate responses had they been present for the old man's performance. But within their own family they make fun of this song, finding it ludicrously overdrawn. They especially ridicule the final, moralizing stanza. "We always dragged out that last line, about 'Beware of jealousy,'" says Helen.[88] "Jealous Lover" is not alone in receiving such parodying treatment. "We'd pretend to cry over poor Little Blossom and the others," says Phydella, "but we would laugh at them, we really did. We really dramatized 'em sometimes, just so they would sound sillier. They were meant to be tragic, definitely they were meant to be tragic. But we couldn't consider them tragedy."[89]

With other songs, only a single line might be rendered humorous by its tortured or inverted syntax, or even a single word could provoke laughter by its seeming exaggeration or inconsistency. "I remember that song though," remarks Phydella, speaking of "The True Young Maid," "that we used to always make fun of was the 'young maid all *in* the garden.' That wouldn't have been sad because it ended up that he was her sweetheart after all. But the words are so silly, in order to get their rhythm and their rhyme in there."⁹⁰ "A Spanish Cavalier" is another song that strikes the sisters as silly, this time for an opening line picturing a gallant who "stood in his retreat." This seems to them oxymoronic—if he's retreating he's not standing; if he's standing he's not retreating. In at least one instance, Phydella's taste for parody inspired her to the composition of an entire song, "The Old Grass Widow," as an "answer" to the already comic "A Stern Old Bachelor."

The dividing line, then—the edge where pathos collapses into bathos—is a wavering, shifting boundary, varying according to situation and individual taste. A collection of tough mountaineers is deeply moved by "Jealous Lover," but a trio of schoolgirls finds the same song comic. Music may serve to elevate life and, by its power, lift character to archetype, casting a heroic or romantic glow over a quotidian event. Observing themselves in song's rigged mirror, a harvest laborer and an Ozark village girl confer high drama upon their lives. But other singers may then turn the tables, using mockery and burlesque to bring the hero back to earth. Here, by simple exaggeration of the song's rhetorical artifice, the schoolgirls tip pathos toward bathos, trade melodrama in for laughter.

She changed her mind after examining the sheets of both songs, but Phydella suggested once in conversation that "Sweet Violets" was a "parody" of "Sweet Bunch of Daisies." She was right, certainly, to withdraw the suggestion of a one-on-the-other influence, but her original sense of the one song's comic exploitation of the other's generic expectations was surely sound. It remains a delicate matter, this ongoing, continually shifting interaction of person and culture, the shaping and reshaping of each by the other. But the point to be emphasized, again, is mutual interdependence, a culture itself recreated and continually redirected even as it is tenaciously preserved by the very persons it in turn nurtures and develops.

The Drunkard's Dream

The Gilbert sisters also know and sing several well-known temperance songs in addition to "Little Blossom"—"Poor Bennie," "The

Drunkard's Dream," and "I'm Alone, All Alone." Without exception these are attributed to their mother. "She was a young woman back when that was going on," says Phydella.

> Well, I remember some Prohibition, but I mean she was with the first movement that started to get it. She was in that era. I don't know that she did any active work. But I'm sure she would have been for it because she was a teetotaler.
>
> Dad was not a teetotaler, but he didn't really approve of getting drunk. He said if you can't use a little temperance, well you just leave it alone. But Mother was a teetotaler. I remember my sister [Alma] telling me when she [their mother] had pneumonia and almost died. They thought she was going to die. Dad said, "I know she'd have a fit if she knew I was giving it to her," but he mixed up a toddy and gave it to her a spoon at a time. It brought her back.[91]

Like almost all his neighbors, Joe Gilbert made his own wine for home consumption. After all, grapes were a major crop in the region, attracting migrant pickers during harvest times. The Gilbert home at Zion stood across the road from a vineyard, and they had their own arbors on each side as well. From their teetotaling mother, then, the Gilbert girls learn several temperance songs. But they are not ardent prohibitionists, and in fact at least Alma was known to enjoy an occasional brandy. What use do they have for these songs? What audience wishes to hear them? The answers are something of a surprise, and the story of their singing is a complex tale.

Thelma and Alma Gilbert, sisters, married Burl and Alex Allen, brothers, dashing suitors with access to the Model T mentioned before in connection with the pyre of love letters. The brothers operated a small coal mine and lived together with their young wives in a house that came with the mining lease and is known in the family as the Coal Mine Place. "They divided it right down the middle," remembers Phydella. Babies soon came. Thelma's son Walter and Alma's son Lloyd were both born in 1928. Alma had another boy, Roy Lee, called Teeny, in 1930, followed by a girl, Bette, in 1931. A radio was purchased, then a record player, and soon new songs by the Carter Family and Jimmie Rodgers were a part of the family repertoire.

But then, just after Teeny's birth, in May 1930, tragedy struck the Coal Mine Place. Thelma died suddenly, some three weeks after suffering a miscarriage with her second child. The family was devastated, and Alma, especially, was overwhelmed: "I was not yet twenty," she wrote, "with two boys and a girl of my own, a nephew hardly four years old, and two men to keep house for." Her husband, Alex, and his now-widowed brother Burl worked hard at their own tasks, but they had little understanding of the burden placed on the household's only woman. "Alex and Burl," wrote Alma, "never once realized how much there was to do, and how hard the ways of doing it. They had their work, and I had mine. It was the way of life at that time, in that place" (*A Way of Life,* 127).

That way of life included occasional poker games, held at the Coal Mine Place. "Alex used to have some of the men come over and they'd play cards," remembers Phydella.

Alex and Alma Allen with Lloyd, Roy, and Bette, Zion, Arkansas, 1932.
Photo courtesy Phydella Hogan and Helen Fultz.

They'd go in the kitchen and get up their card game, and somebody always brought a jug of wine. Everybody around there made
wine, 'cause they had grapes, you know. They'd get to giggling
and drinking their wine, getting a little tipsy in there. . . . We'd
get to singing, me and Helen and Billie, off in the other room,
you see. If we stopped singing, they'd wonder why we quit. We'd
sing those temperance songs, just for pure meanness. Didn't make
any impression on them at all! They just thought it was a pretty
song. Billie'd say, "Let's sing that one." We'd sing it—not a word
out of them. "Boy, that's a pretty song," if they said anything. We
sang every temperance song we knew, just for meanness.[92]

Just for meanness—the phrase recurs in Phydella's telling, but for
her the whole incident is comic and lighthearted. She relates it with
gusto and laughter, presents it as a moment of happy solidarity, singing
womenfolk teasing tipsy menfolk at their play. She was fourteen, maybe
fifteen, then, unmarried, not yet a mother, not yet saddled with a drinking husband of her own. Helen was younger still, perhaps eleven. There
is some evidence, however, that Alma, only six years older but worlds
apart in her experience, may have brought more complex feelings to
these performances. They are not specifically mentioned in her autobiographical reminiscence, but issues at the heart of temperance songs
are given prominent attention.

Alex Allen liked to drink, and he absented himself from his wife
and young children with some frequency on Saturday nights. His wife
makes clear she didn't like it: "Alex was young; too young to want to
stay home with a wife and baby on a Saturday night. The 'boys' were
in town or over at 'Uncle Pete's place' having fun, drinking, playing
poker or shooting craps. I raged and stormed, but on Saturday nights I
went to bed—alone" (*A Way of Life,* 119–20). Sundays, and music,
brought relief and even reconciliation: "By the time church was over
I was once again at peace with the world. I was young and optimistic.
By nightfall I could get my guitar and was as apt to sing 'The Drunkard's
Dream' as I was 'Melancholy Baby.' At the second song, Alex had got-
ten over my sharp words of the early morning or night before, and joining in, together we sang 'Let the Rest of the World Go By' and 'Let
the Lower Lights Be Burning'" (*A Way of Life,* 120–21).

A happy ending, certainly, the young wife successfully coping with "the way of life at that time, in that place." Solaced by her babies, buoyed by her church, consoled by the songs which in their singing quite literally bring the estranged couple back together, she's recovered from Saturday night, ready for Monday morning. A convincing story, certainly, and there seems no reason to doubt it. The detail of "the second song," in fact, may contain a hint of the narration's fundamental accuracy and also an indication of the event's greater complexity, a suggestion of continuing contest within the mended walls.

"The Drunkard's Dream," for one thing, may seem a strange choice for a wife eager to reestablish domestic harmony with a hung over and recently denounced husband. It is a blissful song, certainly, opening with the narrator noting a "happy change" in a certain Edward, soon revealed as the title's dreaming drunk. You look "so neat and clean," the narrator marvels, adding that "I have not seen you drunk about." The encounter evidently catches Edward in the company of his family, too, as the surprised narrator notes that "they look well," even as he recalls that "You used did use them strange." Edward then takes over and attributes his new look to a terrible dream in which he staggered home from a bender to find his wife dead, his children weeping, and "strangers in the room." The drunk cries out his belated promise of reform over the corpse—"Oh, Mary, speak to me once more. / I'll never give thee pain."—and on this cry wakes from his nightmare to find Mary "weeping o'er my bed."

"The Drunkard's Dream," then, bases its vision of family harmony entirely on the husband's reform. He's quit drinking, cleaned up his appearance, and anchored his social life firmly in his family. Everybody's happy. But in the mouth of Alma on a Sunday evening, the song becomes not so much the drunkard's dream as the drunkard's wife's dream. Its singing in this context is hard to imagine as anything other than the battle of Saturday night continued by different means. Her husband, we note, joins in for "the second song." The temperance songs at the poker games, in the light cast by these meditations, would acquire a similar edge, be something in addition to "meanness." They would be the small, indirect voice of protest, its words and thoughts validated by tradition, lifted to an unintrusive but persistent articulation by singing female voices.

Five Generations—Phydella Hogan, *center,* with daughter Martha Estes, *right,* granddaughter Mary Ellen Worton, *top,* great-granddaughter Selena Worton, *second from left,*
and great-great-grandson, Dagan Worton. Family reunion, Goshen, Arkansas, 1994.
Photo by Jim Borden.

These voices are a continuing presence in Gilbert family memories.
A full generation later, the memories of Phydella's daughter Martha Estes
include barn dances hosted by her father: "I remember Daddy having
barn dances, and Mom played for his dances. Daddy always drank—you
know a party to him was drinking and lots of noise and everything. Mom
didn't like that, but the playing—she tolerated it because she liked that,
she liked the music and dancing."[93] The whole scene is remarkably
stable: the men drinking and gambling, the women disapproving and
finding at least refuge and at times even riposte in music.

Massa's in De Cold Ground

The Gilbert collection also contains a good number of items from
the blackface "minstrel show" repertoire. This might at first seem surprising, since there were very few African Americans in all northwest

Arkansas, and none at all in Springdale or in the small communities where the Gilberts lived. "I doubt if we'd seen two black men while we were growing up," says Phydella, though she does go on to recount stories of "some of the Scotts, Grandpa, I guess," being slave owners: "this one, Uncle Mose or Uncle Ben, something, . . . I remember Mother saying that he used to carry 'em on his shoulders to cross the creek down there at Mayfield."[94] Phydella and Helen also recall their mother as having "that old southern way of speaking when she was upset with us." One incident especially stands out in Phydella's memory. She remember that her mother

> was scolding my older sister. . . . She wanted to do something that Mother didn't think she should do. She was pretty young yet. . . . She was ironing, Billie was, and she was talking back to Mother about everybody who got to do whatever it was—I think she wanted to go somewhere, and she was only like twelve or thirteen years old, 'cause I hadn't started school yet. And I remember Mother got Dad's razor strap and was spanking her with it. Her standing there ironing. And Billie was crying, and Mother was saying, "You're not gonna talk to me like I was a coal black nigger."
>
> And that is what stuck with me. Now, I don't remember if I ever heard her say it again. But that really stayed with me, because it was so . . . it was just frightening, to see Mother lose her temper like that.[95]

Joe Gilbert, on the other hand, was a Republican, and his daughters remember not only their father but themselves being teased as "black Republicans" by their "very very Democrat" Scott relatives. "They called him a black Republican," says Phydella. "That was one of the epithets they used for Republicans at that time, because they supposedly had taken up for the blacks when they were freed."[96]

Black Republican he may have been, but Joe Gilbert, of course, had no more intimate acquaintance with black people or black culture than his children, and it's clear enough that issues of race relations are in no way central to the Gilbert family history. The minstrel songs are in their collection not because they feature black protagonists or focus on black life, but because they either overlap nicely with other favorite family types, like sentimental ballads, or were appealing instrumental or comic pieces. "Oh Susanna" and "Camptown Races" are good examples of the latter type, while "Nellie Gray" and "Going from the Cottonfields" are fine instances of the former. "Going from the Cottonfields" especially, with its story of a man forced to move to Kansas, "so many miles away," in search of "gettin' better pay," might have appealed to the Gilberts on more personal grounds. Joe Gilbert was on several occasions forced to leave his home and family for higher paying work in the Oklahoma oilfields. His sons, too, found it necessary to travel in search of work—Buck went to Oklahoma for ranch work, Carl traveled to Kansas for the wheat harvest, and Leslie, the youngest, journeyed all the way to Washington with the Civilian Conservation Corps.

But two distinct attitudes toward racial issues are nevertheless discernible in these songs, the one stressing an alleged fundamental distinction between blacks and whites, operating to the former's social and political disadvantage, the other emphasizing a bedrock shared humanity, operating to connect people across racial lines. Sophia Scott, from her "old southern" perspective, most appreciated songs expressive of the former attitude, where black narrators speak with nostalgic affection of slavery days before "de Yankee troops come down" to spoil the Eden on earth provided by "good old Massa." Massa, even in these songs, is as dead as the world he ruled—he is "in de cold, cold ground" in the song of that title—but "all de darkeys am a weeping" over the loss of such a benevolent owner. (A more sardonic reading to this song is certainly possible. After all, the mourning narrator buries a claim upon holiday under his ostentatious grief—he says he "cannot work before tomorrow cause de teardrop flow"—and suggests instead that spending the day picking his banjo will help to "drive away my sorrow." The song might even be understood as a bit of covert jubilation, the cold ground being exactly where folks like Massa belong. But both Helen and Phydella reject this interpretation as unduly cynical.) "Going from the Cottonfields" articulates equally nostalgic views. Massa's grave "will miss de tender care" of the former slave, whose reluctant departure from the ground of his servitude is directed by economic motives. This number is in fact associated by the sisters with their mother.

In "Nellie Gray" and "Stay in Your Own Back Yard," however, this note of yearning for Massa's loving care is entirely absent. Massa is the clear villain in "Nellie Gray," the "white man" who kidnapped Nellie Gray from her lover and her happy Kentucky home, and "bound her with his chain" to a life of "toil in the cotton and the cane" in Georgia. "Stay in Your Own Back Yard" features the advice of a black mother comforting her crying child over his rejection by white children. The song's content might easily be understood as racist, as favoring a nearly apartheid playground separation of blacks and whites. Even the black mother, absurdly, seems to admire the "skin so white and fair" of the white children and to recognize her child as "a black little coon" who cannot reasonably expect to gain their attention as a playmate. But the song's pathos—and pathos, not social policy, is the business of the song—belongs to the crying black child and the black mother grieved by her baby's tears.

From their songs, then, as from their parents, the Gilbert children had available for their consideration two differing perspectives on appropriate relationships between black and white. They seem to have made their own choices from both camps. Phydella has certainly carried forward the family "black Republican" tradition. "I remember how angry I got," she says, "when they had blacks in the Fayetteville high school and Bill [her oldest son] came home and said Springdale canceled a game because they had a black. They refused to take him out. That's not been that long ago." Phydella also has definite views on the famous Little Rock school desegregation crisis that was, until the 1992 election of its governor to the land's highest office, Arkansas's major claim to national and international fame. "That was absolutely brought on," she says. "It was deliberately brought on. By Faubus. 'Course I hated that man, and I did my level best to talk everybody out of voting for him. Nobody'd listen to me—Bob and Helen, they voted for him."[97]

There may be a glimpse of Helen's views in her brief comment on "Oh Susanna," where she suggests that the omission of the author's name in the *Heart Songs* collection was motivated by fear "they'd get in trouble for saying 'nigger.'"[98] As isolated as she is from contact with African Americans, she nevertheless realizes, even as she resents it, that racial epithets and stereotypes once tolerated in songs and stories are now strongly sanctioned. She has always sung these songs without ever giving a second or even a first thought to their use of racist stereotypes, and she fiercely resists the implication that her family's liking for such songs says anything at all about their attitudes on race. The notion is surely naive, probably indefensible, possibly disingenuous, but she holds it.

What emerges from all this, again, even in an area peripheral to the family's major concerns, is the pervasive presence of music in its life, the varied utilization of communal heritage in the creation of individual values. The songs, again, offer models to compare and contrast, attitudinal building blocks, ingredients of thought. In learning their family's songs, in making songs and singing an integral part of their lives, the Gilbert sisters do not simply inherit a set of attitudes; they also inherit a language, a system of contesting languages and attitudes, which they then use to make their own explorations and construct their own attitudes. They not only learn to talk; they learn to talk back. Their traditional culture, their folklore, serves them most deeply by its open-endedness, by its refusal to present itself as finished. For the Gilbert sisters, songs are tools, not blueprints. They present not one established order, not one tradition understood as authorized to the exclusion of others, but a true marketplace of ideas, understood as open to all the innovations dialogue brings. This function may be especially clear in those instances where the songs address themselves to issues not at the margin of family concerns but at their very center. Here one might choose to begin with a matter already known to be significant in family history and look for its place in the family's songs.

Love and Marriage

An especially prominent theme in Gilbert stories, emerging recurrently in conversation and in Alma's written memoir, is the problem of parental approval for the marriages of children, especially of daughters. The Gilbert sisters married as very young women, even by the standards of the day. Alma married at fifteen, Phydella and Helen at sixteen. In the first instance, at least, their mother was presented with an accomplished fact and was devastated by it. Alma's account of the moment is vivid: "I'll never forget the look on Mama's face as I walked in and, being afraid to speak, handed her our marriage license. 'Oh!' she cried out in a shocked, hurt voice. 'You baby!'" Joe Gilbert, who had given his permission and accompanied the bride and groom to town for the ceremony, apologized to his wife, but gave reasons rooted in family history. "Dad put his arms around her and said, 'I'm sorry Sophia, but ever since the day my sister Addie climbed out the window and ran away to be married, I've vowed when one of my girls asked to be married, I'd not turn them down. I want to keep my girls; I want to be able to play with my grandkids; and that's something my old Daddy never got to do with Addie's children. He had driven her away!'" (*A Way of Life*, 112–13).

Seven years later, in 1934, Phydella sought the permission of both parents for her marriage, but her account makes clear that it was reluctantly given and that her older sister's marriage still rankled:

> He [Bill Hogan] didn't stay only through the berry harvest, and then he left. And he wrote me a letter—couldn't write very well, I should have known! . . . But Oh!, handsome and romantic—he came from Missouri and he'd been all over the country. Strong, macho-type guy. . . .
>
> So I wasn't gonna be like Billie, I wasn't gonna do this without permission, whenever he came back for grape season. . . . He wrote . . . he wanted to come back and would I marry him. I wrote back and said I didn't know whether, . . . I was afraid Mother and Dad wouldn't give permission. Well, he wrote back that we could go without their permission. But I wouldn't have done that for anything because I saw how hurt Mother was when Billie came in and said "I got married." She said, "Well, why didn't you tell me? I would like to have known." And it just hurt her real bad.
>
> So I wasn't gonna do it like that. So I talked to her about it. And Mother said, "Oh, honey I sure wish you wouldn't, I sure wish you wouldn't get married quite so young." But Dad said, "Well, I don't want her doing like Bill did." And that was it.[99]

As Alma makes clear in her memoir, she later experienced firsthand, in her own daughter Bette's marriage, the pain she had caused her mother years before. The scenes are remarkably similar—the young couple enters and the daughter announces her already accomplished marriage to her stunned and dismayed mother. "As they hurriedly left the room after relieving their minds of their secret," writes Alma, "I closed my eyes and saw myself on the day Alex and I were married. Remembered the hurt look on her face as I blithely handed her our marriage license. 'Here,' I thought, 'is payment for the way we did Mama.' And leaning my head on my arms I cried" (*A Way of Life*, 169).

Here, then, is a recurrent, abiding theme in Gilbert family lore. Joe Gilbert's sister Addie is best remembered now for the bitter estrangement following upon her elopement—she "crawled out of a sixteen inch square window" (*A Way of Life*, 40), writes Alma, citing her father's account. This is followed by Sophia Gilbert's enduring sorrow over her daughters' early marriages and is carried to a third generation by Alma's grief at being denied participation in her own daughter's wedding. It comes as no surprise, then, in a family united most deeply in music, to find the same theme recurrent in their songs. At least five numbers in the collection have parental opposition to young lovers at their center. Two of these, "My Horses Ain't Hungry," and "Lolly Truedom" portray young couples who prevail. The Gilbert version of "My Horses Ain't Hungry" ends with Molly ignoring her parents' rejection of her lover and urging him to hurry with his preparations for their elopement: "get ready I pray / And load up your wagon, we'll feed on the way!" In "Lolly Truedom" the maternal opposition is explicitly based on age— "You know you wanta marry, but you know you're too young"—but seems to be economically motivated. Ordering the daughter to defer talk of marriage, the mother tells her to "wash them dishes" instead. By the last stanza, however, the sixteen-year-old daughter is married to "my handsome Sam" and determined to "do the best I can."

In three other songs, however, parental opposition succeeds, with unhappy and even tragic results. "Peter Gray," for example, goes west from his native Pennsylvania "to trade for furs and other skins" when his beloved Lucy Anna's father prohibits his daughter's marriage and packs her off to Ohio. He is soon scalped by Indians, and Lucy Anna, knowing what ballads require of their heroines when news of this sort arrives, promptly takes to her bed and dies. "The Widow's Daughter" is a comic song, but it too tells a story of opposition to young lovers. The obstacle this time is a widowed mother who responds violently to a request for her daughter's hand. Here again the daughter's youth is stressed: "It's a queer thing to me," shouts the broom-wielding widow, "why a girl so young / Can get all the beaus and I can get none." The lover of "Sweet Lorraine" seems to be disliked by her parents on class grounds—they are apparently sending or taking her to "mansions refined and bright" where it is hoped she will soon forget the unsuitable Edgar. Lorraine is apparently resigned, despite her proclaimed love for Edgar: "You know that my parents don't like you, / And darling it breaks my heart."

Here again family history and song interpenetrate—the songs acquire credibility from the very incidents they may have in part inspired, and the stories in turn gain dramatic intensity from the songs. Like the picture of Alma burning love letters, the image of Addie Gilbert climbing from her window comes from a heightened, melodramatic world. Life takes its patterns, learns its roles, and chooses its costumes from the varied repertoire of the songs. Employing their language and gestures, a young woman in a small Arkansas village can conduct her courtships as a ballad heroine, see herself lifted to the "angel," "star," and "queen" of "Sweet Lorraine." Her parents, in their opposition, could be degraded, turned to monsters like the witch-woman of "The Widow's Daughter," whose badge of office is her broom. Once again, as with the temperance songs, the songs about the relationships between blacks and whites, and the "battle of the sexes" songs the sisters sang for their neighbors, a discussion is conducted, varied perspectives are deployed, competing patterns of appropriate behavior are offered.

Never Alone

> But everything, everybody, I'm talking about every nation, every
> human being that came across the earth had a song and sang in some
> way to their god. They could sing in some way in their power.
> —Thomas A. Dorsey

The repertoire of sacred music available to the Gilbert family was enormous, and their knowledge of hymns and gospel songs is far more comprehensive than the approximately twenty-five songs included in their collection. (There are twenty-one songs they classify as "Old Hymns," but several songs they place elsewhere—"A Picture from Life's Other Side," "The White Pilgrim," "Way Over in the Promised Land"—would be recognized by many as gospel songs.) The sisters in fact grew up surrounded by sacred music, in a deeply religious culture sometimes described as "the buckle of the Bible Belt." Their mother was a devout Christian who did her daily work accompanied by her own singing of favorite hymns and gospel songs. "Mother was singing all day long, while she worked," recalled Phydella, who remembered "When the Roll Is Called Up Yonder" and "Blessed Assurance" as among her mother's particular favorites. "Dad's favorite in the gospel line was 'Church in the Wildwood,'" she added.[100]

The Gilberts attended whatever church was available in their home community of the moment. "When we lived at Habberton," Phydella remembers, "the only church there was the Church of Christ . . . and we went to that. The Methodist church was the one that was at Zion. When there were no church services at Zion we would walk over to Oakland to the Baptist church."[101] All these congregations shared a basic Protestant fundamentalism and a devotion to hymn singing. The widely used *Broadman Hymnal,* cited by Helen as the source for "Tell It Again," contains nearly five hundred songs.

In addition to regular church services, the Gilbert sisters attended summer revivals held by holiness and Pentecostal groups. "The Pentecostal church held revivals in the Methodist church [at Zion], and sometimes we went over there. I remember the first time I sang at church—it was long before I went to school, and I was in what they called the Cradle Roll class. . . . We were supposed to sing 'Jesus Loves Me' . . .the twin boys were singing 'Jaysus.' Another time Alma and I were supposed to sing and she got laryngitis. I had to sing by myself."[102]

From a very young age, then, the Gilbert sisters were regular singers in various area churches, contributing "specials" both at regular services and revival meetings. "A special," says Phydella, "is a song that some individual or a group sings for the congregation. It's different from the choir or the songs the whole congregation sings. Usually the specials weren't in the hymn books—gospel, or songs we knew from somewhere else. It's something out of the regular service. Once I sang 'If I Could Hear My Mother Pray Again' with Helen. Seems like you could

Methodist Church, Zion,
Arkansas, 1992.
Photo by the author.

ask the song leader if you had something prepared and wanted to sing. But we were nearly always asked."[103]

Helen especially has continued to sing in church—"When we started going to Habberton Church, our pastor asked Janice and me to go with him one Sunday morning to KFAY and sing before he preached. We sang three songs; I played the guitar. That's my only experience with singing on the radio. Later Bob and I and our oldest son Bobby and his wife, Lois, formed a quartet. Bobby played the guitar, Bob did harmonica, and I played the banjo. We sang every Sunday or Sunday night at revivals for about seven years."[104]

Gospel songs were also regular features on the country music radio shows greatly loved by all the Gilberts, and all their favorite country and bluegrass stars regularly recorded gospel songs. The family's memories of such numbers often combine local and national associations.

Helen Fultz's note to "I'm Gonna Walk and Talk with My Lord," both associates it with a specific well-known singer and stresses its continued local importance: "Martha Carson sings it. We sing it at church now."[105] "The Great Speckled Bird" is for the sisters at one and the same time a church song and a Roy Acuff tune; the much-recorded "I'll Fly Away" was written in 1932 by the prolific Oklahoma gospel composer Albert E. Brumley, but the Gilberts remember learning it from "radio programs featuring current gospel groups."[106] The Bailes Brothers were from West Virginia, but they were stars of the *Louisiana Hayride* from its beginnings in 1948 and were "immensely popular in the Arkansas-Louisiana-Texas region," according to country music historian Bill C. Malone.[107] "Dust on the Bible" was one of their most popular tunes, and Phydella to this day remembers it as theirs and associates it with that favorite show. They of course know "Peace in the Valley," but associate it with recorded versions by Tennessee Ernie Ford and Elvis Presley instead of its composer, Thomas A. Dorsey. Even "I Saw the Light" is remembered more as a radio song performed by regional gospel groups than as a Hank Williams tune.

From a vast regional repertoire, then, the Gilbert sisters learn a great many religious songs. But for their family collection they choose a relatively small group. For no other type of music is their standard so selective. The "Old Hymns" section of their collection, more than any other, consists of true family favorites. Here, perhaps more obviously than in other places, their songs reveal their hearts and minds, delineate the shape of their faith, and describe the way they understand the tie between man and God and the link between heaven and earth. First by the songs they include, and second by the songs they omit, the Gilberts participate in local theological debates and articulate their own positions.

They are not, for example, much interested in hell or damnation. "The Great Judgment Day" does include "prayed too late" stanzas, but the emphasis, even here, is reserved for the glories of heaven. Several other songs—"Why Will You in Bondage Stay," "Come Unto Me," "Drifting Away"—consist almost entirely of more or less impassioned invitations to share in the immediate benefits of faith. "Bring your cares to Jesus and he will give you rest" says "Come Unto Me"; "let Him loose your fetters" urges "Why Will You in Bondage Stay." Christianity as celebrated in Gilbert song understands those outside its company as not so much damned to hell after death as bound and imprisoned in this life. The stress, in song after song, is on invitation, on God's persistence in the offer of His grace, above all on the immediate benefits of acceptance. "He now opens the prison wide," says "Why Will You in Bondage Stay," "so come to the light while you may." "Come Unto Me" is even more succinct: "Bring your cares to Jesus, He will give you rest."

Also conspicuous by their absence from the Gilbert collection are the countless apocalyptic visions, hell-fire and brimstone numbers, marches of the church militant. "No Hiding Place," "Bring Down the Latter Rain," "He Will Set Your Fields on Fire," the Methodist hymnal's "Day of Wrath"—all these are absent, as are "Onward Christian Soldiers" and "Faith of Our Fathers." These are mostly familiar songs, known to the Gilberts, but not one of them, as they put it, is "one of ours."[108]

To the threat of hell they prefer the promise of heaven, the "land far away, mid the stars, we are told, / where they know not the sorrow of time" of "The Evergreen Mountains of Life," or the "land of never ending day" of "Summer Land of Love." "Home of the Soul," "Where the Soul Never Dies," "As the Life of a Flower"—all these also feature glimpses of "the radiant shore / where the sun never sets."

And what of this heaven? What is it like? How are its joys made palpable? A closer look reveals that the songs of the Gilbert collection not only favor celebrations of heaven over fears of hell, but describe that heaven in terms of a rural, pastoral world. Heaven, it turns out, is the green world of earth, an Eden with the Fall undone. The songs describe a place of streams and valleys, an "evergreen mountain of life," a "summer land of love." The place bears a striking resemblance to the hills of northwest Arkansas. The Gilberts, it turns out, imagine their heavenly home by idealized remembering of their earthly one, by making eternal the bright perfections of an Ozark summer day.

In fact, this type of imagery is used interchangeably between the two realms. God's creation, Nature, is presented as a material testament, a divine Work with messages entirely in harmony with the divine Word. In song after song, the beauties of creation are celebrated in openly prelapsarian terms. The well-known "How Great Thou Art" offers a spectacular example, its opening stanza describing a scene of "lofty mountain grandeur" so lovely it prompts the soul to songs of praise. "Church in the Wildwood" makes the tie between sanctified earth and naturalized heaven especially vivid. The lovely "wildwood," a "vale" where "wild flowers bloom," is presented as an obviously appropriate spot for God's church. Here heaven touches earth even as earth reaches heaven. In the wildwood church, the two realms unite, making possible the lovely prayer of the final stanza where the flight from "this spot of my childhood" to the celestial "mansions of light" seems a journey of no great distance.

It should be noted here that the terms of this picture are not automatic; other visions of heaven were available. Many well-known hymns portray a decidedly urban paradise, with its riches imaged in predominantly architectural terms, a mineral rather than botanical ideal. Pearly gates, walls of jasper, streets of purest gold—these are staples of the celestial city described in scores of religious songs. A well-known hymn is titled "Jerusalem the Golden," "When We All Get to Heaven" looks to a time when "the pearly gates will open, We shall tread the streets of gold," and the visions of "I Will Sing You a Song" reveal a "fair city" with "bright jasper walls."

Songs like these are known to the Gilberts, but they too are omitted from the collection. "These are the ones we liked so well we sang 'em at home too," says Phydella. "Some of them—'No, Never Alone,' 'Why Will You in Bondage Stay,' 'As the Life of a Flower'—I don't remember seeing them in any hymnbooks. 'Home of the Soul'—I don't remember it being in the hymnal, though it was a family song. Where we got it I don't know, unless it was Church of Christ or somewhere they [her parents and older siblings] lived and learned it that had a different set of hymnals."[109]

Also conspicuous by their absence are songs centered on the shortcomings of others—"Dust on the Bible," for example, with its censorious account of a most unneighborly visit. For all its popularity and familiarity, it was never included as "one of ours" by the Gilbert singers. An especially revealing omission in this vein is "Farther Along," a great favorite among southerners despite (or perhaps in some instances because of) its spectacular mean-spiritedness. Full of starchy rectitude, the song gets off to a whining start in which the "we" who sing are "oft made to wonder why others living about us" are "never molested though in the wrong." A second stanza continues in the same vein: "Then do we wonder why others prosper / Living so wicked year after year." Even the single stanza apparently centered upon the counter-balancing joys awaiting the godly—all such trials will "be as nothing" once we "sweep through the beautiful gates"—has an implied vindic-tiveness at its heart. No doubt the triumphant entry of the blessed will only be enhanced by the absence from their company of those worldly "others" whose undeserved short-term prosperity was so bitterly resented. Their feet shall slide in due time, says this grim little favorite, and the sooner the better.

"Farther Along," perhaps the best-known song of this type in the southern repertoire of religious music, is a striking omission from the Gilbert collection. Surely they knew the song? Of course they did; the whole family knew it. "But we didn't sing it at home," Phydella said. "It wasn't one of our favorites."[110] The major distinction here is revealed, as it is in numerous other instances, as founded in place, in locale. In church the Gilberts sang the same hymns that everybody else sang—the Church of Christ songs in Habberton, songs from the Baptist hymnal in Oakland, Methodist hymns in Zion. But at home they sang the "family hymns," the songs they cherished as their own regardless of their source.

When these songs that were their favorites turn attention to neigh-bors outside the faith, they do so to stress very different concerns than those of "Farther Along." They focus not upon rebuke but upon relief, the open availability of faith's unfailing comforts. The question is never why do the heathen prosper; the question is always won't you come? "Let the Lower Lights Be Burning," perhaps the single song most cher-ished by the Gilbert sisters, the one remembered by Phydella as most often sung at evening's end, before the family went to bed, is classified by *The Broadman Hymnal* as a song of "Social Service." To the "poor sailor tempest tossed, / trying now to make the harbor," the Christian "brother" trims his lamp, sends a saving "gleam across the wave." The loss of even one soul from the company of the blest is a cause not for satisfied self-congratulation but for lament. "Be saved," urges "Drifting Away," "why will ye die?"

A world not only fallen but plagued by sickness, war, and economic depression is by such a faith's radical Arminianism rendered bearable.

Life's burdens are real and heavy, but God is a saving help who answers every call. The nights of the soul can be dark indeed. For Phydella Hogan the death of her father was so shattering an event that even forty years later she communicated it indirectly, by loaning her copy of Alma's autobiographical memoir. But the consolations of faith, especially as those consolations are set to music, are equal at last to every dark omen. "Lean on the Lord till the morning," says "Home of the Soul." Grace is amazing; salvation is free. "No, Never Alone"—that is both a title and the heart of the matter, for the Gilberts.

In several of these leanings, it turns out, the predilections of the Gilberts are in line with those of rural southerners generally. Malone, for example, mentions songs filled with "the martial imagery of missionary Protestantism" only to note that southern religious music was "more often gentle, bucolic, nostalgic, and sentimental." Heaven is "sometimes described as a city of gold, but more often as an abundant Beulah Land." "The nostalgic evocation of home as a bastion of virtue and security," however, which Malone calls "almost the central theme of southern gospel music," is strikingly absent from the Gilbert collection.[111]

Home and family are obviously of central importance to the Gilberts. Their annual family reunions, their long history of mutual assistance and continued close association, the very existence of a family ballad book assembled as a conscious inheritance for children and grandchildren —all these testify to the enduring strength of family ties. But such ties are not stressed, indeed are not in evidence at all, in their favorite religious songs. "Precious Memories" (mentioned in this context by Malone) is absent, as are other such staples as "The Wayfaring Stranger," "The Family Who Prays" and "My Mother's Prayer." All these, with their double celebration of home and family and the joys of heavenly reunion, would at first seem surprising omissions.

But only at first. The Gilbert vision, in its repeated insistence upon God's grace as freely offered, in its recurrent urging of grace's acceptance, reveals itself as open and generous far beyond regional and denominational norms. Grace so understood cannot with good logic or in good conscience focus its attention upon a single nuclear family. The lamp must be kept burning, the lifeline thrown out again and again. Home, properly understood, is indeed evoked as "a bastion of virtue and security" in the Gilbert collection's hymns and gospel songs, but "home" here reaches far beyond the family gate to encompass the whole idealized Ozark landscape that is for them a Beulah Land, a Bunyanesque "desired country" open to all. It's a loving, gentle theology, articulated in lovely, comforting song.

The Local Tradition

Richly documentable family musical traditions like that of the Gilberts, providing opportunities for close-up observation of the intimate, continually changing relationships between singers and songs as they develop and endure in specific situations, are a treasure for folklorists and ethnographers of widely varied particular interests. There is, for example, a great deal of valuable material relating to geographic or regional characteristics of traditional music. The Gilbert text of "Home Sweet Home," for example, would seem at first glance to have a word missing from its final stanza. "So now you know the reason / Why I'm compelled to roam," concludes the cowpoke in exile, "A murderer of the deepest / Is far from home, sweet home." A murderer of the deepest what? Helen and Phydella are sympathetic, but have no answer. "I know it sounds wrong," says Helen, "but that's how we learned it. I'm almost sure."[112]

Things are not so simple, as it turns out. The last of three versions of "Home Sweet Home" included in Vance Randolph's *Ozark Folksongs* as "The Wandering Cowboy" is a version obtained in 1941 from Mrs. Dorothy Freeman of Natural Dam, Arkansas. Mrs. Freeman's final stanza is nearly identical to the Gilbert version: "Now boys, you know the reason / That I'm compelled to roam, / I'm a sinner of the deepest, / And far from home, sweet home."[113] Natural Dam is in Crawford County, just to the south of the Gilbert's home in Washington County. "Home Sweet Home," then, is reported in at least one other collection in the apparently defective form used by the Gilberts, and reported in that form in both a time and a place close to their own acquisition of the song. It is at least possible, therefore, that Helen's memory is entirely correct, that the apparently defective line is in fact a regional variant.

"How we learned it" doesn't necessarily count for everything with traditional singers, but it usually counts for a great deal. The sisters are perfectly aware of the penchant in old songs for archaic and "fancy" language, and they have great tolerance for phrasings which now seem to them unclear or even incoherent. Phydella and Helen are both puzzled, as already noted, by the phrase "stood in his retreat" in "A Spanish Cavalier." This seems to them comic—is one to picture a retreating soldier ending his flight, making a "stand?" If so, his guitar strikes them as an ineffectual weapon. Even if, as seems probable, the "retreat" is a noun, not a verb, a place instead of an action, a fortress or hideout, the comedy of his guitar and standing position remains. A good bit of laughter has surrounded discussions of this question, but in the face of all this hilarity the song is still sung in the old way. Phydella's jocular commentary makes clear that the last stanza (and others) of "The True Young Maid," where the returning lover "raised her up like a kind brother / The kisses he gave her one, two, three," is also perceived as unintentionally comic, but here too the phrasing is unchanged in family singing.[114] "How we learned it" continues to direct performance, at least in these instances.

Another apparently idiosyncratic feature of the Gilbert collection would be the use of "Holy Boly" as a title for the widely known song more commonly titled "Johnny Sands." This song appears again and again in the major regional collections—Belden's *Ballads and Songs Collected by the Missouri Folk-Lore Society,* Randolph's *Ozark Folksongs,* and Ethel and Chauncey O. Moore's Oklahoma collection, *Ballads and Folk Songs of the Southwest,* all print versions—but "Holy Boly" does not appear as a title, or even as a refrain. But idiosyncrasy, like omission, may prove more apparent than real. When Theodore Garrison assembled "Forty-Five Folk Songs Collected from Searcy County, Arkansas" for a Master's thesis at the University of Arkansas in 1944, he included a song called "The Old Woman in Ireland," sung by Mrs. Daisy Turner of Zack, Arkansas, in July 1942, which Garrison says is "often confused" with 'Johnny Sands'" in Searcy County. Mrs. Turner's song features a two-line nonsensical refrain after each verse—"Hody-oddy-inktum, hody-oddy-a, / Hody-oddy-inktum-day."[115] This has not exactly arrived at "Holy Boly," but it's clearly well on the way. Once again, as with the apparent dropped word in "Home Sweet Home," another instance can be found sufficiently close in time and place to make at least plausible the suggestion of a local or regional tradition embodied in the apparently idiosyncratic Gilbert version.

The Gilbert version of "Holy Boly" is also unusual (unique in the versions consulted) in providing for the survival of the would-be murderess: "And now my song is ended / I can't sing any more / But don't you know that silly old fool / Came a-swimmin to the shore." But here, too, despite the different result, the Gilbert conclusion resembles very closely that of another Arkansas version, so that once again what seems at first glance to be an idiosyncratic version of a widely distributed song may on closer examination reveal itself as fitting a regional subtype. "Rich Old Lady," another "Johnny Sands" variant recorded for W. K. McNeil by Kenneth Rorie of Batesville, Arkansas, in 1979 also ends with an epilogue: "Now my little song is over / And I won't sing it no more. / But wasn't she a blamed old fool / For not swimming to the shore."[116]

A more obvious example of such a tradition occurs with the Gilbert version of the Child ballad usually called "The Sweet Trinity," "The Lowlands Low," or "The Golden Vanity." The Gilberts call their version "The Green Willow Tree," and Phydella is quite specific in tracing it to her mother-in-law, Margaret Hogan, and in locating her learning of the song in Nevada, Missouri. Belden includes three Missouri versions, and four of the five Randolph versions are also from Missouri. None is called "The Green Willow Tree," though one of Belden's and two of Randolph's (including the one from Arkansas) are called "The Merry Golden Tree."

These variations have mostly to do with ship names, since nearly all variants of the song include two named vessels. In the Gilbert version, for example, a ship called the *Green Willow Tree* is sunk by a brave adventurer from another ship called the *Turkey Shivaree*—he bores holes in its side with some sort of auger—in return for his captain's promise of gold and "my lovely little daughter your wife for to be." The captain betrays him, of course, refusing to take him back on board, but the hero refuses to "do you like I just did them," and is left to drown in "the lowlands, lonesome low."

Other versions change ship names—"The Merry Golden Tree" is the hero's home ship in two of Randolph's versions and the single Oklahoma text printed in *Ballads and Folk Songs of the Southwest,* and also the victim ship in one of Belden's. In some versions, moreover, the hero proves less gallant and *does* sink the second ship as he did the first (this happens to the *Turkish Revelry,* the home ship in Belden's C version). The song as the Gilberts knew it fits quite nicely into this regional tradition. Its closest overall resemblance is to Randolph's A text, from Cyclone, Missouri, but once again the only version to share its title with the Gilberts' comes from their immediate neighborhood. Irene Carlisle's 1952 University of Arkansas M.A. thesis, "Fifty Ballads and Songs from Northwest Arkansas," includes three versions of this ballad, including one called "The Green Willow Tree" collected in 1951 from Mrs. Rachel Henry of Spring Valley, Arkansas. Mrs. Henry's version also uses the same ship names as the Gilbert version (though *Turkey Shivaree* becomes *Turkey Shevelee,* and home ship and victim ship are reversed). Thirty years earlier, in 1921, in the year of Helen's birth, the Gilberts were living in Spring Valley.

Sometimes not just the shape of a song, but even its very presence may be in large part a matter of local event or taste. "Chingaling Chan," for example, at first proved difficult to locate. No versions were found in the major regional collections, but when the song was found in another repertoire it was not only close to home but reported as deriving from an identical source. In 1985, when Julie Hefley sang "China Man" for Lucille Burdine and William B. McCarthy in Mount Judea, Arkansas, she noted that she and her sister Susie Campbell had "learned it when they were in school in the 'twenties, apparently from their teacher."[117] The sisters, in their songbook, remember how they learned "Chingaling Chan": "Learned at Zion. At school, from a teacher."

Past and Present

The family music tradition is never in stasis; it changes unceasingly, grows as new material is added and shrinks as new custodians find old favorites uncongenial to their own developing tastes. And it continues to function as it has always functioned—as a center of family entertainment and family history, a frame for memory, and a guide for behavior. Thus Jeanie Fultz Miller, singing with her mother and her aunt Phydella in her mother's kitchen one June afternoon in 1990, strums the last accompanying chords of "Bill Vanero" and then listens intently as the two older women remember sitting up all night with a desperately sick child, Jerry, Phydella's youngest, then just a baby, six weeks old.

"We thought he was dying, but neither of us would ever say so," says Phydella. "He was too weak to nurse," adds Helen. "We gave him sugar water and medicine every fifteen minutes, out of a dropper." Gradually, in the quiet exchange of their conversation, the whole somber scene builds again. The hot night in the summer of 1945, Phydella just back from Missouri, her marriage ended, living with Helen in the Coal Mine Place at Zion. Bob Fultz gone too, a Navy man on a battleship in the Pacific. The tiny infant barely living, the women themselves small and vulnerable with no men and eight young children. It was a harrowing night in a harrowing time, the sisters pulling the baby back from death's threshold as much by desperate will as by their poor medicine.

By morning though, the child had rallied, and the sisters "danced and sung around the room" in relief and celebration. "We were hysterical," says Phydella in summary, in closure, to Helen's nods and Jeanie's smiles.[118] We all know Jerry, a grown man now, the center of this vivid story made happy at its end by the image of his mother and aunt singing and dancing in a room ablaze in warm light.

This is a favorite story, told so often in the family that Helen has given it a comic title: "The Night We Got Historical." But what made it resurface here? "Bill Vanero," with its tale of the cowboy/lover slain by "Apache Indians" on his way to Little Bessie, would seem an unlikely candidate. The presence of Jeanie, Jerry's cousin, another child of the two sisters who so often shared their lives even as both centered those lives on raising children? The heat in Helen's kitchen this June day? The room's soft light? A letter or call from Jerry yesterday or this morning? Some or all of the above, in intangible combination? Or none of the above?

Exactitude here is impossible, not even desirable. There are songs so strongly attached to particular persons and situations for the sisters that the song's performance must inevitably summon the person's memory, the situation's recollection. Or, reversing the direction, the thought of the person, recollection of the situation, will in most cases trigger rememberings of the song. But "Bill Vanero" is not one of these. On another occasion it might be sung without any thought of Jerry, or the

Coal Mine Place, or the summer of 1945. What does emerge, however, time and again, is the association of present music with past music, past events and their music in association with present events and their music.

Music itself, over and over, disclosed in surprising and myriad ways, shows at the family's heart. It's an abiding presence, its power in the distant past evident in the sisters' memories of childhood reunions at their Grandmother Scott's home in Mayfield, its power in the present obvious in the setting of the 1990 retelling of "The Night We Got Historical" story, its power in the future suggested by Jeanie Miller's determination to save recordings of her mother's singing, or Bill Hogan's and Martha Estes's very different efforts to develop their own singing and playing out of the heritage provided by their mother.

Alma suffered a serious stroke in 1986, which ended her active participation in the songbook project, though she lived until 1992. But Phydella and Helen continue even now to tinker with their collection, considering new material and reevaluating old. They still look eagerly for additional verses for their old songs, sometimes trying to remember as perfectly as they can which ones were a part of the versions sung by their father or mother, aunt or brother, but at other times simply adding a new verse because they like it.

Even in the 1990s, attempting to help yet another researcher with his enthusiasms, as they had helped Mary Celestia Parler with hers thirty years earlier, the sisters are not simply historians, their interest focused on the past. They are singers, with their interest focused on good songs. In 1990, for example, the Child ballad "Lord Lovel" was removed from the collection as it was being prepared for publication because, as Phydella explained, "I copied it out because I thought maybe Helen or I would learn to sing it, but we never did. It's not one of ours." "Geisha Girl" was also removed, at about the same time, for similar reasons. "I sang that one in Nebraska," says Phydella, "but none of the others sing it. It's not one of the family's."[119]

At least one song that does remain in the collection, the tragic dying-child ballad "Put My Little Shoes Away," is not sung by all family members. Helen Fultz, for one, finds it too painful. "I just can't sing it," she says, searching for words and finding them inadequate. "It's about a little child, children are special to me. It's too much."[120] Here the problem is not that pathos collapses into bathos, as it does with

"Jealous Lover." Here pathos continues to lift, intensifying at last to the unbearable. Almeda Riddle, reminded of "The Four Marys" when she heard it in 1964 in California, remembered singing it as a child with her older sister Claudy, who died in 1904. "But I think maybe when she died, I just stopped singing that song, because it reminded me of her . . . the shock of Claudy's dying. . . . I think I blocked off that song—you can do things like that."[121]

The remarkable openness of the family tradition to new materials is nicely illustrated by two stories, one involving a proposed addition to the collection in 1964 or soon thereafter, and the other a song on a family tape from the 1970s. The earlier instance occurred when Phydella sent to her sisters for their consideration a new version of "The House of the Rising Sun," identified as "sung by The Animals." Phydella was living in Lincoln, Nebraska, then, helping her just-divorced eldest son, Bill, raise his four children and playing with him "all round Lincoln" in a band called Country Strings. "We already knew the song," she remembers, "but that one had some verses we didn't sing, and we all liked the new version better."[122]

The second example comes from a tape made in 1974 as a birthday present to her sister Phydella by Helen Fultz. Included among the selections, all performed solo with banjo accompaniment by Helen, is "Looking out My Back Door," which is introduced at some length:

> It's hard to know, you know, what kids like these days; it's just almost impossible to figure out what they would like. . . . Richard might remember this one because it was one of the kind that the kids liked back, what shall we say, four or five years ago. At any rate it's a Creedence Clearwater. . . . This is the kind of thing that Mac used to like. This was more a peppy one that came out, and it got real popular with a lot of people, not just kids. Like I told Bill when I played it for Timmy and Kyle, I think it was probably about an LSD trip, but we'll just not go into that. It's kind of cute anyway.[123]

That every performance of a traditional song is a new recreation is by now a commonplace of scholarly commentary, but the Gilbert sisters, in these instances of acquiring new songs and recasting old ones or altering their tonal shape, provide examples of several levels of creative

Phydella Hogan,
Lincoln, Nebraska,
about 1967.
*Photo courtesy
Phydella Hogan.*

redeployment of the inherited tradition. Even the songs, mostly Alma's, that they claim as their own creations exhibit their traditional roots in their meter, their imagery, and their world view. Traditional culture, then, even as it earns its much-remarked reputation for conservatism by such practices as the "How we learned it" rationale for phrasings recognized as nonsensical, exhibits at the same time a much less emphasized capacity for adaptation and innovation. "Jealous Lover" as sung by the Gilbert sisters is a different song than the piece of the same title sung by Vance Randolph's rough mountaineers. Nothing is fixed. Meanings are not inherent, but are continually refashioned out of ongoing negotiations between singers and audiences in ever altering circumstances.

But this whole scene, in all its complexity, its mixing of traditional and popular elements, is one that would have set the old-school folk music scholars spinning in their graves—imagine MacEdward Leach or, closer to home, H. M. Belden, confronted with three Ozark grandmothers blithely adding popular rock and roll songs to a family collection exhibiting in many respects an excellent fit with the "ballet book" familiar to collectors of traditional song. Such scholars, of course, would have known exactly what to do—they would have immediately excised such material as "untraditional" and therefore out of place in a "folk music collection." Even Mary Celestia Parler did not hesitate to turn off her recorder when informants insisted on performing the popular pieces she dismissed as "hillbilly junk."

But in fact such violations of generic boundaries have always been characteristic of the Gilberts. On several occasions, at least one going back to the 1930s, they put music to poems they'd liked in popular magazines and newspapers. "The Malibu Trail" came from *Western Story,* for example, while "Wishing Rug" was from the *Kansas City Star.* "Let the Rest of the World Go By" is one of the family's most beloved songs, long associated with the sisters' most treasured memories of musical evenings together with their parents, but Phydella Hogan did not for all this hesitate to rewrite its lyrics as a fiftieth anniversary wedding present for her sister Helen and her husband. In this too the Gilberts are in no sense unique: when collector D. K. Wilgus visited Ollie Gilbert in Stone County in 1965, the famous ballad singer treated him to a sprightly version of "Blue Suede Shoes." Songs in family tradition are treasured, and many factors encourage their faithful preservation. But they are above all used, employed in the business of living, not tucked away in some scrapbook as mere relics of a revered though vanished past.

They Wanted to Interview Me

She had no idea. She didn't know a thing so rucked in the
vernacular could have such an epic quality.

—Don DeLillo

It was in Lincoln, while she was living in Nebraska, that Phydella found in the public library the *Heart Songs* anthology credited so often in the sisters' collection. She was looking for "Sweet Evelina," a favorite of her mother's, "because we didn't have all of it." The *Heart Songs* version had two verses not sung by Sophia Gilbert—"She sang the first and the last of these. Billie sent them to me, but these two we couldn't remember. . . . That's why I got the book, was that so many of the songs, I'd go through, I'd say, 'Gee, there's got to be more to 'em than this.' So I got the *Heart Songs* book and started looking 'em up. And some of them would spark a memory. I'd think, 'Oh yeah, I remember hearing that now.'"[124]

By 1965, however, the year she remembers looking for "Sweet Evelina" in *Heart Songs,* Phydella already knew something about versions and variants in traditional song. Ten years earlier, perhaps as early as 1952 or 1953, she had been a folklorist's informant for the first time. "That was when I was in Fayetteville, cooking for Jug Wheeler at the drive-in. He hired student help, nearly all—he had a core crew and the rest of it was student help that worked around their schedules. There was two or three students who had discovered I sang this type song, and so they wanted to learn some of 'em, they wanted to interview me for their folklore class."[125]

These student interviews brought Phydella to the attention of Mary Celestia Parler, who taught folklore classes in the English department at the University of Arkansas and collected at least as assiduously among her students and other area residents as did her more famous husband, Vance Randolph. Phydella remembers:

> Finally she called me, and she said, "I got your name from one of my students," said "all my students keep getting so much material from you, I'd like to meet you.". . . So then's when I invited her out to the reunion, and she went out to the reunion with us and Uncle Huston and all of 'em sang for her, see?
>
> We had it at Helen's house that year. . . . She stayed afterward and we sang till we were just absolutely so hoarse we couldn't sing any longer. . . . She said, "You know, if I didn't know better I'd swear you were making them up. Nobody knows that many songs." I said, "Well, we could sing all night if our voices'd hold out."[126]

According to the notes filed with her collections, now housed at Mullins Library at the University of Arkansas, Mary Parler recorded fifty-nine songs from the Gilbert sisters on three occasions in 1960 and

1961. She also, recalls Helen, arranged for them to sing for her classes and to perform at a folk festival held in Fayetteville:

> We sang at the Agri Park. We were going to [sing together] but Phydella's voice quit that day and I had to sing all of 'em by myself, I think, except maybe one. We sang "The Shadow of the Pines" I'm almost sure. . . . That song about, I don't know whether we know a name to it or not, about "an old woman, in London she did dwell. She loved her old man dearly, another twice as well." . . . It's funny. "Holy Boly," it's called.
>
> But we didn't sing very many 'cause there was so many people there. Max Hunter was there, and a woman, Jo-Ann something, from Missouri, that sang so beautiful. All I remember is she sang about that "Willie got drownded in the deep blue sea." And I thought that Almeda Riddle was there.[127]

By 1955, then, if not a bit earlier, Phydella was gradually made aware of herself as a "folk" singer and "informant." Students, and later their teacher, were interviewing and recording her. By 1960 Helen was getting the same treatment. Events like the folk festival in Fayetteville brought them both into contact with the full flower of the "folklore" business as practiced at that time. Almeda Riddle, from Heber Springs, Arkansas, was already a widely acclaimed traditional singer and was on her way to becoming a seasoned festival performer; Max Hunter was an energetic collector from Springfield, Missouri, who articulated extremely rigorous "authenticity" standards. From contacts like these and from Mary Celestia Parler, Phydella especially learned the ideas about folksongs and folksinging which pop up occasionally in her comments and in her conversation.

It seems obvious, then, that the brief flurry of attention Helen and Phydella received in the late 1950s and early 1960s served to stimulate their interest in and respect for their family musical heritage. Even Alma, home for a family reunion in 1961, was recorded on one occasion by Mary Parler. It would seem to be no accident that the systematic gathering of their songs followed soon upon these encounters.

It is no less clear, however, that the influence of folk festivals and folklorists upon the Gilbert sisters was in many ways superficial. They did not become regular festival performers, and there is no evidence

whatever in their collection of that bias in favor of older songs so common in the folksong publications of the period. Phydella and Helen will
often compare their "version" of a song with one found in a songbook,
but they do not speak of "variants" or "oral transmission." Francis James
Child is unknown to them, but Jimmie Rodgers, the Carter Family,
Mac Wiseman, and Gene Autry are frequently cited. "The Green
Willow Tree" and "Barbara Allen" appear in their collection, and the
latter especially is recognized by them as "one of the old folk songs,"
but neither song is especially prized on account of age or alleged folk
origin. The sisters have a wonderful version of the Child ballad usually
known as "The Farmer's Curst Wife" or "The Old Man under the
Hill," but they know it as "Ty-Oh-Rattle-Ding-Day" and for them it
is simply "one of Dad's songs." The song they know as "Jinny Fer
Jinny" provides another example—it is a version of Child 277, more
often known as "The Wife Wrapt in Wether's Skin" or "Dandoo," but
Phydella and Helen did not know this, and they cherish it as a song
their mother sang when they were very young.

For every such old folksong, moreover, the Gilbert collection contains at least four or five with origins in nineteenth-century popular
music or twentieth-century recordings. The early years of commer-
cially recorded country music are especially well represented in their
repertoire. The Gilbert collection thus stands as a vivid corrective to
the Child-and-other organizational scheme of the major folksong collections from the period. What does matter about a song, in the sisters'
judgment, is first of all its connection with their family history, and sec-
ondly their personal sense of its loveliness as a piece of music. The loose,
four-part organization of their collection reflects these priorities, with
the large first section encompassing a wide variety of songs united for
the Gilberts as "family favorites."

The Gilbert repertoire emerges from such comparisons with other
collections as less dominated by songs usually recognized as "folk," and
at the same time richer than most in popular songs from the 1920s and
especially the 1930s, the music the sisters heard on their wonderful new
radios and record players and then sang for their appreciative neighbors.
Analysis also reveals a rich vein of comic pieces, songs from the minstrel
repertoire, cowboy ballads, and temperance weepers. This varied and

more popular repertoire made them less attractive to academic researchers and folk festival promoters, but it made them more appealing in their own communities.[128]

Though they still sing for these communities—Helen and Bob Fultz with their daughter Jeanie and her family in church, and Phydella and her family with the Fultz family at Zion reunions—the sisters intended a narrower audience, centered on their children and grandchildren, when they undertook to gather their songs. Phydella's memory of the songbook's genesis is precise both in regard to immediate cause and to time and place: "I was the one that started it," she says. "Then Helen and Bill got into it just as heavy. My motive was that they ought to be saved for our children." The immediate cause was the remark by Mary Celestia Parler already cited in connection with her visit to a family reunion. "Mary Parler had said, 'Nobody can know that many songs,' and I had a typewriter so I just started writing down what I could remember. That was the year I had pneumonia so bad, 1959, and I was in the house, it's gone now, right behind Jug Wheeler's drive-in on Dickson Street."[129]

Musicianship continues to flourish in the Gilbert family. Helen and Phydella continue to perform regularly at area churches, retirement homes, and home demonstration clubs, Helen with a string band called the Brush Creek Girls, and Phydella as a banjo picker with several local bands. They speak proudly of the talents of children and grandchildren. Helen's daughter Jeanie is not only a member of the Brush Creek Girls, but also, writes Phydella, "sings with Helen and Bob's gospel group when they perform at Hindsville or at church."[130]

Phydella's oldest son, Bill, the one who played with her in Nebraska with the Country Strings, not only continues to play and sing himself, but has passed the gift on to his children. "His children can all play an instrument," writes Phydella. "Richard, the oldest, is the only one who plays in a band. He started as drummer for his dad at age fourteen. Now plays guitar as well as drums and is an excellent singer, performs regularly."[131]

Martha Hogan Estes, writing from her perspective as Phydella's daughter, interrupts a roll call of musical siblings and cousins to label herself and her cousin Janice (Helen's oldest) "the least talented of the

Bob Fultz, Jeanie Miller, Dale Miller. Mayfield Church, Mayfield, Arkansas, May, 1994. *Photo by the author.*

entire family," adding that despite her best efforts to play the banjo Walter Allen made her for a birthday present, "Roy Clark needn't worry." Janice, for her part, once purchased a tambourine when a friend told her that "anyone" could get music from a tambourine. "I only got a sore hip." she reported.

These exceptions made, Martha Estes's list provides a vivid indication of music's enduring hold on the family. "Helen's oldest son Bobby sings and plays the guitar; her younger daughter Jeanie has the sweetest voice you'd ever hope to hear and plays the guitar as well as her mother does; the middle son Larry has a wonderful voice . . . and does great renditions of Roger Miller songs; Mac, the youngest boy and baby of the family, plays guitar . . . and is a fine bluegrass banjo picker." Even Janice, hip sore from her tambourine, "has a sweet and smooth alto voice and sings hymns and old gospel songs."[132]

If the elders look with pride upon the accomplishments of children and grandchildren, the children are in turn devoted to parents and grandparents, revering them in lucid recognition as the sources of their personal sense of a niche in existence, a place of their own in the wide

Bill Hogan, Lincoln, Nebraska, about 1973.
Photo courtesy Phydella Hogan.

wide world. Bill Hogan still presents the single occasion when he sat
and played with his uncle Buck Gilbert at a family reunion in Goshen
as "one of the most meaningful experiences of my life." Buck Gilbert
was in poor health then—"he couldn't drive any more, but he could
still pick," Bill remembers—but he played mandolin to his nephew's
guitar in a group that he remembers also included his mother, Phydella,
his aunt Helen, and his cousin Jeanie. "I didn't think I'd ever get to see
him again," Bill says. "It was something to remember. I'd listened to
him play when I was about eight or nine years old, and Mom and Aunt
Helen were always praising him, but that was the only time I actually
got to pick with him. I got to give him his due, tell him he was something special. He was about half embarrassed."[133]

Here, on the edge of the twenty-first century, the family musical
traditions continue not only in depth but in breadth. Where in the early
1900s Sophia Scott loved hymns and sentimental "Oh my God" songs
and Joe Gilbert preferred comic and nonsense numbers, now they have
grandchildren devoted both to gospel songs—the favorites of Helen's
daughter Jeanie Miller and Phydella's son Joe Hogan—and to Roger
Miller tunes. Jeanie Miller may worry now about her son Nathan's love

Family Reunion, Goshen, Arkansas, 1994. *Left to right,* Bill Hogan, Jeanie Miller, Phydella
Hogan, Helen Fultz, Ruth Gayer, Pat Fultz.
Photo by Jim Borden.

for a "rock music" that seems to her mere noise, but she might find
comfort in remembering her mother Helen's and her aunt Phydella's
liberties with "Jealous Lover," or their adoption of the Animals' 1964
version of "The House of the Rising Sun" and Creedence Clearwater's
1970 "Looking out My Back Door" as their own. Jerry Hogan now
reveres his mother's music, but remembers with some chagrin a time
when he felt very differently: "After we moved to California in 1961,
I went through a phase where I thought country music and banjos were
'uncool' even though I once made a feeble attempt to learn how to
play. In 1963, my mother and I made a bus trip from California back
to the midwest and Arkansas. She took her banjo along, naturally, and
I recall how embarrassed I was because I had to carry it for her. It was
just too much of a hick thing for a hip eighteen year old California kid
to handle."[134]

It's a given that the tastes of the children will at times confound and
appall their elders, but it's no less true that those same children soon end
up cherishing and passing on to their own children the music they

learned from their parents and now cannot separate from their most fundamental sense of who they are. Jerry Hogan now makes a point of asking his mother to play his favorite banjo tunes every time he comes to visit her. And what are those favorites? "Cripple Creek" and "Blue Bells of Scotland"—the latter being of course the same song cherished by his sister Martha, and long before that the special favorite of Jerry's grandfather Joe Gilbert, the song he wanted his son Buck to play at his funeral.

As for Nathan Miller, the rock and roll son whose musical tastes his mother, Jeanie, finds so worrisome—on Sunday mornings he can even now be seen singing with her in the church at Mayfield while his father, Dale, and his maternal grandparents, Bob and Helen Fultz, sit listening from the pews. It's a nearly empty church on a chill and rainy day, but the Fultz family is here, worshipping the Lord by raising their voices in song. The old family homeplace, maybe three miles west, may

Joe Gilbert with his grandson Jerry Hogan, Mayfield, Arkansas, 1947. Photograph by Walter Allen.

Photo courtesy Phydella Hogan and Helen Fultz.

Family reunion, Goshen, Arkansas, 1994. *Left to right,* Ashley Hogan, Mike Hogan, Phydella Hogan, Jerry Hogan, Brandon Hogan, Bill Hogan.
Photo by Jim Borden.

be fallen into ruin, and Phydellia Stringfield Scott, its keeper, who was the family matriarch for Alma and Phydella and Helen, has been buried in the cemetery at Goshen for half a century. But if by a miracle of resurrection three-quarters of this century were to vanish, and the family ancestors going back five generations were to gather in these nearly empty pews for today's service, they would be very much at home, would often need no hymnal to join their voices with great-great-grandson Nathan's in the morning's song.

The family thus gathered, that would seem so fragile to an outsider's eye, so dwarfed by the inclement weather and the emptiness of the small church, reveals itself upon closer inspection as attending quite successfully to its own continuance, passing on through its singing a whole way of life. The tradition the family loves changes continually, but in such changing abides, lives on at a center it in turn provides.

One August afternoon in 1992 or 1993 I sat at Helen Fultz's table with her and Phydella Hogan and talked again about songs. Bob Fultz came in for his lunch, and as she poured her husband's coffee and cut his pie she reminded him that he'd taught her "Nighttime in Nevada," a song we'd discussed earlier. "Remember?" she said, "you learned that out in New Mexico, before we got married. You were out there working with your uncle George and aunt Magna. You learned it from their girls, and when you came back you taught it to me. You said it made you so homesick, made you miss me so much when they sang it."[135] Bob Fultz didn't say much, he was busy with his pie, but I suddenly saw him, with his wife, as a man and woman who had succeeded, who built a life together and raised a family so successfully that four of their five children have built homes for their own families on land from the old homeplace. He and his wife, like Phydella, and like their parents before and children after, built good lives in times that were often hard, on ground that was often stony. And music, then and now, lives at the center of that building. The Gilberts, I realized, are people for whom

Grave of Phydellia Scott, Goshen, Arkansas, 1993.
Photo by the author.

Family Reunion, Goshen, Arkansas, June 1994. *Left to right (foreground)*, Mac Fultz, Andrea Fultz, Bob Fultz, Helen Fultz, Larry Fultz, Jeanie Miller.
Photo by Jim Borden.

the lovely blessings of the old Romanian New Year's carol ring vividly true. They are "as hard as stone, as strong as steel, as tough as song."[136]

I remembered too the stories Phydella and Helen had told me before about another time of separations. At the beginning of 1945, in the final year of the Second World War, Phydella and her husband split up. She was in Nevada, Missouri, then, pregnant with Jerry and working in a cafe. Bob Fultz was a Navy man, serving somewhere in the Pacific, but Helen was at home in Zion. She told Phydella to come— the Coal Mine Place had held two Gilbert families before, and it could do it again.

"My brother Leslie sent us bus fare for the trip," recalls Phydella, "and I took my three children and moved in with Helen and her four." Her memories of this time, as of other times, are filled with music: "If we hadn't had singing to get us through we would have both gone crazy. Of course we sang to the kids every night, and we sang as we did the never-ending chores connected with seven small children under ten years—eight after Jerry was born—as well as the gardening, canning, and house work."

The highlight of the week, cherished alike by adults and children, was a now-famous radio show, described in loving detail by Phydella: "every Saturday night we had four hours of the Grand Ole Opry at Nashville, Tennessee, with the Solemn Old Judge, Roy Acuff, Bill Monroe, and Grandpappy Jones along with the Fruit Jar Drinkers and a host of others." Phydella's account here is wholly celebrative, centering on her son Bill's struggles to stay awake long enough to hear his great favorite, Roy Acuff: "He would drape a blanket across two chairs and say, 'I'm just gonna lay down a minute. If I go to sleep, wake me when Roy Acuff comes on.' Gabriel himself couldn't have wakened that boy but he would be so mad at us next morning and swear we hadn't even tried."

But there were tough times, too, for the two women. Phydella was a woman without a husband, and Helen's husband was gone in harm's way. "Bob was on a battleship," Phydella remembers, "and sometimes Helen wouldn't hear from him for weeks, then she might get a whole stack of letters at once. She would be in seventh heaven until she'd read them all and then the fear would start creeping in again. Was he still all right when she got the letters? Maybe something had happened before

"The Coal Mine Place," Zion, Arkansas, 1993.
Photo by the author.

they even got mailed. All the dreads that hang over women in wartime would be there."[137]

That Helen Fultz turned to her music in these dark hours comes as no surprise. When the First Man of Navajo myth prepares for his dangerous journey up Giant Spruce Mountain his wife First Woman worries about him: "the devouring ones will surely set upon you," she says. "Surely you will be devoured like so many others have been." But he replies with confidence: "Do not be afraid," said he. "Nothing will go wrong. For I will surround myself with song. . . . You may be sure that the words of my songs will protect me."[138]

So Helen Fultz, as remembered by Phydella: "I could always tell when fear began to get her down. She'd grab her old guitar and head out the back door, or if the weather was bad she'd go into the back bedroom and shut the door. . . . I don't know if there were any special songs she sang, but after awhile she would come back in and be especially kind to the children, telling stories or playing games or singing to them, or maybe just fixing them something special to eat."[139]

Martha Hogan Estes, from the perspective of the child she then was, remembers her mother, Phydella, turning to her music for support in her own hard hours: "she sang and played when Daddy was gone with his buddies at night—as I recall, that was often. I realize now that she sang for companionship, to combat loneliness, frustration, anger, and fear, but as a kid I only knew that Mama sang." Her remembrance then turns to recollected economic hardship, but then returns, in characteristic family fashion, to close in music: "I remember times when she was out of cigarettes and would re-roll the stubs of old cigarettes, sometimes using brown paper; boil a cup of coffee, sometimes from reused coffee grounds; and pick that banjo and sing to us kids. We didn't know she was sad, lonely, or scared; we loved it."[140]

I thought again of all those times, of the stories and songs of those times, while I watched Phydella and Helen fussing over Bob Fultz, teasing him about his pie and remembering "Nighttime in Nevada." I saw too that Phydella and Helen accomplished the raising of their children as Bob and Helen accomplished their courtship and marriage, as the Gilbert family accomplished almost everything, with the help of music, by the use of song. They used "Nighttime in Nevada" to help their courtship, I thought, just as Helen and Phydella used Roy Acuff songs to raise Bill, and as Phydella sang "The Shadow of the Pines" to get her daughter Martha to comb and brush her hair. They all used music to communicate their devotion, to battle time and space and fear and illness and loneliness, to keep themselves together. They are still using it, I thought, right here, right now.

And then I spoke too quickly, without thinking: "You used that song to stay together, to overcome separation, didn't you?" I said. "You did it with songs, didn't you? You did everything with songs."

It was a strange outburst. I was too far gone in my scholar's frenzy, lost in my admiration for their wit and persistence and its lovely achievement. The joy of these recognitions, the sudden patterning of what had just before been isolated anecdote, however vivid, mere incident, however striking—I always forget that not everyone shares it. Bob Fultz didn't even look up, and even Helen and Phydella, who know me better and had witnessed such enthusiasms before, looked at me with some bewilderment. Of course, their looks seemed to say, what are you after all this interviewing and recording anyway—feebleminded? But finally Helen spoke, told me the truth: "We were always serious about our music," she said.

Helen Fultz, Bob Fultz, Mayfield, Arkansas, 1993.
Photo by the author.

Coda

INITIATED IN 1989, *Singing In Zion* was substantially complete by 1994, though of course any "ending" for such a project is necessarily arbitrary. In the winter of 1995, with only the notes and song annotations still incomplete, I went to Korea for a semester as a Fulbright lecturer. In April a letter arrived with news of Bob Fultz's death—he had been in failing health for several years. The family gathered to bury him in the Goshen cemetery, and dressed him, Phydella Hogan wrote, in the overalls he'd worn all his life.

In 1996 Phydella herself, weakened by illness, gave up her apartment in Fayetteville and moved in with her daughter and son-in-law, Kirby and Martha Estes. But in that same year Helen Fultz surprised and delighted everyone by marrying neighbor widower Chester Morris, a longtime friend with whom she shared a love for country and gospel music. I was back home by then—my daughter Masie and I attended the wedding at the Mayfield church and the party afterwards at the community building in Goshen.

There are also new arrivals in the family. At last count, as 1998 opens, Phydella Hogan has thirteen grandchildren, thirteen great-grandchildren, and two great-great-grandchildren, while Helen Fultz is not far behind with eleven grandchildren and sixteen great-grandchildren. And, of course, the latest news included music: Bob and Helen Fultz's youngest son, Mac, has a fine band, the Rhythm Method, fronted by the singing of his wife, Pat, and their youngest daughter, Andrea, only fourteen, is already playing electric guitar and starting a band of her own. Phydella's son Bill is still playing occasional gigs at weddings and nursing homes, though his oldest son, Richard, is too busy with his job on the police force to play with him much any more. Helen and daughter

Jeanie are of course still playing and singing in church, and sometimes husband and father Dale still joins in on harmonica.

Come back in fifty or one hundred years, all this suggests, and you'll find some things to recognize under all the change. The generations are born and pass on, but the family endures; the book comes to an end, but the music abides.

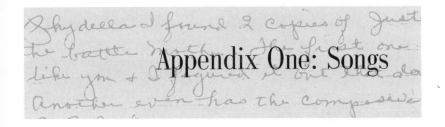

Appendix One: Songs

> *There is remembrance, and communion, altogether human and unhallowed. For families will not be broken. Curse them and expel them, send their children wandering, drown them in floods and fires, and old women will make songs out of all these sorrows and sit in the porches and sing them on mild evenings.*
>
> —Marilynne Robinson, *Housekeeping*
> (New York: Bantam Books, 1982), 194

ONLY SONGS mentioned in the text are discussed here—a complete list of the song titles in the Gilbert family songbook is found in Appendix Two. Songs are in order of their mention in the text, and are printed as they appear in the songbook manuscript, with indicators of "chorus" or attributions to *Heart Songs*, for example, left unaltered. Scores are provided for songs where taped performances were available, though no harmonization between printed text and taped performance is attempted. The Gilbert sisters wrote out their songs from memory, just as they sang them from memory. Their tradition is oral and aural at its core; variation is to be expected. Songs mentioned but not included in the family songbook are identified. Annotations by Phydella Hogan and Helen Fultz both in the original songbook manuscript and in early drafts of this book are included. My own annotations are bracketed and indented. These are in no way exhaustive and are intended as guides to currency in local and regional tradition and as aids to readers concerned with particular songs. For songs lacking local and/or regional variants, I have sometimes given references from further afield. For full bibliographic citations, see the References following the scores, song texts, and annotations.

I have made every effort to respect copyright; in several instances copyright restrictions forbid the printing of lyrics.

I Could Not Call Her Mother

The marriage rites were over
    And oh, I turned aside
To keep the guests from seeing
    The tears I could not hide.
I wreathed my face in smiling
    And led my little brother
To greet my father's chosen
    But I could not call her mother.

They've moved her dear old picture
    From its old accustomed place
And placed beside my father's
    A young and fairer face.
They've made my mother's chamber
    The boudoir of another
But I will not forget you
    My dear, my angel mother.
Tonight I heard her singing
    A song I used to love
When its sweet notes were uttered
    By her who sings above

It pained my heart to hear her
    The tears I could not smother
For every note was hallowed
    By the voice of my dear mother.

I know my father gives her
    The love he bore another
But if she were an angel
    I could not call her mother.

Remember how Mother's voice quavered when she sang this? I thought it was one of the most beautiful songs she sang. Do you think maybe it was because we know that mother was apt to go at any time, and yet, she kept right on with the business of living and serving her family as if she had all the time in the world, and went on living her religion as if today would be her last, that made us love this sort of thing? Whatever the reason, they don't sound the same when anyone else sings them. [P.H.]

[Randolph has this as "The Stepmother" (*Ozark Folksongs,* 4: 196–98). An early version from Arkansas appears in a 1928 newspaper article by Lilith Shell, "Folk Songs Furnished Most of Mountain Entertainment," *Arkansas Gazette*, March 11, 1928, sect. 2, 16. This number has popular music roots—it was twice copyrighted in the 1850s.]

Kitty Wells

I never shall forget the day
When we together roamed the dell
I kissed her cheek and named the day
That I would marry Kitty Wells.

CHORUS

The birds were singing gaily in the morning
The myrtle and the ivy were in bloom
The sun on the hilltops was a-dawning
It was there we laid her in the tomb.

Oh, death came in my cabin door
And stole from me my joy and pride
And when I found she was no more
I laid my banjo down and cried.

Oh, springtime has no charm for me
There's gloom and sadness in the dell
No brightness in the sun I see
Since I have lost my Kitty Wells.

I can't copy this song without adding the comments of Alma Allen, who sent the first full copy:

> Mama sang this ever since I can remember. I always used to listen for the sort of "waver" in her voice in this particular song. NOT a "quaver" like an old person would have, but a sort of broken, or up and down way of saying a word.

My apologies "Bill" for quoting you so exactly. Most of the comments I have sort of generalized, as they could be and usually are sentiments or memories held by all of us. I too, can remember the little trilly waver that mother used in this one, but I wouldn't have known how to express it if you hadn't thought of it first. Since lots of people may see these songs in years to come, and mine, yours and Helen's copy will be the same, well I say, "let 'em read and wonder at some of those unnecessary comments after the songs." They may be Greek to strangers, but to the Gilbert Clan they will make perfect nonsense, eh Helen? I thought you'd both agree.
P. H.   1960

Aren't you glad you made the comments? By now you'd probably have forgotten a lot of it? [H. F., note added in her draft copy of songbook, December 1993]

[Authorship of this mid-nineteenth-century piece is disputed, but most often ascribed to Charles E. Atherton. It has been much recorded by country singers, including Ernest Stoneman and Vernon Dalhart. Almeda Riddle learned it as a child from a school friend (Abrahams, *A Singer and Her Songs*, 57–59); versions also appear in Dugaw ("Dreams of the Past," 29–31), McNeil (*Southern Folk Ballads: Volume II*, 166–68), Owens (*Texas Folksongs*, 145–48), and Stilley ("The Stilley Collection: Part Two," 106–7).]

Dirty Faced Brat

Please let me scrape the snow from your door
No, get out! you dirty faced brat
And he went with one of his glossy curls
Sticking out through a hole in his hat.
But he turned once and said with a tear in his eye
Please, mister, my mother is poor
I told you once, No, take your shovel and go
And don't you return anymore.

His face was the picture of hunger and want
His heart was a stranger to joy
And he looked as he wiped the tears from his brown eyes
Like the wreck of a beautiful boy.
It is a blessing not all are the same
Not hard as the man in the store
For that night he went home and made his mother's heart glad
By driving the wolf from her door.

He told his poor mother how he had gone in
And asking to shovel the snow
The gentleman called him a dirty faced brat
And ordered him out of the store.
As he'd walked down the street, he was hailed by the nicest little girl
Who had wanted to know
"If you will wait there a minute little boy
Mama says won't you shovel the snow."

God bless that good woman, his poor mother cried
She's an angel on earth in disguise
As the little boy knelt by his bedside to pray
She watched him with tears in her eyes.
They were tears of love and affection for her child
They were tears from her brow of joy
Tears proud to know, that a mother had raised
A Christian and a dutiful boy.

That boy is no longer a boy, but a man
And his poor mother died years ago.
His beautiful wife is the sweet little girl
Who asked him to shovel the snow.
He is now taking care of a wreck of a man
In his home, who is blind as a bat
And he never will know his friend shoveled the snow
Or was ever the dirty faced brat.

Mama sang this one when we were all small and once when Ernest made fun of it, Aunt Myrtie gave him a scolding for laughing at a poor little boy whose hair stuck through a hole in his hat.

You couldn't hardly get those fit in when you were playing an instrument. Now she [mother] sang without an instrument so if she wanted to drawl something out she did. . . . That one ["Dirty Faced Brat"] was the hardest thing to do. I tried to do it for you didn't I one day? And I couldn't get the words in the lines to fit in. And then there was that other one . . . "Little Home in Sunny Tennessee." That was the hardest thing. [H. F., taped interview, Mayfield, Arkansas, January 22, 1991]

Another of Mother's favorites, and how she could sing it! [H. F., note added in her draft copy of songbook, December 1993]

[This is one of the collection's great puzzles. No other version of this song has been located.]

My Horses Ain't Hungry

My horses ain't hungry, they won't eat your hay
So, fare you well Molly, I'm going away.

Your people don't like me, they say I'm too poor
They say I ain't worthy to enter your door.

I know they don't like you, but why do you care
You know I'm your Molly, you know I'm your dear.

So why are you waiting, get ready I pray
And load up your wagon, we'll feed on the way!

This is one of the old songs Dad used to sing. I'm not sure if there is any other verse or not, but I can't "hear" his voice singing any other words. Is that the way you remember the old songs? I "listen" and in my mind I can see Mama or Dad when they sang these songs and I know exactly how they sound. I mean the way their voices went up and down, how the old-time tunes wavered, they had a kind of quaver you know; all of them nearly. (Please excuse sentence structure, I must write as I think, and I'm sure you'd not be able to understand me if I didn't!)

These comments are Billie's, about 1960. Uncle Huston also sang it. [P. H.]

[Randolph has this as "Texas Cowboy" (*Ozark Folksongs*, 4: 216), and Owens has it twice, as "Some Say I Drink Whiskey" (*Texas Folksongs*, 161–63) and "On Top of Old Smoky" (178–79). Another Ozark version is the bizarrely titled "Fair U-Well-Lizza" in High (*Old, Old Folk Songs*, 22–23).]

Fair Nottingham Town

As I went down to fair Nottingham town
A riding a horseback on my daddy's grey mare
With a white mane and tail and a list on her back
And not a hair on her but what was coal black.

She stood still and threw me off in a ditch
She bruised my shirt and dirtied my skin
With my saddle and stirrups I mounted again
And with my ten toes I rode off of the plain.

And as I rode on to fair Nottingham town
I met a strange company a riding around
A king and a queen and a company more
All riding a horseback and walking before.

A stark naked drummer a beating his drum
With his heels in his pockets before them did run
It made them so mad that they scarcely looked down
When I asked them the way to fair Nottingham town.

When I got there not a soul could I see
The streets were all crowded a lookin' at me
I sat myself down on a hot frozen stone
Ten thousand around me and me all alone.

I asked pretty Polly to fancy me now
And let us be married tomorrow right now
So married we were and I lived all alone
A family we raised, not a child of our own.

Our Grandfather Gilbert's family came from England to Texas when he was just a boy. This is an old song they brought with them. Grandpa taught it to Dad and he taught it to us.

[This is in Randolph as "Nottingham Fair" (*Ozark Folksongs*, 3: 201–2), and Ritchie has it as "Nottamun Town" (*Singing Family of the Cumberlands*, 115–17). Another Ozark version was collected by Max Hunter as "Adam Haw Town" (folksong collection, no. 17).]

Blue Bells

Not in the songbook collection, though a family favorite. An instrumental piece, without lyrics. Ernest Scott, who learned the piece in Mayfield from an old-time fiddler, claimed that the song was properly known as "Blue Bells of Scotland," but Phydella Hogan remembers the two as different songs. A tape she's heard of "Blue Bells of Scotland" has accompanying lyrics. [P. H., telephone conversation, April 12, 1998]

Turkey in the Straw

Not in the songbook. This popular fiddle tune, originally known as "Zip Coon" or "Old Zip Coon," goes back to 1834. It's sometimes credited to Bob Farrell, sometimes to George Washington Dixon.

Buffalo Gals

As I went lumbrin' down the street, down the street, down the street
A lovely girl I chanced to meet, Oh she was fair to view.
Oh Buffalo gals will ye come out tonight, will ye come out tonight,
    will ye come out tonight
Buffalo gals will ye come out tonight and dance by the light of the
    moon.

I asked her if she'd have some talk, have some talk, have some talk
Her feet covered up the whole sidewalk as she stood by side of me.

CHORUS

I'd like to make that gal my wife, gal my wife, gal my wife
And I'd be happy all my life if I had her by my side.

Heart Songs, p. 366

I know a different version but this is probably the original one. [H. F., note added in her draft copy of songbook, January 1994]

Yes—we sang it differently. Don't know how *this* copy got in without ours. I remember:

As I was walkin' down the street, down the street,
    down the street,
A pretty little girl I chanced to meet, oh she
    was fair to see.

CHORUS
Buffalo gals won't you come out tonight
Come out tonight, come out tonight?
Buffalo gals won't you come out tonight,
And dance by the light of the moon?

I danced with a gal with a hole in her stockin'
And her toes kept a-rockin', and her knees kept a-knockin'.
I danced with a gal with a hole in her stockin'
And we danced by the light of the moon.

[P. H., note added in her draft copy of songbook, August 1994]

[Randolph has four versions of this well-known play party piece (*Ozark Folksongs*, 3: 332–34). Another Ozark version is in Stilley ("The Stilley Collection: Part One," 16–18).

Old Dan Tucker

Old Dan Tucker went to town a ridin' a billy goat
A leadin' a hound, the hound he barked and the
billy goat jumped, throwed old Dan right a-straddle of
a stump.

CHORUS
Get outta the way for old Dan Tucker, he's too late to get
his supper, supper is over and breakfast a-cookin'
Old Dan Tucker a standin' a-lookin'.

Old Dan Tucker he got drunk, fell in the fire and
kicked up a chunk, A coal of fire got in the heel of
his shoe, and Lord God Almighty how the ashes flew.

Old Dan Tucker is a fine old man washed his face in the
frying pan, combed his head on a wagon wheel and died
with the toothache in his heel.

CHORUS
Get outta the way for old Dan Tucker, he's too
late to get his supper, supper over and the dishes washed
you'll get no supper here by gosh.

Must have always known this one. [H. F., note added in her draft copy
of songbook, January 1994]

[This celebrated number from the minstrel show and play party repertoire was
written by Dan Emmett in the early 1840s. Randolph has five versions (*Ozark Folksongs,*
3: 301–4). It's also in Stilley ("The Stilley Collection: Part One," 32–34).]

Green Corn

You be the dray horse, I'll be the rider
We'll go to grandad's and get some cider
Green corn . . . hard corn . . .
Bring along your demijohn I say.

CHORUS

Green corn, hard corn, bring along your demijohn
Green corn, hard corn, enough to choke the devil on
Green corn . . . hard corn . . .
Bring along your demijohn I say.

I come to the river and I couldn't get across
Jumped on an alligator, thought he was a hoss
Green corn . . . etc.

He smacked his jaws and I begin to holler
Opened up my demijohn and give him a swaller
Green corn . . . etc.

Got across the river, run across the fields
Durned ole alligator right on my heels
Green corn . . . etc.

Gonna pick a little cotton, make a little money
Buy a jug of cider and take it to my honey
Green corn, hard corn,
Bring along your demijohn I say.

All I know about this song is we played the music to it on the banjo! [H. F., note added in her draft copy of songbook, January 1994]

And I can't remember, but I think Ernest sang this. I already knew the first two verses and the chorus. The last three verses I made up for use in a skit some of my students did at a nursing home in Van Buren [Arkansas], about 1979. [P. H., note added in her draft copy of songbook, August 1994]

[Randolph has this as "I'll Meet You in the Evening" (*Ozark Folksongs*, 2: 342–43). His B version is titled "Green Corn," though both variants are markedly different from the Gilbert text. It's also in Owens (*Texas Folksongs*, 238–40).]

Cripple Creek

I got a gal at the head of the creek
Go up to see her 'bout the middle of the week.
Kiss her on the mouth just as sweet as any wine
Wraps herself around me like a sweet pertater vine.

CHORUS

Goin' up Cripple Creek, goin' in a run
Goin' up Cripple Creek to have a little fun
Goin' up Cripple Creek, goin' in a whirl
Goin' up Cripple Creek to see my girl.

Girls on Cripple Creek about half grown
Jump on a boy like a dog on a bone
Roll my britches legs to my knees
Wade old Cripple Creek whenever I please.

CHORUS

Cripple Creek's wide and Cripple Creek's deep
I'll wade old Cripple Creek afore I sleep
Roads are rocky and the hillside's muddy
I'm so drunk that I can't stand studdy*.

CHORUS

---

* steady

Learned to play the tune on the banjo when we were kids. Only knew words of the chorus. Found the rest in some old songbook I think. P. H.

So did I. [H. F., note added in her draft copy of songbook, January 1994]

[I think this piece is widely known, though it's missing from most of the regional collections. There is a version in Stilley ("The Stilley Collection: Part One," 34).

I'm a Little Wildwood Flower

Not in the songbook. I have found no trace of this number in the regional collections.

Jesus at the Well

Our Saviour once wandered this earth
As a man footsore and weary through Samaria land
The story he told most wondrously great
Salvation through Jesus for poor sinful men.

Then sing (yes, we'll sing) the sweet song (the sweet song)
The glo-rious (the sweet and glorious song, the sweet song) song
Of Jesus who died on the tree
He died (he died on the cruel cross, died on the tree) on the tree

For you and for me
He died on Mt. Calvary for you and for me
Then sing the sweet story
Salvation is free

Both footsore and weary he came to a well
And there to a woman his story did tell
She heard it with joy that her soul could be free
Salvation through Jesus for you and for me

CHORUS

Now brothers let's sing the sweet story so true
Salvation through Jesus for me and for you
Let every glad heart the great message now tell
The same and sweet story
There told at the well.

Another of Mother's favorite hymns. Billie called this "The Savior at Samaria."

I don't think this is in any songbook. My mother taught it to me. [H. F., Mullins Library tapes, 1960]

[I've not been able to locate this lovely piece in any hymnal.]

Summer Land of Love

There is a land of never ending day
Where saints shall forever with the Saviour stay
My spirit now is happy on the way to that summer land of Love.

CHORUS

No night (no night mars) mars the beauty of the day
No sor-row (no sorrow, grief or woe) shall drive the joy away
For ev-er (forever in that land) with Jesus I shall stay
In that summer land of love.

Though sorrow often may sweep around me here
And sometimes I'm almost overcome by fear
My soul shall rest where all is wondrous clear
In that summer land of love.

I'm serving Jesus as I onward go
By driving away the clouds of sin and woe
Sweet peace and rest my spirit soon shall know
In that summer land of love.

Now we did that one as a "special" too. I think we had a special song-book with all these odd one in it at home that we may have picked up somewhere. I don't know whether it was just some church's book that we had got or what, but they were not in the Methodist hymnal. "Summer Land of Love" is kind of lilty and happy sounding for a church song. And these are where you repeat with the alto—these in the parentheses. [P. H., taped interview conducted by Elizabeth Foster, Fayetteville, Arkansas, May 15, 1992]

The lines in brackets [parentheses] are for the alto or other harmony singer. Have no idea where it came from but was a family favorite ever since I can remember. [P. H., note added in her draft copy of songbook, August 28, 1994]

[This is missing from the regional folksong collections, and I have failed to locate it in any hymnal.]

Sally Goodin

Not in the songbook. This popular fiddle tune has been much recorded—Arkansas native Eck Robertson's 1922 version is often cited as the first country music record. It's in Stilley ("The Stilley Collection: Part Two," 80).

Dusty Miller

Not in the songbook.

Four in the Middle

Four in the middle and I can't jump (?) Josie
Four in the middle and I can't get around
Four in the middle and I can't jump Josie
I love Susie Brown.

Another old song we used to sing was something like this. There were a lot of verses to this but I can't remember what they were. They may have been just descending numbers until the set had been performed once. Anyway, the four girls stood in the middle and the boys joined hands and danced in a circle around them until some signal when one girl was claimed—or maybe they all grabbed a partner, like in a Paul Jones, I can't remember now. But someone always came up with enough verses to continue until everyone had got a partner and danced. Only, of course, it wasn't called dancing! And I always wondered what they meant by "jump Josie," but that is what they sang.

[Randolph prints nine versions of this popular play party piece (*Ozark Folksongs,* 3: 309–13).]

The Frozen Girl

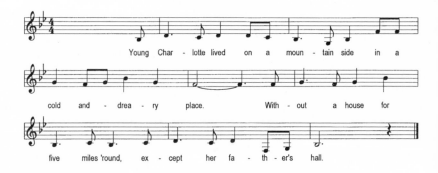

Young Charlotte lived on a mountain-side
In a cold and dreary place
Without a house for five miles round
Except her father's hall.

In a village sixteen miles away
Was a merry ball that night
Although the wind was freezing cold
Her merry heart was light.

Oh, daughter dear, the mother said
This blanket around you throw
For oh, the wind is freezing cold
And you'll catch your death of cold.

Oh, mother dear, the daughter cried
And she laughed like a gypsy queen
To ride in a blanked muffled up
I never should be seen.

Oh no, my cloak is warm enough
You know it's lined throughout
I have besides my silken scarf
To bind my neck about.

Into the sleigh she quickly sprang
And away they sped so fast
Young Charles ne'er thought as he tucked her in
This ride would be her last.

What a night, cried Charles, I never knew
These reins I scarce can hold
She replied in a low and frozen tone
I am exceedingly cold.

He cracked his whip, he urged his steed
Still faster than before,
Through five more miles of dreary cold
In silence they did go.

How fast, cried Charles, the frozen snow
Is gathering on your brow
She murmured in a low and trembling tone
I'm growing warmer now.

At last they arrived at the lighted hall
The people gathered round
Young Charles stretched forth his arms to help
Pretty Charlotte to the ground.

She made no move, she made no sound
Young Charles excited grew
Why sit ye there like a monument
That has no power to move.

He chaffed her hands, he smoothed her cheek
He kissed her marble brow

And his thoughts went back to when she said,
"I'm growing warmer now."

Learned from mother.

[This well-known American ballad (Laws, *Native American Balladry*, G17) shows up in many regional collections, often as "Young Charlotte." Randolph has eight versions (*Ozark Folksongs*, 4: 105–11), and it's also in Belden (*Ballads and Songs*, 308–17), Moore and Moore (*Ballads and Folk Songs of the Southwest*, 327–31), Owens (*Texas Folksongs*, 98–100), High (*Old, Old Folk Songs*, 32–33), Rainey (*Songs of the Ozark Folk*, 46–47), and Stilley ("The Stilley Collection: Part Two," 91–93).]

Poor Bennie

Fa - ther dear fa - ther come home with me now, the
clock in the stee - ple strikes one. You
said you were com - ing right home from the shop as
soon as your day's work was done. Come
home come home. Fa - ther dear fa - ther come
home. Come home, Come home Please
fa - ther dear fa - ther come home.

Father, dear father, come home with me now
The clock in the steeple strikes one
You said you were coming right home from the shop
As soon as your day's work was done.

CHORUS

Come home, come home, please father, dear father, come home.
Come home, come home, please father, dear father, come home.

The fire is all out and the house is so dark
And mother's been waiting since tea
With poor brother, Bennie, so sick in her arms
And no one to help her but me.

Father, dear father, come home with me now
The cock it is crowing for dawn
And this is the message Ma sent me to bring
Come quickly or he will be gone.

Yes, we are alone, for poor Bennie is dead
And gone with the angels of life
And these are the very last words that he said
"I want to kiss papa good night."

Mother used to sing this and all us kids would cry and then beg her to sing it again.

[This was written by Henry Clay Work—he titled it "Come Home, Father" and published it in 1864. Randolph prints it as "Father, Dear Father, Come Home With Me Now" (*Ozark Folksongs*, 2: 396–97), and Eleanor Henderson's 1950 University of Arkansas M.A. thesis collection has a version (titled "The Drunkard's Daughter") obtained from Mrs. T. M. Davis (87–88). Burdine and McCarthy list a version titled "Poor Benny" ("Sister Singers," 409).]

The Blind Child

They tell me Father, that tonight
You wed another bride
And that you'll clasp her in your arms
Where my dear mother died.

They say her name is Mary too
The name my mother bore
But Father is she kind and true
Like the one you loved before.
And is her step so soft and low
Her voice so sweet and mild
And father will she kindly love
Your blind and helpless child.

Please Father do not bid me come
To greet your loving bride
I could not meet her in the room
Where my dear mother died.
Her picture's hanging on the wall
Her books are lying there
And there's the harp her fingers touched
And there her vacant chair.
The chair where by her side I knelt
To say my evening prayer
Dear father, it would break my heart
I could not meet her there.

And when I cry myself to sleep
As now I oft-times do
Then gently to my chamber creep
My new mama and you
And bid her gently press a kiss
Upon my throbbing brow
Just like my own dear mother did
But father you're weeping now.
Now let me kneel down by your side
And to our Savior pray
That God's right hand may lead you both
Through life's long weary way.

The prayer was murmured soft and low
I'm tired now, she said
He raised her gently in his arms
And laid her on the bed
Then as he turned to leave the room
One joyful cry was given
He turned to see the last sweet smile
His blind child was in Heaven
They laid her by her mother's side
And raised a marble there
On it engraved these simple words
"There'll be no blind ones there."

One of Mother's songs, and the one Joe always wanted me to sing. When he was about 3 or 4 he called it "The Girl With the Bandage On Her Eyes." [P. H., note added in her draft copy of songbook, August 1994]

[This piece has been much collected in the Ozarks. Randolph prints three versions (*Ozark Folksongs*, 4: 191–93). It's in the Henderson collection (again from Lula Davis) as "The Blind Girl" ("An Ozark Song Book," 66–67), and Rainey (*Songs of the Ozark Folk*, 43) calls it "Little Blind Child." It's also in Belden (*Ballads and Songs*, 275–76) and the Brown collection from North Carolina (2: 392–94). Almeda Riddle knew this as "Blind Child's Prayer" (Abrahams, *A Singer and Her Songs*, 52–55).]

Don't Go Out Tonight, My Darling

Not in the songbook. Not sung by the Gilberts.

Old Grey Beard and His Leggins

My mammy told me to open the door
Ha-ha I won't have him,
I opened the door and he fell in the floor
With his old grey beard and his leggins

My mammy told me to get him a chair
Ha-ha I won't have him,
I got him a chair and he called me his dear
With his old grey beard and his leggins.

My mammy told me to fetch him a stool
Ha-ha I won't have him,
I fetched him the stool and he acted like a fool
With his old grey beard and his leggins.

My mammy told me to bring him some fish
Ha-ha I won't have him,
I brought him some fish and he swallowed the dish
With his old grey beard and his leggins.

My mammy told me to put him to bed
Ha-ha I won't have him,
I put him to bed and he stood on his head
With his old grey beard and his leggins.

My mammy told me to cover him up
Ha-ha I won't have him,
I covered him up and he whined like a pup
With his old grey beard and his leggins.

My mammy told me to tell him to go
Ha-ha I won't have him,
I told him to go but he went mighty slow
With his old grey beard and his leggins.

My mammy told me to get her the gun
Ha-ha I won't have him.
I got her the gun and you oughtta seen him run
With his old grey beard and his leggins.

When we were children (very small ones too) we used to go to Grandma's every fall. We went in a wagon, or buggy and later in a "T" model Ford and it was quite a treat. We always sang at these gatherings in the afternoon and sometimes as many as a hundred people would be there. Seemed like everyone in our family and quite a few of the neighbors played a stringed instrument of some sort or a "French harp" or maybe a "Jew's Harp" which we pronounced "Juice Harp." When I tried to play one it WAS rather juicy. Anyhow, we young'uns used to sing this old ditty and act it out for the older people and we thought we were really actors.

Here's another old song acted out with appropriate gestures. [P. H., Mullins Library tapes, 1960]

I can remember us acting out all those old silly songs like "Old Grey Beard and His Leggins" and all of those, you know. We'd act those out every time we went to Grandma's or went to somebody's house. [P. H., taped interview conducted by Elizabeth Foster, Fayetteville, Arkansas, October 15, 1991]

Our granddaughter loves this (Andrea). [H. F., note added in her draft copy of songbook, January 1994]

[This is all over the regional collections, under many titles. Randolph calls it "The Old Black Booger" (*Ozark Folksongs*, 1: 291–94), though his B version, from Van Buren, is titled "Shoes, Boots, and Leggins." In Belden it's "The Old Man's Courtship" (*Ballads and Songs*, 264); Moore and Moore call it "The Old Man Who Came Over the Moor" (*Ballads and Folk Songs of the Southwest*, 253–54), and Owens has it as "Old Shoes Boots and Leggins" (*Texas Folksongs*, 217). Four Ozark versions appear in the Hunter collection (folksong collection, no. 687) and Rainey (*Songs of the Ozark Folk*, 6) also has it. The Brown North Carolina collection prints five versions (3: 17–20).]

My Mother Was a Lady

Three drummers sat at dinner in a grand hotel one day,
While dining they were chatting in a jolly sort of way.
And when a pretty waitress brought them a tray of food,
They spoke to her familiarly in a manner rather rude.

At first she did not heed them or make the least reply
Until at last a remark was made that brought teardrops to her eyes,
Then facing her tormentors with cheeks now burning red,
She was a perfect picture as appealingly she said:

CHORUS

My mother was a lady, like yours you will allow
Perhaps you have a sister who needs protection now
I've come to this great city to find a brother dear,
And you wouldn't dare insult me, sir, if Jack were only here.

They sat there, stunned, in silence until one cried in shame,
Forgive me, Miss, I meant no harm, pray tell me what's your name.
She told him and he cried again, I know your brother too,
We've been friends for many years and he often speaks of you.
He'll be so glad to see you, and if you'll only wed
I'll take you to him as my wife for I love you since you said:

Repeat chorus

This is a song my brother, Carl, found in a magazine. I'm not sure just when but probably just before the 1920s or thereabouts. Since he didn't know the tune to the song he made one for it. We have since heard the original tune but always liked Carl's better and sang it to that tune. P. H.

They found that first in the *Comfort Magazine,* and my brother [Carl] liked it so well, and we didn't have any music to it, so he made a tune to go with it. It is a song with a tune because we found it later. But by then they were so used to his that we'd rather have it. [P. H., taped interview conducted by Elizabeth Foster, Fayetteville, Arkansas, May 15, 1992]

In later years some country singer put this out on a record. Seems like it was Red Sovine but I'm not sure. [H. F., note added in her draft copy of songbook, January 1994]

[This 1896 piece by Edward B. Marks with music by Joseph W. Stern is rarely found in the regional collections. Almeda Riddle knew it, evidently as "The Two Drummers" (Abrahams, *A Singer and Her Songs,* 187), and the Max Hunter collection also has it (folksong collection, no. 425).]

Empty Cot in the Bunkhouse

There's an empty cot in the bunkhouse tonight
There's a pinto's head hanging low
His spurs and chaps they hang on the wall
Limpy's gone where all good cowboys go
There's a ranch for every cowboy
Where the foreman takes care of his own
There will be an empty saddle tonight
But he's happy up there I know.

He was riding the range last Saturday noon
When a norther had started to blow
With his head on his chest, heading into the West
He was stopped by a cry soft and low.
There a crazy young calf had strayed from his ma,
And was lost in the snow and the storm
And he lay in a heap at the end of the draw
Huddled all in a bunch to keep warm.

Limpy hobbled his feet, threw him over the back
And started again for the shack
But the wind got cold and the snow piled up
And poor Limpy strayed from the shack.
He arrived at three in the morning
And he put the maverick to bed
Then he fell on his bunk unable to move
Next morning old Limpy was dead.

There's a cot unused in the bunkhouse tonight
There's a pinto's head hanging low—
His spurs and chaps they hang on the wall
Limpy's gone where all good cowboys go
There's a place for every cowboy
Who has that kind of a love
And someday he'll ride on pinto again
On the range up there above.

Old song of the '30s or '40s. Another one learned from the grape pickers—guitar picker named Harold played a seventh on this song, C7, first time I ever knew there was such a thing. H. F.

[Written in 1934 by Gene Autry, this number is missing from all the regional folk-song collections. There is a good discussion of it by Jim Bob Tinsley (*He Was Singin' This Song*, 104–6).]

The Derby Ram

As I went down to Derby town upon a market day
I saw the biggest ram, sir, that ever fed on hay.
The ram was fat behind, sir, the ram was fat before
He measured ten yards round, sir, I think it was no more.
Hubelocus, tubelocus, you may think I lie
But you can go to Derbytown and see the same as I.

The wool grew on his back, sir, it reached to the sky
And there the eagles built their nests I heard the little ones cry.
The wool grew on his belly, sir, and reached to the ground
'Twas sold in Derbytown, sir, for forty thousand pounds.
Hubelocus, tubelocus, you may think I lie
But you can go to Derbytown and see the same as I.

The wool upon his tail, sir, filled more than fifty bags
You had better keep away, sir, when that tail shakes and wags.
The horns upon his head, sir, were as high as man could reach
The Quakers built a pulpit there to have a place to preach.
Hubelocus etc.

And he who knocked the ram down was drownded(?) in his blood
And he who held the dish, sir, was carried away in the flood.
Then all the boys in Derbytown came beggin' for his eyes
To kick about the street, sir, as any good football flies.
Hubelocus etc.

The mutton from this ram, sir, gave all the army meat
And what was left I'm told, sir, was served out to the fleet.
Oh, as I went to Derbytown upon a market day
I saw the biggest ram, sir, that was ever fed on hay.
Hubelocus etc.

Learned from my father-in-law, Bill Hogan Sr., Nevada, Missouri about
1940. P.H.

[This English song has been widely printed in American folksong collections.
Randolph has three versions (*Ozark Folksongs,* 1: 393–400); Belden (*Ballads and Songs,*
224–25) and Owens (as "Derby's Town," *Texas Folksongs,* 230–31) also have it. It's in

Brown's North Carolina collection (2: 439–40), Leonard Roberts's Kentucky collection (*Sang Branch Settlers,* 101–2), and Jean Ritchie's *Singing Family of the Cumberlands* (41–43). Max Hunter's Ozark collection includes four versions (folksong collection, no. 136).]

When I Was a Little Boy

When I was a little boy, to London I did go
To set upon a picket like a feller at a show.
Tum-a-row-tum-a-ring-sty-deedle-all-a-day.

I set right there till a giant passed by.
He looked down on me and his head touched the sky.
Tum-a-row-tum-a-ring-sty-deedle-all-a-day.

I bantered for a wrestle with a hop-skip-run.
I threw him for the sport and killed him when I was done.
Tum-a-row-tum-a-ring-sty-deedle-all-a-day.

The people all seen this deed I done.
They give me gold and silver that'd weigh three ton.
Tum-a-row-tum-a-ring-sty-deedle-all-a-day.

I built a little box just three acres square,
And all the money that I got I put it right there.
Tum-a-row-tum-a-ring-sty-deedle-all-a-day.

When I traveled I traveled like an ox,
And in my jacket pocket, well I packed my little box.
Tum-a-row-tum-a-ring-sty-deedle-all-a-day.

I bought a little hen and her color was fair.
I set her on a mussel shell she hatched out a hare.
Tum-a-row-tum-a-ring-sty-deedle-all-a-day.

The hare turned to a horse sixteen hands high,
And if anybody beats this they tell a big lie.
Tum-a-row-tum-a-ring-sty-deedle-all-a-day.

This is an old Irish ballad sung by my father-in-law who was so *very* Irish that when he was "mad" or drunk his brogue became so pronounced you could hardly understand him. Copied 1960—by Phydella Hogan

Well, I don't know what the name of this is. My father-in-law used to sing it up in Missouri. [P. H., Mullins Library tapes, 1960]

Learned from my father-in-law, Bill Hogan, Sr. at Nevada, Missouri about 1936–37. I don't know if it has a title. He just called it "When I Was a Little Boy." [P. H., Fayetteville, Arkansas, October 28, 1993]

[Randolph includes two Missouri versions (*Ozark Folksongs*, 3: 47–48), but this piece is not found in the other regional collections.]

The Green Willow Tree

There was a ship sailed from the North Country
Crying over the lowlands low
There was a ship sailed from the North Country
And the name of the ship was the Turkey Shivaree
When she sailed o'er the lowlands, lonesome, low
Where she sailed o'er the lowlands low.

She hadn't been a-sailin but weeks two or three
Crying o'er the lowlands low
She hadn't been a-sailin but weeks two or three
Till she hove in sight of the Green Willow Tree
Lying anchored in the lowlands, lonesome low
Lying anchored in the lowlands low.

I'll give you gold I'll give you a fee
Crying o'er the lowlands low
I'll give you gold, I'll give you a fee
And my lovely little daughter your wife for to be
If you'll sink her in the lowlands, lonesome low
If you'll sink her in the lowlands low.

He bared his breast and off swum he
Crying o'er the lowlands low
He bared his breast and off swum he
Till he came in sight of the Green Willow Tree
Lying anchored in the lowlands, lonesome low
Lying anchored in the lowlands low.

He had a tool which he meant for to use
Crying o'er the lonesome low
He had a tool which he meant for to use
To lay against the cabin and eleven holes to push
To sink her in the lowlands lonesome low
To sink her in the lowlands low.

They grabbed for their hats and they grabbed for their caps
Crying o'er the lonesome low
They grabbed for their hats and they grabbed for their caps
And they all began stopping up the salt water gaps
But he sank her in the lowlands, lonesome low
He sank her in the lowlands low.

He bowed his breast and back swam he
Crying o'er the lowlands low
He bowed his breast and back swam he
Saying now I'll have the wife the captain gave me
For I sank her in the lowlands lonesome low
I sank her in the lowlands low.

O captain, captain take me on board
Crying o'er the lowlands low
Captain o captain take me on board
And be unto me as good as your word
For I sank her in the lowlands lonesome low
I sank her in the lowlands low.

I'll give you no gold and I'll give you no fee
Crying etc.
I'll give you no gold and I'll give you no fee
And my daughter will never be wed to thee
Tho you sunk 'em in the lowlands lonesome low etc.

If it wasn't for the virtue of all your men
Crying etc. and repeat 1
I'd do you like I just did them
I'd sink you in the lowland, lonesome low
I'd sink you in the lowland low.

Then he bowed his breast and off swum he
repeat as before
And he bid farewell to the Turkey Shivaree
As she sailed in the lowlands, lonesome low
Etc.

Learned at Nevada, Missouri from my mother-in-law, Margaret (Meg) Hogan. P. H.

I think she called it "Sinking in the Lowland Sea." She sang it unaccompanied. She never did sing with music, but she had a wonderful voice. This one had all sorts of minors in it, and she'd get every one. I usually sang with an instrument, and I didn't know any minor chords, so I just slid all around 'em when I tried to sing. [P. H., Fayetteville, Arkansas, December 14, 1993]

[This Child ballad (286) is very strong in Ozark tradition, appearing in many collections under a variety of titles. Randolph (under "The Lowlands Low") prints five versions (*Ozark Folksongs*, 1: 195–201), Belden (as "The Golden Vanity") has three (*Ballads and Songs*, 97–100), while Moore and Moore call it "The Sweet Trinity" (*Ballads and Folk Songs of the Southwest*, 134–35). Irene Carlisle's 1952 University of Arkansas M.A. thesis prints three versions ("Fifty Ballads and Songs," 45–51); one came from T. M. Davis as "The Turkish Reveille," and another is reprinted in McNeil (*Southern Folk Ballads*, 1: 34–37). Stilley has it as "The Merry Golden Tree" ("The Stilley Collection: Part One," 4–6). See also the Brown collection from North Carolina (2: 191–95). Almeda Riddle knew it under several titles (Abrahams, *A Singer and Her Songs*, 141–46), and Max Hunter's Ozark collection has five versions, also under various titles (folksong collection, no. 623).]

Way Over in the Promised Land

Colie, colie, scrootch tum a nairy
Colie, colie, scrootch tum a nairy
Colie, colie, scrootch tum a nairy
Si oh! Clo-poka-lo-shalla-hay.

Where oh where are the Hebrew children
Where oh where are the Hebrew children
Where oh where are the Hebrew children
Way over yonder in the promised land.

Colie, colie, skin my finnikin
Colie, colie skin my finnikin
Colie, colie skin my finnikin
Si oh! Clo-poka-lo-shalla-hay.

Where oh where is the prophet Daniel
Where oh where is the prophet Daniel
Where oh where is the prophet Daniel
Away (Way?) over yonder in the promised land.

Colie, colie, cong go nolie
Colie, colie cong go nolie
Colie colie cong go nolie
Si oh! Clo-poka-lo-shalla-hay.

Where oh where is good old Moses
Where oh where is good old Moses
Where oh where is good old Moses
Way over yonder in the promised land.

Clynie watcha cly watcha cly nah twyo
Clynie watcha cly watcha cly nah twyo
Clynie watcha cly watcha cly nah twyo
Si oh! Clo-poka-lo-shalla-hay.

By and by we'll go and see them
By and by we'll go and see them
By and by we'll go and see them
Way over yonder in the promised land.

Written down from memory in 1960 by Phydella Hogan and Alma (Billie) Allen. Our dad learned this Indian Version of "Way Over In The Promised Land" while he lived in what is now the state of Oklahoma but was then called Indian Territory. I believe the Indians he learned it from were Cherokee, and we have tried to put the words down as they sounded to us. The English words are below each stanza, so that if anyone knows Cherokee they can tell if we have it right. We think it has a beautiful chantlike tune and rhythm.

We loved to get Dad to sing this. [H. F., note added in her draft copy of songbook, January 1994]

[This is an old song with a mystery at its center. The *Original Sacred Harp* calls it "Hebrew Children" (other sacred harp collections title it "The Promised Land") and credits it to Peter Cartwright, a clergyman from Virginia. The mystery is its acquisition of the "Indian" association. Of Belden's two versions (*Ballads and Songs*, 457–59), the B variant is titled "Indian Song," while Brown's North Carolina collection (3: 685) includes a "Cherokee Hymn." Almeda Riddle's version is called "Nishi"—she also associates the songs with "Cherokee Strip" Indians (Abrahams, *A Singer and Her Songs*, 50–52, 175–76). Max Hunter's Ozark collection includes two versions (folksong collection, no. 710).]

Twilight A-Stealing

Not in the songbook. For a good discussion, see W. K. McNeil's *Southern Mountain Folksongs* (112–14, 211–12). McNeil's version is from Almeda Riddle.

There Was an Old Woman and She Had a Little Pig

Not in the songbook.

How Tedious and Tasteless the Hours

Not in the songbook.

Jerry, Go and Ile That Car

Oh, it's ring the bell and blow the whistle
And Lurie go ile the car-r
The handle up, the handle down
Tight clutchin' to the bar.

Raise me up so I can see the old handcar
Before I die
These were the very words
Poor Lurie he would cry . . .

    Alma
Come all ye railroad section men
And listen to my song
It is of Larry O'Sullivan
Who now is dead and gone.
For twenty years a section boss,
He never lost a car-r
Oh it's 'g'int ahead and cinter back
An' Jerry go an ile that car-r-r.

For twenty years a section boss
He worked upon the track
And be it to his credit
He niver had a wrack.
For he kept iver j'int right up to the p'int
Wid the tap of the tampin' bar-r
And while the byes was a-shimmin' the ties
It's Jerry wud yez ile that car-r-r.

'Twas in November, in the winter time
An' the ground all covered wid snow
'Come put the handcar-r on the track
An' over the section go!
Wid his big sojer coat buttoned up to his throat
All weathers he would dare—
An' it's Paddy Mack, will yez walk the track,
An' Jerry, go and ile that car-r-r.

"Give my respicts to the Road-masther,"
Poor Larry he did cry
And lave me up that I may see
The ould hand-car-r before I die."
They lay the spike-maul upon his chest
The gauge an' the ould claw-bar-r
And while the byes do be fillin' the grave,
"O, Jerry, go an' ile that car-r-r!"

I'm not quite sure, but I think the tune is almost the same as your version, and I bet they both came from the same Irish folksong. All of them get changed as they spread through the country.
P. H.

Never heard of it. [H. F., note added in her draft copy of songbook, January 1994]

[This American ballad (Laws H30) is rare in regional collections. Belden has it as "The Old Section Boss" (*Ballads and Songs,* 445–46). Norm Cohen's *Long Steel Rail* includes a thorough discussion (543–46).]

Washed My Hands in Muddy Water

I learned this from a couple in Lincoln, NE. who used to sing it with our group, "Country Strings," in the 1960s. Their name was Hyslop—the man's name was Joy. I can't recall her name for sure but I think it may have been *Jean* or *June.* I really liked the song. Am not sure if Helen ever sang it but I did. [P. H., note added in her draft copy of songbook, August 28, 1994]

[A five-stanza version of this song appears in the Gilbert songbook, but copyright restrictions do not allow for its printing here.]

[This is a 1960s piece, written by Joe Babcock, and recorded by country singer Stonewall Jackson (in 1965) and pop singer Johnny Rivers (in 1966). There is a version in the Max Hunter collection (folksong collection, no. 716).]

Old John Bull

Another War Eagle song to the tune of Yankee Doodle.

Once on a time old Johnny Bull
Flew in a raging fury
And said that Jonathan should have
No trial, sir, by jury.
That no elections could be held
Across the briny waters
And now, said he, we'll tax the tea
Of all her sons and daughters.

Then down he sat in burly state
And blustered like a grandee
And in derision made a tune
Called "Yankee Doodle Dandy."

Yankee Doodle, these are facts
Yankee Doodle Dandy
My son of wax, your tea I'll tax
Yankee Doodle Dandy.

John sent the tea from o'er the sea
With heavy duty rated
But when it reached the Boston shore (Well, they rhyme anyway!)
Its cargo was ill-fated.

Then Jonathan to pout began
And raised a strong embargo
We'll drink no tea, dear sir, said he
Threw overboard the cargo.

Yankee Doodle keep it up
Yankee Doodle Dandy
We'll poison with a tax, your cup
Yankee Doodle Dandy.

A long war then they had in which
John was at last defeated
And Yankee Doodle was the March
To which his troops retreated.

Yankee Doodle keep it up
Yankee Doodle Dandy
(We didn't drink your poison cup) (This also rhymes!)
Yankee Doodle Dandy!

So . . . you forgot two lines in fifth verse and one in last chorus. Never let it be said we can't improvise! Billie's.

I don't remember this at all. [H. F., note added in her draft copy of songbook, January 1994]

Neither do I. But the older kids must have sung it since Billie remembered it so well. [P. H., note added in her draft copy of songbook, August 1994]

[This number is missing from the regional collections. S. B. Luce's *Naval Songs: A Collection of Original Selected and Traditional Sea Songs* has it as one of several pieces titled "Yankee Doodle" (24), and attributes the lyrics to "Gen. Geo. P. Morris, 1802–1864."]

Nighttime in Nevada

Not in the songbook. Helen Fultz made a tape of this song as a birthday present for her sister Phydella Hogan in 1974.

Bad Companions

Come all you young companions and listen unto me
I'll tell you a sad story of some bad company
I was born in Pennsylvania among the beautiful hills
And the memory of my childhood is warm within me still.
I had a kind old mother who often would plead with me
And the last advice she gave me was "Son seek God in need."
I had two loving sisters as kind and good as could be
And down on their knees before me they prayed and wept for me.
But I did not like my father, I did not like my home
I had in view far rambling so far away did roam
I bid adieu to my loved ones, to home I said farewell
And I landed in Chicago, the very depths of hell.
Twas there I took to drinking, I sinned both night and day
And yet within my bosom a feeble voice would say
Farewell, farewell my loved one, may God protect my boy
And blessings ever be with him throughout his manhood joy.
I courted a fair young maiden, her name I will not tell
For I would never disgrace her as I am doomed for hell
Twas on one beautiful evening, the stars shone in the sky
And with a fatal dagger I bid her spirit fly.
Then justice overtook me, you all can plainly see
My soul is doomed forever throughout eternity
And now I'm on the scaffold, my moments are not long
You may forget the singer but don't forget the song.

I think Carl taught us this one when we were all small.

[Randolph prints two versions as "Taney County" (*Ozark Folksongs,* 2: 139–41), though his B text is titled "Bad Companions." There's a text in John Lomax's pioneering *Cowboy Songs and Other Frontier Ballads* of 1910 (81–82), and Laws also includes it (E15). Carl T. Sprague, the Carter Family, and Vernon Dalhart, among others, made early country music recordings.]

Rovin' Gambler

I am a roving gambler, I've gambled all around
Wherever I meet with a deck of cards I lay my money down
I lay my money down, I lay my money down.

I've gambled out in Washington, I've gambled down in Spain
I'm going back to Georgia to gamble my last game.

I hadn't been in Washington not many more weeks than three
When I fell in love with a pretty little girl she fell in love with me.

She took me in her parlor, she cooled me with her fan
And she whispered low in her mother's ear, I love that Gamblin' man

Oh daughter, my dear daughter, how can you treat me so
To leave your dear old mother and with a gambler go.

Mother my dear mother, you know I love you well
But the love I have for the gambling man no human tongue can tell.

Oh mother my dear mother, I'll tell you if I can
If you ever see me comin' back again it will be with my gamblin' man.

I hear the train a comin', it's comin' around the curve
A whistlin' and a blowin' and strainin' every nerve.

I've gambled out in Washington I've gambled down in Spain
So I'm goin' back to Georgia to gamble my last game.

I believe we learned this from Carl—don't know when he learned it.

[This is in Laws (H4) as "The Gambling Man." Randolph has this in three versions as "The Guerrilla Man" (*Ozark Folksongs,* 4: 356–60), and Belden calls it "The Guerrilla Boy" (*Ballads and Songs,* 374–77). Almeda Riddle learned it from her husband but "sung it very little," as she considered it a "man or male type" song (Abrahams, *A Singer and Her Songs,* 185). Other versions are in Owens (*Texas Folksongs,* 183–85), Stilley ("The Stilley Collection: Part One," 24–25), the Brown collection from North Carolina (3: 78–79), and the Max Hunter Ozark collection (folksong collection, no. 544).]

Home Sweet Home

We were lying out on the prairie
On Franklin's range one night
With our heads upon our saddles
The fire was burning bright.
Some were telling stories
And some were singing songs
Others were idly smoking
As the hours rolled along.

At last they fell to talking
Of distant friends so dear
One boy raised his head from his saddle
And brushed away a tear.
This boy was young and handsome
His face bore the look of care
His eyes were the color of heavenly blue
He wore light wavy hair.

They asked him why he left his home
Which was to him so dear
He said, now boys I'll tell you why
I left old Kansas' shore.
I fell in love with a pretty little girl
Her face was soft and white
But another fellow loved her too
So it ended in a fight.

The other fellow was Tom Smith
We'd been good friends for years
And Tom and I shared each other's joys
Our sorrows and our fears.
Oh how it makes me shudder
When I think of that sad night
When Tom and I were first quarreling
I struck him with my knife.

[How still and white he lay there
With blood gushing from his head.

Said Bob old boy you'll be sorry
When you see me laying here dead.]

Oh yes, I will forgive you
As you've asked to be forgiven
We've been good friends on earth, now
Let's be good friends in heaven.
So now you know the reason
Why I'm compelled to roam
A murderer of the deepest
Is far from home, sweet home.

Carl learned this one in Kansas while we lived at War Eagle in the early 1920s. Probably 1921. Carl had gone to harvest wheat in Kansas that year.

We sang this a lot as it was well liked as a "cowboy song." When we sang for people someone invariably asked, "Do you know any cowboy songs." [H. F., note added, with fifth stanza in brackets above, in her draft copy of songbook, December 1993]

[This is "The Wandering Cowboy" in Randolph (*Ozark Folksongs,* 2: 204–7), the same title Laws uses (B7). It's also found in McNeil (*Southern Folk Ballads,* 1: 157–59, 213) and (as "Franklin Slaughter Ranch") in Glenn Ohrlin's *The Hell-Bound Train: A Cowboy Songbook* (159). Brown's North Carolina collection has it as "A Jolly Group of Cowboys" (2: 619–21), while Eleanor Henderson's 1950 University of Arkansas M.A. thesis collection calls it "Home Sweet Home," like the Gilberts ("An Ozark Song Book," 24–25).]

Little Green Valley

All night long in my dreams I see a spot far away
Nestled in the hills in the land that I love
Stormy weather may come but whether the sky is blue or gray
I keep dreaming of sunlight streaming from heaven above;

I see a candlelight down in the little green valley
Where morning glory vines are climbing round my door
Oh how I wish I were there tonight down in the little green valley
For then my homesick heart would trouble me no more.
There's only one thing ever gives me consolation
And that's the dream that I'll be going back some day
And every night down upon my knees I pray the lord to please
        take me
Back to that little old green valley far away.

It's not hard to see just what's wrong with me all the time
When I tell you I'm homesick, lonesome and sad
There's a deep regret I can never get off my mind
That I went to roam, left the only home I ever had;

I hear a mockingbird down in the little green valley
I know he's singing out his heart to welcome me
And someone waits by the garden gate down in the little green valley
When I get home again how happy she will be.
Down by a babbling brook together once more we'll wander
And in a shady nook we'll while the hours away
And there I'll leave all my cares behind, go where I know I'll find
        sunshine
Back to that little old green valley far away.

I learned this song from some boys named Carnes in 1935. They were
named Odell and Odean. [H. F., note added in her draft copy of songbook, December 1993]

[This piece is from the early country music repertoire. Carson Robison wrote it
and recorded it. Bradley Kincaid remembered hearing Grandpa Jones sing it (Jones,
Radio's Kentucky Mountain Boy, 155).]

Blue Ridge Mountain Home

Not in the songbook. Carson Robison wrote "My Blue Ridge Mountain Home" in 1927; Vernon Dalhart recorded it.

The Girl I Loved in Sunny Tennessee

I was speeding on a train that would bring me back again
To the old homestead in sunny Tennessee
As the great wheels rolled along seemed to me they hummed a song
Of the sweetheart who was waiting there for me.
It was just a few short years since I'd kissed away her tears
And I left her by my dear old mother's side
And each day we've been apart she's grown dearer to my heart
Since the night that I asked her to be my bride.

CHORUS

I could hear the darkies singing as she said farewell to me
Far across the fields of cotton, my old homestead I could see
As the moon rose in its glory, there I told life's sweetest story
To the girl I loved in sunny Tennessee.

As the train pulled in at last, old familiar scenes were passed
And I met my mother at the station door
As old friends gathered round, tears on every face I found
But I missed the one I'd been longing for to see
And I whispered, Mother dear, where is Mary, she's not here
All the world seemed lost and sadness came to me
As she pointed to a spot in our churchyard's little lot
Where my sweetheart sleeps in sunny Tennessee.

REPEAT CHORUS

One of Mother's favorites. Probably from the late 1800s.

H. F.: We learned it from Mother. . . . Mother sang it, . . . that's why I have such a time with the tune when I'm trying to sing it, because there's a line that goes in that . . . she always sung in there, that hadn't oughta go in there. You're repeatin' that same . . . something over again and then you can't get the tune to fit. But she did it. P. H.: She was raised in Church of Christ; she sang a capella most of the time. [H. F. and P. H., taped interview, Mayfield Arkansas, January 22, 1991]

These old songs had such lovely music to them. [H. F., note added in her draft copy of songbook, January 1994]

[This turn-of-the-century vaudeville number is credited as "The Girl I Left in Sunny Tennessee" to Henry Berdan and Frederick J. Redcliffe, and alternatively as "The Girl I Loved in Sunny Tennessee" to Harry Braisted and Stanley Carter. The date given in both attributions is 1899. It was recorded early by country musicians— Charlie Poole's North Carolina Ramblers cut it in 1925. Randolph includes one text from a manuscript copy (*Ozark Folksongs*, 4: 333); the Max Hunter collection also has it (folksong collection, no. 212).]

Dear Charlie

I received your letter, dear Charlie
The last one you wrote to me.
I've read it over and over
And of course my dear friend, I'll agree.

Here are your letters, dear Charlie
I burned mine as they came.
And I hope without reading them over
You'll submit them at once to the flame.

You do not need them, dear Charlie
To remind you of vows untrue,

But as you've required them of me
I'll send them at once to you.

Here is your picture, dear Charlie
It's almost faded away,
Because I've kissed it so often,
And this you may tell Miss Gray.
Here is your ring, dear Charlie
Don't give it to her, I pray
Unless you tell her 'twas once mine
One year ago today.

One year ago today, dear Charlie
One bright happy day to us both
You vowed you'd never deceive me
But I find you untrue to your oath.

And now I must say goodbye
My letter is near to an end,
But I hope you'll remember, dear Charlie
I'm forever and ever your friend.

Now where in the world do you suppose we picked this one up?
Probably from Aunt Myrtie, I think it sounds like some of the ones she
used to sing. Don't you agree, "Dear Charlie"?

HA HA   HA HA   HA HA   HA HA   P. H.

There was an answer, one stanza that ended "affectionately yours
Charlie Brooks," we three used to laugh at. He wrote *asking* for his letter so maybe this song is the *answer*. [H. F., note added in her draft copy
of songbook, December 1993]

[Randolph has this as "Charley Brooks" (*Ozark Folksongs,* 4: 210–13). Other versions are in Dugaw ("Dreams of the Past," 17–18) and Max Hunter's Ozark collection
(folksong collection, no. 96). Almeda Riddle reported learning this "as a small child"
(Abrahams, *A Singer and Her Songs,* 189).]

Goin' to See My Truelove

Not in the songbook.

Twenty-One Years

The judge said, "Stand up, boy, and dry up your tears.
You're sentenced to Nashville for twenty-one years."
So kiss me goodbye, babe, and say you'll be mine,
For twenty-one years, babe, is a mighty long time.

Go beg that governor, babe, on your sweet soul.
If you can't get a pardon, try and get a parole.
If I had that governor where the governor's got me,
Before Tuesday morning, that governor'd be free.

Six months have gone by, babe, I wish I were dead.
This dirty old jailhouse the floor for a bed.
It's rainy, it's hailing, the moon gives no light.
Oh, babe, please tell me why you never write.

I've counted the days, babe, I've counted the nights,
I've counted the minutes, I've counted the lights.
I've counted the footsteps, I've counted the stars,
I've counted a million of these prison bars.

I've counted on you, babe, to get me a break,
But I guess you've forgot, babe, I'm here for your sake.
For you know who's guilty, you know it too well,
I'll rot in this jailhouse before I will tell.

Come all you young fellows with hearts brave and true,
Don't trust in a promise, you're beat if you do.
Don't trust in a woman, no matter what kind,
For twenty-one years, boys, is a mighty long time.

A prison song. We learned this from a transient grape cutter, I think
about 1933–1934. It was on a record too. It was really popular for
awhile—we sang it a lot when it first came out. [P. H., Fayetteville,
Arkansas, November 2, 1993]

[Country songwriter Bob Miller wrote this in 1932, and it started showing up in
folksong collections soon afterward. It's in Laws (E16), and Randolph prints five versions (*Ozark Folksongs,* 2: 156–59). Almeda Riddle knew it (Abrahams, *A Singer and Her
Songs,* 184). Other versions are in the Brown collection from North Carolina (3:
417–18) and Max Hunter's Ozark collection (folksong collection, no. 639).]

Frankie and Johnny

Frankie and Johnny were sweethearts,
Oh, lord, how they did love.
They swore to be true to each other,
As true as the stars above.
He was her man, he wouldn't do her wrong.

Frankie went down to the corner
Just to get a bucket of beer.
Frankie said, "Mr. Bartender,
Has my lovin' Johnny been here?
He is my man, he wouldn't do me wrong."

I don't want to cause you no trouble,
But I don't want to tell you no lies.
I saw your man about an hour ago
With a girl called Nellie Blye.
He is your man, but he's doin' you wrong.

Frankie looked over the transom,
Saw there to her surprise,
There sat her loving Johnny
Makin' love to Nellie Blye.
He was her man, but he was doin' her wrong.

Frankie drew back her kimona,
Drew out a new forty-four.
Root-a-toot-toot, three times she shot
Right through that hardwood door.
She shot her man, he was doin' her wrong.

Roll me over Frankie, roll me over slow,
Turn me on the other side,
That bullet hurts me so.
I was your man and I done you wrong.

Frankie said to the warden,
What are you goin' to do?
The warden said to Frankie,
It's the electric chair for you.
You shot your man, he was doing you wrong.

This story has no moral,
This story has no end.
This story only goes to show
There ain't no good in men.
He was her man, and he done her wrong!

From older family members—brothers and sisters? Dad? Uncle Huston?
[P. H., written note, Fayetteville, Arkansas, November 2, 1993]

I think I learned this from Billie after she got married. Bill Hogan also sang it, with an unprintable verse or two added. [P. H., note added in her draft copy of songbook, August 28, 1994]

[The origins of this widely known piece (Laws I3) have been much debated (and even litigated). It is frequently found in folksong collections, including Randolph (*Ozark Folksongs,* 2: 127–36) and Belden (*Ballads and Songs,* 330–33). Brown's North Carolina collection prints nine versions (2: 589–97).]

Seven Years with the Wrong Woman

Seven years with the wrong woman
Is more than a man can stand.
Seven years with the wrong woman.
Will ruin most any good man. [Will drive most any man mad.]
Seven years with the wrong woman
Will age you and turn your hair grey.
So make up your mind and search till you find
A face you can stand every day.

Learned this and the counterpart at Zion, but can't remember who we learned them from. [P. H., note added in her draft copy of songbook, August 28, 1994]

[Written by country songwriter Bob Miller in 1932, this piece is missing from the regional folksong collections.]

Seven Years with the Wrong Man

Seven years with the wrong man
Is a long time to live.
Seven years with the wrong man
To take but not give.
If I had my druthers,
Girls you'll understand,
I'd rather have ten babies
Than to have the wrong man.

[This is another Bob Miller novelty piece from the 1930s, according to Bill Malone and Judith McCulloh's *Stars of Country Music* (343).]

The Miner's Child

Not in the songbook. Randolph has this as "The Dream of the Miner's Child" (*Ozark Folksongs,* 4: 386). The song has English origins —"Don't Go Down in the Mine, Dad" was composed by Robert Donnelly and Will Geddes, and published in London in 1910. Vernon Dalhart recorded an American version by Andrew Jenkins in 1925. A thorough discussion is Archie Green's *Only a Miner* (113–49).

The Great Titanic

Not in the songbook. Randolph prints two versions (*Ozark Folksongs,* 4: 144–45), and three variants (including one performed by Lula Davis) appear in Irene Carlisle's 1952 University of Arkansas M.A. thesis ("Fifty Ballads and Songs," 80–86).

Utah Carrol

My friend you've asked the question
Why I'm silent, sad and still
Why my brow is always darkened
Like a cloud upon a hill.
Rein in your pony closer
And I'll tell to you a tale
Of Utah Carrol my pardner
And his last ride on the trail.

Mid mesquite and the cactus
In a western fairyland
Where the cattle roam by the thousands
In many a bunch and brand
There's a grave without a headstone
Without either a date or a name
Where my pardner sleeps in silence
It's the land from where I came.

Long we rode the range together
We had ridden side by side
I loved him like a brother
And I wept when Utah died.
Together we rode the roundups
Cut out and burned the brands
When dark and stormy weather came
We joined the night-herd's dreary band.

When the stampedes came so quickly
Each cowboy worked with a will

It was Utah Carrol to the front
For his voice rang loud and shrill
Twas his voice controlled the stampedes
For it rang out loud and clear
And when the cattle heard it
It o'ercame their maddened fear.

We were rounding up one morning
And the work was nearly done
On the right the cattle started
In a wild and maddened run.
The boss's little daughter
Was holding on that side
Rushed in to stop the cattle
And that's where Utah died.

On the saddle of the pony
Where the boss's daughter sat
Utah Carrol, that morning
Had placed a red blanket.
That the saddle might ride easy
For Lenore, his little friend
But the blanket that he placed there
Brought my pardner to his end.

As Lenore rushed in with her pony
To turn the cattle to the right
The blanket slipped from under her
And caught in her stirrup tight.
When the cattle saw the blanket
Almost trailing on the ground
They were maddened in an instant
And charged it with a bound.

When Lenore saw her danger
She turned her pony's face
And leaning from the saddle
Tried the blanket to replace.
While leaning from the saddle
Fell in front of that wild tide

Lie still, Lenore, I'm coming
Were the words my pardner cried.

About fifty yards behind her
Utah came riding fast
Little did he think that moment
That ride would be his last.
Many times from out the saddle
He had caught the trailing rope
To raise Lenore at full speed
Was Utah's only hope.

As the horse approached the maiden
Footsteps sure and stately bound
Utah leaned from his saddle
To raise Lenore from the ground.
Such a weight upon his cinches
Had never been felt before
The hind cinch snapped asunder
And he fell beside Lenore.

Utah picked up the blanket
And waving it o'er his head
He started across the prairie
Again, Lie Still, he said.
As he started across the prairie
Every cowboy held his breath
For we knew the run he was making
Either meant his life or death.

Quickly from out his scabbard
For he was bound to fight
While dying like a cowboy
True and tried.
His pistol flashed like lightning
The report rang loud and clear
As the herd rushed in upon him
He dropped the leading steer.

When the herd closed in around him
My pardner had to fall

Never more to lead the roundup [. . . to cinch a bronco]
Nor to give the cattle-call.
He must die upon the ranges
His fate was awful hard
I could not make the distance
In time to save my pard.

When we broke in the circle
On that never forgotten day
From a dozen wounds and bruises
His young life ebbed away.
I went in and knelt beside him
Though I knew his life was o'er
And I faintly heard him murmur
I'm coming, lie still, Lenore.

These were Utah Carrol's last words
He had gone the endless trail
At the call of what was his duty
With a nerve that could not fail
Then closing his eyes in remembrance
At the Master's dread command
The tears rolled down in silence
As I closed my pardner's hands.

Some day in that grand, bright future
I've heard the preacher say
I know that my young pardner
Won't be lost on that great day
For as a true cowboy
He was willing here to die
And I know that my young pardner
Has a home beyond the sky.

One of our "most requested" songs and we loved to sing it. [H. F., this and bracketed line in thirteenth stanza above added in her draft copy of songbook, January 1994]

I think Helen is right. The line should read, "Never more to cinch a bronco." But the song was too long and the tune too monotonous for

me to enjoy singing it. [P. H., note added in her draft copy of songbook, August 1994]

[This American ballad (Laws B4) is widely reported in the regional collections,
beginning with John Lomax's 1910 *Cowboy Songs and Other Frontier Ballads* (66–68).
Randolph has it as "Utah Carl" (*Ozark Folksongs,* 2: 239–41), the same title reported
by Moore and Moore (*Ballads and Folk Songs of the Southwest,* 325–27). McNeil (*Southern
Folk Ballads,* 1: 154–56, 212) gives a version from Almeda Riddle, and provides a fine
headnote describing a 1927 recording by Carl T. Sprague and movie performances by
Ken Maynard. Other versions appear in Irene Carlisle's 1952 University of Arkansas
M.A. thesis ("Fifty Ballads and Songs," 95–98), in Theodore Garrison's 1944 University
of Arkansas M.A. thesis ("Forty-Five Folk Songs," 118–21), in Owens's *Tell Me a Story*
(98–101), and in Max Hunter's Ozark collection (folksong collection, no. 664).]

Jealous Lover

Way down in a low green valley
Where the shy little violets bloom
There sleeps a beautiful maiden
In a cold and silent tomb.

She died not broken hearted
Nor sickness ever befell
But in one moment parted
From the one she loved so well.

One night when the moon shone brightly
And lightly fell the dew
To this young maiden's cottage
Her jealous lover drew.

Come love, and let us wander
In the meadow bright and gay
Come love, and let us ponder
Upon our wedding day.

No, Edward, I am weary
And do not care to roam
For roaming is so dreary
I'd rather stay at home.

This raised his jealous anger
And a solemn vow he made
Saying in one moment's parting
In death you shall be laid.

Down on her knees before him
Thus pleading for her life
But in her snow-white bosom
He plunged the fatal knife.

Oh, Edward, I'll forgive you
If this be my last breath
I never have deceived you
And she closed her eyes in death.

Oh, God in heaven pity
For I have taken her life
And God only knows how I loved her
And she would have been my wife.

Now I am tired of living
From living I must part
With the same cold bloody dagger
I'll pierce my jealous heart.

Down on his knees beside her
The solemn vow he made
And in his own white bosom
He plunged the fatal blade.

Come all you jealous lovers
Take warning now from me
If ever you have a true lover
Beware of jealousy.

Another song all families seem to know. The ones, that is, that ever sang or collected songs. [H. F., note added in her draft copy of songbook, December 1993]

[This American ballad (Laws F1) appears in many of the regional collections, including ten versions in Randolph (*Ozark Folksongs*, 2: 44–53) and eighteen in Belden, where its title is "Florella" (*Ballads and Songs*, 324–30). It's also found in Owens (*Texas Folksongs*, 100–102), Burdine and McCarthy ("Sister Singers," 409), and Rainey (*Songs of the Ozark Folk*, 47). Eleanor Henderson's 1950 University of Arkansas M.A. thesis includes a variant titled "The Weeping Willow" ("An Ozark Song Book," 20–21), and it's also listed as known by Almeda Riddle (Abrahams, *A Singer and Her Songs*, 184). Max Hunter's Ozark collection includes three versions (folksong collection, no. 176), and Lilith Shell's 1928 *Arkansas Gazette* article includes another ("Folksongs Furnished," sect. 2, 16).]

A Little Rosewood Casket

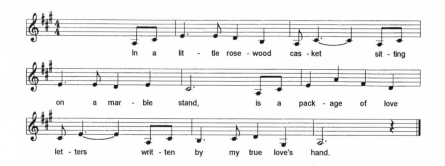

In a little rosewood casket
Sitting on a marble stand
There's a package of love letters
Written by my true love's hand.
Go and bring them to me, brother
And read them o'er to me
I have often tried to read them
But for tears, I could not see.

Go and bring them to me, brother
And sit upon my bed
Lay your head upon my pillow
For my aching heart's most dead.
Read them to me gently, brother
Until I fall asleep
Fall asleep to wake in Heaven
Oh dear brother, do not weep.

I thought I saw him Sunday
With a lady by his side
And I thought I heard him whisper
Asking her to be his bride.
When I'm dead and in my coffin
And the people gathered round
He will come and look upon me
In my snow-white wedding gown.

Oh, for the pining heart that wasted the poor dears(?) away! Do you suppose the lover even came to the funeral and if he did, did he recognize the "snow white wedding gown?"

I suppose every family knew this song. Our "group" still sings it. [H. F., note added in her draft copy of songbook, January 1994]

[This often collected weeper originated as a pop song in 1870, written by Louis P. Goullaud and Charles A. White and titled "A Package of Old Love Letters." Randolph prints three versions (*Ozark Folksongs,* 4: 269–72). Belden (*Ballads and Songs,* 220), Owens (*Texas Folksongs,* 181–83), Stilley ("The Stilley Collection: Part One," 23–24), McNeil (*Southern Folk Ballads,* 1: 123–25, 200–201), and Rainey (*Songs of the Ozark Folk,* 53) also have it. Shell ("Folk Songs Furnished," sect. 2, 16) and Brown's North Carolina collection describes twenty-four (2: 631–35). There were early country music recordings by Vernon Dalhart and Bradley Kincaid.]

Church in the Wildwood

There's a church in the valley by the wildwood
No lovelier spot in the vale
No spot is so dear to my childhood
As the little brown church in the dale.

CHORUS

(Bass lead) Oh, come, come, come, come
Come to the church in the wildwood
Oh, come to the church in the vale
No spot is so dear to my childhood
As the little brown church in the dale.

How sweet on a clear Sabbath morning
To list to the clear ringing bell
Its tones so sweetly are calling
Oh come to the church in the dell.

To the church in the valley by the wildwood
To the place where the wild flowers bloom
Where the parting hymn will be chanted
We will weep by the side of the tomb.

To the church in the valley by the wildwood
When day fades away into night
I would fain from this spot of my childhood
Wing my way to those mansions of light.

This was Dad's favorite song. We sang it at his funeral. [P. H., taped interview conducted by Elizabeth Foster, Fayetteville, Arkansas, May 15, 1992]

Dad's favorite. In most hymnals as well as *Gospel Favorites*. [P. H., note added in her draft copy of songbook, August 29, 1994]

[Composed by William S. Pitts, this number is no. 39 in *Joy To the World* and no. 145 in *Devotional Hymns*, two hymnals owned by Phydella Hogan.]

The True Young Maid

A young maid all in the garden
A young soldier chanced to meet
He stepped up, proposed a bargain
Asking her his bride to be.

Oh no, kind sir, you are too hasty
You're not the one I wish to see
So don't impose on a fair young maiden
By asking her your bride to be.

I have a true love all in the army
He has been gone for four long years
And if he's gone for seven longer
No other man shall dry my tears.

He raised his hands and thus he lingered
What his feelings were no one can tell
A golden ring upon his finger
And suddenly to his feet she fell.

He raised her up like a kind brother
The kisses he gave her, one, two, three
I am your own true-hearted lover
Returned home to marry thee.

This true young maid was probably in the garden about the time of World War I. And since she was ALL in it, it is to be presumed that the lover who was ALL in the army had changed considerably while there or perhaps he had left a part of him in it? The army I mean. Doubtless she thought he had when he raised her up like a kind *brother* and then kissed her three times, after proposing to her first! P. H.

[This in Randolph (*Ozark Folksongs*, 1: 258–61) as "The Maiden in the Garden," in Belden as "A Sweetheart in the Army" (*Ballads and Songs*, 148–51), and in Owens as "A Pretty Fair Maid" (*Texas Folksongs*, 90–92). Eleanor Henderson's 1950 University of Arkansas M.A. thesis includes two versions as "Pretty Little Miss" ("An Ozark Song Book," 52–55).]

A Spanish Cavalier

A Spanish Cavalier stood in his retreat
And on his guitar played a tune dear
The music so sweet would oft-times repeat
"The Blessings of my Country and You dear."

CHORUS

Oh, say, darling say, when I'm far away
Sometimes will you think of me dear?
Bright sunny days will soon fade away
Remember what I say and be true dear.

I'm off to the war, to the war I must go
To fight for my country and you, dear
And if I should fall, in vain I would call
For the blessings of my country and you, dear.

And when the war is o'er, to you I'll return
Back to my country and you, dear
But if I am slain, you will seek me in vain
For upon the battlefield you will find me.

(Spanish-American War song)

I can't remember when we *didn't* sing this so we must have learned it early in life. [H. F., note added in her draft copy of songbook, January 1994]

[This piece is missing from the regional collections. I learn from W. K. McNeil that it was written in 1881 by William D. Hendrickson.]

The Old Grass Widow

by Phydella Gilbert Hogan

(not a women's libber)

I live in a crummy apartment, from menfolks I am hid
I do not have to feed a man or tend to a kid.

CHORUS

Dear old apartment, I pay a mint for thee
But I'm an old grass widow from matrimony free.

I have a stove that's worth nine cents and a table worth fourteen
I cook my grub in TV trays and seldom keep things clean.

I go to bed whenever I please and sometimes not at all
I buy my clothes at the Goodwill store and change them every fall.

I can spend my time writing stuff like this altho' it is a shame
Or I can flirt with the garbage man with no one to complain.

And when I die and go to hell like all grass widows do
I'll simply yell, "Throw on more coal cause my ex is a-comin' too!"

With darned few apologies to the menfolks in the family . . . I just couldn't resist! You will also notice that I went one better on "The Stern Old Bachelor" . . . one extra stanza.

A Stern Old Bachelor

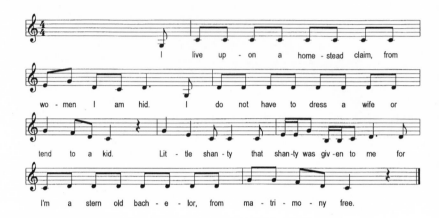

I live upon a homestead claim, from women I am hid,
I do not have to dress a wife, or tend to a kid

CHORUS

Little shanty, that shanty was given to me
For I'm a stern old bachelor, from matrimony free.

I have a stove that's worth ten cents and a table worth fifteen
I cook my grub in an oyster can and I always keep things clean

I go to bed whenever I please and get up just the same
I change my socks three times a year with no one to complain.

And when I die and go to heaven like all old bachelors do
I will not have to trouble myself if my wife don't get there too.

Repeat chorus after each verse or if too long that way, after each two verses.

Dad sang this song too, as far back as any of us can remember. P. H.

[This is rare in the regional collections, but it is in Randolph (*Ozark Folksongs,* 3: 246).]

Sweet Violets

There once was a farmer who took a young miss
Out back of the barn where he gave her a . . . lecture
On horses and chickens and eggs
And told her she had the most beautiful . . . manners
That suited a girl of her charms,
A girl that he wanted to take in his . . . washing
And ironing, and then if she did
They could get married and raise lots of SWEET VIOLETS.

CHORUS

Sweeter than all the roses,
Covered all over from head to toes
Covered all over with SWEET VIOLETS.

The farmer decided he'd wed anyway
And started in planning for his wedding . . . suit
Which he purchased for only one buck
And then he found out he was just out of . . . money
And so he got left in the lurch
Standing and waiting in front of the . . . end of the story
Which just goes to show that all a girl wants
From a man is his SWEET VIOLETS.

Repeat chorus

I could get the rest of the words to this song—O.K.? [H. F., note added
in her draft copy of songbook, January 1994]

[This is missing from the regional folksong collections. It was written by Joseph K.
Emmet in 1892. There is a brief reference to obscene versions in Randolph, *Roll Me in
Your Arms* (192).]

Sweet Bunch of Daisies

Sweet bunch of daisies, brought from the dell
Kiss me once darling, daisies won't tell
Give me your promise, oh sweetheart do
Darling I love you, will you be true?

Sweet bunch of daisies how dear to me
Bring back to memory love of thee
When we together roamed through forest green
Gathering the daisies growing by the stream.

Sweet bunch of daisies treasures more than gold
Bring back sweet memories of days of old.

These are the words to an old-time waltz, a beautiful fiddle tune. [H. F. note added in her draft copy of songbook, January 1994]

[This is a popular piece from 1894, composed by Anita Owen. It's missing from the regional folksong collections.]

Little Blossom

Not in the songbook, though obviously well known in the Gilbert family and frequently mentioned in conversation by both Phydella Hogan and Helen Fultz. Randolph has three versions (*Ozark Folksongs,* 2: 403–7). There are recordings by Mac Wiseman and Dolly Parton, among others.

The Drunkard's Dream

My, Edward, you look happy
Your dress so neat and clean
I have not seen you drunk about
Pray tell me where you've been.

Your wife and children they look well
You used did use them strange
But now you've kinder to them grown
How come this happy change?

It was a dream, an awful dream
From Heaven sent to me
To snatch me from a drunkard's life
From want and misery.

I dreamed once more I staggered home
There seemed a silent gloom
I missed my wife, where could she be?
And strangers in the room.

I heard them say, "Poor thing she's dead
Oh, what a wretched life
Shame and grief have broken her heart
To be a drunkard's wife."

My children they came weeping 'round
And scarcely drew their breath
I gently touched her once warm cheeks
But they were cold in death.

She is not dead, I fainter grew
And rushed to where she lay
I gently kissed her once warm lips
But they were cold as clay.
"Oh, Mary, speak to me once more
I'll never give thee pain
I'll never grieve your lovely heart
I'll never drink again."

Oh, Mary, 'tis Edward's call
I know she's come
When I awoke my Mary dear
Was weeping o'er my bed.

One of the old temperance songs which were so popular in the early 1900s.

I can't remember ever singing this but probably Mother did. [H. F., note added in her draft copy of songbook, January 1994]

Yes, Mother sang it. I don't think we did it unless it was at Billie's house when they had a card game going. [P. H., note added in her draft copy of songbook, August 1994]

[Randolph prints three versions (*Ozark Folksongs*, 2: 393–96), and Belden has one (*Ballads and Songs*, 469–70). Henderson's M.A. thesis includes a text from Lula Davis ("An Ozark Song Book," 89–90), and Max Hunter's Ozark collection also has one (folksong collection, no. 164).]

I'm Alone, All Alone

I'm alone, all alone, my friends have all fled
My father's a drunkard, my mother is dead
I'm a poor little girl, I wander and weep
For the voice of my mother to sing me to sleep.

She sleeps on a hill in a bed made of clay,
How cold it did seem to lay mother away
She's gone with the Angels and none do I see
As dear as the face of my mother to me.

We were so happy till father drank rum,
Then all of our troubles and sorrows begun
Mother grew paler and worked every day,
Baby and I were too hungry to play.

Slowly she faded until one summer's night
They found our sweet faces all solemn and white
And with the big tears slowly dropping I said,
Father's a drunkard and mother is dead.

Last night in my dreams she seemed to draw near
She kissed me as fondly as when she was here
She kissed my cheek and fondled my brow
And whispered sleep on, I'm watching you now.

Another of Mother's favorites which made us cry. [H. F., note added
in her draft copy of songbook, January 1994]

[Randolph has this as "The Drunkard's Lone Child" (*Ozark Folksongs*, 2: 398–402),
though he groups what seem to be several distinct songs under this title. This piece was
also in Almeda Riddle's repertoire (Abrahams, *A Singer and Her Songs*, 187, 190). It is
included in Brown's North Carolina collection (3: 50–51), and in Henderson's 1950
M.A. thesis ("An Ozark Song Book," 85–86).]

Melancholy Baby

Not in the songbook. Composition rights have been matters of liti-
gation, but this popular and much recorded piece from 1912 is usually
credited to George A. Norton with music by Ernie Burnett.

Let the Rest of the World Go By

Are the struggles and strifes we find in this life
Really worthwhile after all
I was wishing today I could just run away
Out where the west wind calls
With someone like you, a pal good and true
I'd like to leave it all behind and go and find
Some place that's known to God alone
Just a spot to call our own
Then we'd build a little nest somewhere out in the west
And let the rest of the world go by.

Is the future to hold just struggles for gold
While the real world waits outside
Way out on the breast of the wonderful west
Across the Great Divide.
With someone like you, a pal good and true
I'd like to leave it all behind and go and find
Some place that's known to God alone
Just a spot to call our own
There we'd find perfect peace where joys never cease
Out there beneath the kindly skies
And we'd build a little nest somewhere out in the west
And let the rest of the world go by.

We loved to sing this song. On Bob's and my 50th anniversary Phydella
gave us a framed copy of a version of this song she had re-written about
our lives! [H. F., note added in her draft copy of songbook, January
1994]

[This number is missing from the regional folksong collections. It's a 1919 piece
written by J. Keirn Brennan with music by Ernest R. Ball.]

Let the Lower Lights Be Burning

Brightly beams our Father's mercy
From His lighthouse ever more
But to us He gives the keeping
Of the lights along the shore.

CHORUS
Let the lower lights be burning
Send a gleam across the wave
Some poor fainting, struggling seaman
You may rescue, you may save.

Dark the night of sin has settled
Loud the angry billows roar
Eager eyes are watching, longing
For the lights along the shore.

Repeat chorus

Trim your feeble lamp my brother
Some poor sailor, tempest-tossed
Trying now to make the harbor
In the darkness may be lost.

Repeat chorus

Bob, I looked this up in an old hymnal just to be sure I hadn't forgotten it. It was an old book I had left with Helen and she had sent back to me and Billie when I was in California, and she had marked this song at the top "Our Song." She had marked several of our favorites in the book, and I thought you might like to look at it. Remind me when you are here again, and I'll get the book out for you. [P. H., note added in her draft copy of songbook, April 16, 1992]

Was in our hymnal at Zion. We sang that a lot at church, we really did. And we loved it. I always thought it was so pretty. We nearly always ended up singing "Let the Lower Lights Be Burning"—we used to go out on the front porch in the summertime and sing (in the winter we sang in the living room), right after supper when the sun'd go down and it'd start getting cooler. We'd sit out on the porch and we'd sing until bedtime. When we finally wound down we usually ended up with hymns. That would be the one that we usually ended up with, I think. Now Helen's got it that we sang something else. See, you remember differently. [P. H., taped interview conducted by Elizabeth Foster, Fayetteville, Arkansas, May 15, 1992]

[This shows up in many hymnals, credited to P. P. Bliss. In the *Broadman Hymnal* it's no. 262, in *Melodies of Praise* it's no. 243, and in the 1933 Stamps-Baxter *Song Service and Revival* it's no. 127.]

Oh Susanna

I come from Alabama with my banjo on my knee
I'm gwine to Louisiana my true love for to see
It rained all night the day I left, the weather it was dry
The sun so hot I froze to death, Susanna don't you cry

CHORUS

Oh Susanna, now don't you cry for me,
I've come from Alabama with my banjo on my knee.

I jumped aboard the telegraph and started down the river
The lectric fluid magnified and killed five hundred nigger
The bullgine bust the horse run off, I really thought I'd die
I shut my eyes to hold my breath Susanna don't you cry.

I had a dream the other night when everything was still
I thought I saw Susanna a comin' down the hill
The buckwheat cake was in her mouth, the tear was in her eyes
Says I, "I'm comin' from the south, Susanna don't you cry."

I soon will be in New Orleans and den I'll look around
And when I find Susanna I will fall upon de ground
And if I do not find her dis darkey'll surely die
And when I'm dead and buried, Susanna don't you cry.

Heart Songs, p. 172   no author given

Probably afraid they'd get in trouble for saying "nigger." [H. F., note
added in her draft copy of songbook, January 1994, in reference to the
"no author given" citation in the original songbook manuscript]

[This is one of Stephen Foster's better-known minstrel songs, from 1848. The
regional folksong collections exclude it, but Owens's *Tell Me a Story* notes it as sung at
a Texas German *Saengerfest* (205). For a detailed treatment, see Ken Emerson's *Doo-
Dah!: Stephen Foster and the Rise of American Popular Culture*.]

Camptown Races

De Camptown ladies sing dis song, Doo-dah, doo-dah
De Camptown racetrack nine miles long, Oh doo-dah day,
I came down dar wid my hat caved in, Doo-dah, doo-dah
I go back home wid a pocket full of tin, Oh doo-dah day.
Gwine to run all night, gwine to run all day
I'll bet my money on de bobtail nag, somebody bet on de bay.

De longtailed filly and de big black hoss, doo-dah, doo-dah
Dey fly de track and dey both cut across, oh doo-dah day
De blind hoss stickin' in a big mudhole, doo-dah, doo-dah
Can't touch bottom wid a ten foot pole, oh doo-dah day.

CHORUS

Old muley cow come onto de track, doo-dah, doo-dah
De bobtail fling her over his back, oh doo-dah day
Den fly along like a railroad car, doo-dah, doo-dah
Runnin' a race wid a shootin' star, oh doo-dah day.

CHORUS

See dem flyin' on a ten mile heat, doo-dah, doo-dah
Round de racetrack den repeat, oh doo-dah day
I win my money on de bobtail nag, doo-dah, doo-dah
I keep my money in an old tow bag, o doo-dah day.

Heart Songs, p. 352

[This is another Stephen Foster number. It's missing from the regional folksong collections.]

Nellie Gray

There's a low green valley by the old Kentucky shore
Where I've whiled many happy hours away
Just a sitting and a singing by the little cabin door
Where lived my darling Nellie Gray.

When the moon had climbed the mountain and the stars were
  shining too
Then I'd take my darling Nellie Gray
And we'd float down the river in my little red canoe
While my banjo, sweetly I would play.

Last night I went to see her, she has gone the neighbors say
The white man has bound her with his chain
He has taken her to Georgia for to wear her life away
To toil in the cotton and the cane.

FIRST CHORUS

Oh my darling Nellie Gray, they have taken you away
And I'll never see my darling anymore.
I am sitting by the river and I'm weeping all the day
For you're gone from the old Kentucky shore.

My canoe is under water and my banjo is unstrung
And I'm tired of living anymore
My eyes they shall look downward and my song shall go unsung
While I stay on the old Kentucky shore.

My eyes are getting blinded and I cannot see my way
Hark! there's someone knocking at my door
I hear the angels calling and I see my Nellie Gray
Farewell to the old Kentucky shore.

LAST CHORUS

Oh my darling Nellie Gray, up in heaven there they say
That they'll never take you from me anymore
I am coming, coming, coming as the angels clear the way
Farewell to the old Kentucky shore.

We used to sing the first chorus after each verse, but it makes for an awfully long song. Also, I used to think this was an old Stephen Foster song but found in an old song collection that it was written in 1856 by Benjamin Russell Hanby. He sent it for publication to Oliver Ditson & Co. of Boston who published it. The song was an immediate hit, and the Ditson Co. paid Hanby off with a measly ten copies of the sheet music. When he complained, they told him that he had earned the fame but that Ditson earned the money, and he was never able to collect a cent for this popular classic of old-time music.

I still sing this sometimes. I think it is beautiful. [H. F., note added in her draft copy of songbook, January 1994]

[Phydella Hogan's "old songbook" might be the *Heart Songs* collection she mentions in other places. "Darling Nelly Gray" is included there (116–17). It is missing from the regional folksong collections, though Bradley Kincaid knew it as "an old plantation song" (Jones, *Radio's Kentucky Mountain Boy,* 149), and it's also included in a paperback soldier's songbook, *Popular Songs of the A.E.F.* (64).]

Going from the Cottonfields

I'se a goin' from de cottonfields, I'se a goin' from de cane
I'se a goin' from de old log hut dat stands down in 'de lane
I'se gwine to join de expedition headed for 'de Norf
And de boat is on de ribber dat's gwine to take me off.

CHORUS

I'se goin' from de cotton fields and oh it makes me sigh
For when de sun goes down tonight I'se gwine to say goodbye.

They say dat up in Kansas so many miles away
De colored folks is flockin' round and gettin' better pay
I don't know how I'll find it dere but I is bound to try
So when de sun goes down tonight I'se gwine to say goodbye.

I dread to leave de dear old place where I was borned and bred
To leave de friends dat I have made and de graves of dem dat's dead
De flowers dat bloom on Massa's grave will miss de tender care
No hands like mine will take de pains to keep dem bloomin' dere.

Now Dinah she don't wanta go, she says she's gettin' old
She says she's 'fraid we'll freeze to death de country am so cold
But I'se bound to help my chillun some befo I'se called to die
So when de sun goes down tonight I'se gwine to say goodbye.

I'se sold de old log cabin and de little patch of ground
Dat good old Massa gave to me when de Yankee troops come down
My heart is sad and sore now, de tears are in my eyes
For when de sun goes down tonight I'se gwine to say goodbye.

One of mother's old songs.

I remember when "Bill" came to see us from California and we all three
worked on this song trying to get the lines right. We sat at the kitchen
table down in our old house—must have been about '61. [H. F., note
added in her draft copy of songbook, December 1993]

I remember that, too. But to use Billie's language about "hearing" the
way a song was sung, I think the last two lines of the first stanza are
reversed. I can "hear" Mother singing, "the boat is on de ribber dat's
gwine to take me off. / I'se gonna join de expedition headed for de
Norf." [P. H., note added in her draft copy of songbook, August 1994]

[This is missing from the regional folksong collections, but there is a version very
similar to the Gilberts' under the title "I'm Gwine From the Cotton Fields" in Byron
Arnold's *Folksongs of Alabama* (115).]

Massa's in De Cold Ground

Round de meadows am a-ringing de darkey's mournful song
While de mockingbird am singing happy as de day is long
Where de ivy am a creeping o'er de grassy mound
Dare ole Massa am a sleeping, sleeping in de cold, cold ground

CHORUS
Down in de cornfield, hear dat mournful sound
All de darkeys am a weeping, Massa's in de cold, cold ground

When de autumn leaves were falling when de days were cold
Twas hard to hear old Massa calling cause he was so weak and old
Now de orange trees am a blooming on de sandy shore
Now de summer days am coming Massa neber calls no more.

Massa makes de darkeys love him cause he is so kind
Now dey sadly weep above him mourning cause he leave dem
    behind
I cannot work before tomorrow cause de teardrop flow
I try to drive away my sorrow pickin' on de old banjo.

Heart Songs, p. 350   Stephen Foster

We didn't know all the verses to this, but I recall the first verse and the
chorus. I think Mother sang them. [P. H., note added in her draft copy
of songbook, August 28, 1994]

[This Stephen Foster piece from 1852 is missing from the regional folksong collections, but it does appear (as "Massa's In the Cold, Cold Ground") in the paperback
soldier's songbook, *Popular Songs of the A.E.F.* (28), and is discussed in Charles Hamm's
Yesterdays (213–15).]

Stay in Your Own Back Yard

Roses bloomin round the door, lilacs round the gate
Mammy in the little cabin door
Curly-headed pickininny comin' home so late
Cryin' cause his little heart is sore
All the chillin' playin' 'round has skin so white and fair
None of them with him will eber play
So Mammy in her lap, takes the little weeping chap
And croons in her kind old way

CHORUS

Now Honey, jus stay in yo own back yard,
Doan mind what dose white childs do
What fo you suppose deys gwine to think
Ob a black little coon lak you
So stay on dis side ob dat high board fence
And honey doan cry so hard
Go out and play, jus as much as you please
But stay in your own back yard.

Learned this part of the song from Red Foley. There is another verse—
the child dies and Mammy croons to her old black self. Chorus. [H. F.,
note added in her draft copy of songbook, January 1994]

[This is a number from 1899 with words by Karl Kennett and music by Lynn
Udall. The regional folksong collections don't have it, but David Ewen's *American
Popular Music* calls it "one of the first successful songs discussing racial problems. It stoi-
cally accepted segregation and racial discrimination as realities, and considered these
problems as they affect a child"(369).]

Lolly Truedom

As I started out one morning bright and clear
Lolly true dum true dum truda lolly day.
As I started out one morning bright and clear
I heard an old lady talking to her daughter dear
Lolly true dum true dum truda lolly day.

Now, wash them dishes and stop your clattering tongue
Lolly true dum true dum truda lolly day.
Wash them dishes and stop your clatterin' tongue
You know you wanta marry, but you know you're too young
Lolly true dum true dum truda lolly day.

Well, I'm sixteen and this you must allow
Lolly true dum true dum truda lolly day.
Well, I'm sixteen and this you must allow
If I'm agonna marry I'm agonna marry now
Lolly true dum true dum truda lolly day.

If you're gonna marry where'll you find a man
Lolly true dum true dum truda lolly day.
If you're gonna marry where'll you find a man

Lord Godamighty there's my handsome Sam
Lolly true dum true dum truda lolly day.

What if Sam'd slight you like he did before
Lolly true dum true dum truda lolly day.
What if Sam'd slight you like he did before
Lord Godamighty I can get a dozen more
Lolly true dum true dum truda lolly day.

There's tinkers and tailors and men for the plow
Lolly true dum true dum truda lolly day
There's tinkers and tailors and men for the plow
They all wanta marry and they wanta marry now
Lolly true dum true dum truda lolly day.

There's doctors and lawyers and men of high degree
Lolly true dum true dum truda lolly day
There's doctors and lawyers and men of high degree
They all wanta marry and they wanta marry me
Lolly true dum true dum truda lolly day.

Well now I'm married I'll do the best I can
Lolly true dum true dum truda lolly day
Now I'm married I'll do the best I can
I'm livin' all alone with my handsome Sam
Lolly true dum true dum truda lolly day.

This is one we learned from Mother, and she and all the aunts sang it when they were quite small.

I don't remember *when* we learned it. All I remember is washing dishes and singing it, because there's something in it about washing dishes, and that's what we'd sing when we washed dishes. [H. F., taped interview, Mayfield, Arkansas, January 22, 1991]

So did we—sing it with great gusto as we washed the dishes! [H. F., note added in her draft copy of songbook, January 1994]

[This is included in Randolph as "Rolly Trudom" (*Ozark Folksongs*, 3: 77–79), in Belden as "Mother and Daughter" (*Ballads and Songs*, 266), and in Owens as "Rolly Troodum" (*Texas Folksongs*, 214–16).]

Peter Gray

Once on a time there was a man, his name was Peter Gray
He lived way down in that there town called Penn-syl-van-i-a
Blow ye winds of the morning, blow ye winds heigh-ho
Blow ye winds of the morning, blow, blow, blow.

Now Peter Gray he fell in love, all with a nice young girl
The first three letters of her name were L–U–C, Anna Quirl.
Blow ye winds of the morning, blow ye winds heigh-o
Blow ye winds of the morning, blow, blow, blow.

But just as they were going to wed, her papa he said, "No!"
And consequently she was sent way off to Ohio.

CHORUS

And Peter Gray he went to trade for furs and other skins,
Till he was caught and scalp-y-ed by the bloody Inji-ins.

CHORUS

When Lucy Anna heard the news, she straightway took to bed,
And never did get up again until she di-i-ed.

CHORUS

Heart Songs, p. 359

I heard Uncle Huston do this way back when I was little.

[Most regional folksong collections lack this piece, though Max Hunter did record a version (folksong collection, no. 497). *Heart Songs* provides no author attribution.]

The Widow's Daughter

A sweet thing I courted, I thought for to wed
Her mother a widow, her father was dead
When I asked for her hand I dodged from the blow
Her mother she screamed, as she answered me "NO!"

My daughter, my daughter, my daughter, cried she
To think that my daughter should go before me
It's a queer thing to me why a girl so young
Can get all the beaus and I can get none.

I know you're a widow whose pockets are large
I know you're a widow who bears a great charge
A widow! cried she, you scorn my name
And up with the broomstick and at me she came.

Come all you young men and take warning from me
And never a widow's daughter go to see
For as sure as you do you'll meet with your doom
And carry the marks of the widow's old broom.

Mother's. Heard it all my life anyway. P. H.

[This American ballad (Laws H25) is called "The Widow's Old Broom" by Randolph (*Ozark Folksongs,* 3: 107–9) and "Courting the Widow's Daughter" by Belden (*Ballads and Songs,* 248–49).]

Sweet Lorraine

The bright lights were gleaming from heaven
The skies were all mingled and blue
The sea it was bronze and azure
They remind me Lorraine of you.

CHORUS

Give me your answer, today sweet Lorraine
Tell me that you love me, don't turn away
For you are my angel, my star and my queen
Give me your promise, today, sweet Lorraine.

To the city they tell me you're going
To the mansions refined and bright
Lorraine I'm afraid you'll forget me
And the dear ones you're leaving behind.

Lorraine I don't know why I love you
When I know that you don't care for me
You've broken your promise to marry
And I find you're untrue to me.
Dear Edgar, you know that I love you
That's the reason why we must part
You know that my parents don't like you
And darling it breaks my heart.

Repeat CHORUS

I don't remember when we learned this one, but we sure did wear it
out singing it at Zion didn't we?
Phydella Hogan, 1960

Yes, and that's where I remember learning it, again from "Bill." [H. F.,
note added in her draft copy of songbook, December 1993]

[Owens has this as "Lorene" (*Texas Folksongs*, 185–88). Hamm's *Yesterdays* lists
this as the twenty-fifth most often recorded song in the United States from 1900 to
1950 and gives composer credit to Mitchell Parrish, with music by Cliff Burwell (488).
Randolph's "Lorena and Paul Vane" (*Ozark Folksongs*, 4: 257–59) is a different song.]

A Picture from Life's Other Side

In the world's mighty gallery of pictures
Hang the pictures that are taken from life
A picture of love and of passion
A picture of beauty and strife
A picture of life and of beauty
Old age and a blushing young bride
All hang on the wall but the saddest of all
Is the picture from Life's other side.

CHORUS

It's a picture from life's other side
Someone has fallen by the way
A life has gone out with the tide
That might have been happy some day
Some poor old mother at home
Watching and waiting alone
Waiting to hear from a loved one so dear
Tis a picture from Life's other side.

The first scene is that of a gambler, who has lost all his money at
   play
Draws his dead mother's ring from his finger that she wore on her
   wedding day
His last earthly possession, he stakes it and bows his head that his
   shame he might hide
When they lifted his head, they found he was dead, tis a picture
   from life's other side.
The next tells a tale of two brothers whose paths in life differently
   lead
While one is in luxury living, the other one begged for his bread
One dark night they met on the highway, your money or life the
   thief cried
Then he took, with his knife, his own brother's life
Tis a picture from life's other side.
The last is a scene by the river of a heartbroken mother and babe
Neath the harbor lights see her shiver, an outcast whom no one will
   save

Yet she was once a good woman, somebody's darling and pride
God help her, she sleeps, and there's no one who weeps
Tis a picture from Life's other side.

I remember Mother sang this, at least part of it. I later got the rest of the words as Porter Wagoner sang it. [H. F., note added in her draft copy of songbook, December 1993]

[This tear-jerker is a popular music piece by Charles E. Baer, who published it in 1896. It is often found in the sacred music repertoire. Randolph has a version (*Ozark Folksongs*, 4: 31–32), and Almeda Riddle also knew it (Abrahams, *A Singer and Her Songs*, 187). Max Hunter's Ozark collection has two versions (folksong collection, no. 500).]

The White Pilgrim

I came to the spot where the White Pilgrim lay
And pensively gazed at his tomb
When in a low whisper, a voice seemed to say
How sweetly I sleep here alone.

The tempest may howl and the loud thunder roll
And gathering storms may arise
But calm are my feelings, at rest is my soul
The tears are all wiped from my eyes.

I wandered a stranger, an exile from home
To publish salvation abroad
Endeavoring the trump of the gospel to blow
Inviting poor sinners to God.

I left my companion, deserted, alone
I bade all my kindred farewell
I left my poor children who for me now mourn
In a far distant region to dwell.

But when among strangers and far from my home
No companion, no relative nigh
I met with contagion and sank in the tomb
My spirit ascended on high.

Go tell my companion and children most dear
To weep not that James is now gone
The same hand that led me through scenes dark and drear
Has kindly conducted me home.

I came to the place of the mourner below
I entered the mansion of grief
Most freely the tears of deep sorrow did flow
I tried but could give no relief.

I spoke to the widow concerning her grief
I asked her the cause of her woe
And why there was nothing to give her relief
Or to soothe her affliction below.

She looked on her children then looked upon me
That look I shall never forget
More sorrowful far, than a seraph might be
She spoke of the trials she'd met.

But why should I murmur, Why should I complain
Why think that my portion is hard
For what is my loss to his infinite gain
He has entered the joys of his Lord.

A song which my father-in-law, William Hogan, used to sing at Nevada, MO in the mid-1930s. My sister, Helen Fultz, later (1960) found a copy in some magazine and copied it for me. She also found a mention of the White Pilgrim in Ripley's Believe It Or Not which told the story of a man who was called the "White Pilgrim" and wandered as a missionary all over the U.S. until he caught some kind of fever and died. His name was James but I have forgotten the last name as the original clipping was lost, which told of his accomplishments. The man lived in the early 1800s I believe. P.H.

My grandfather was a typical Irish laborer, but he sang, sang a lot. He sang one song we all just loved to hear him sing. It was actually a religious song—now this man had no religion, it was just a pretty song, had nothing to do with what he believed. Anyway I think it was called "The White Pilgrim," but it had a line in it that after we were grown we realized it was "how sweetly he sleeps," I suppose meaning he's dead. Grandpa sang it "how sweet lie he sleeps." I know he had a broadside, but he could read so poorly. . . . He always sang that song that way—it was funny." [Martha Hogan Estes, taped interview conducted by Amy Kreitlein, Fayetteville, Arkansas, November 21, 1993]

[Randolph has four variants (*Ozark Folksongs,* 4: 56–57). Almeda Riddle calls it "The Lone Pilgrim" (Abrahams, *A Singer and Her Songs,* 92–93, 177), and Shell includes a brief text ("Folk Songs Furnished," sect. 2, 16). For a thorough discussion, see D. K. Wilgus's article, "'The White Pilgrim': Song, Legend, and Fact."]

When the Roll Is Called Up Yonder

Not in the songbook. This number does appear in *Melodies of Praise* (no. 182), with words and music credited to J. M. Black.

Blessed Assurance

Not in the songbook. This famous song was written by Fanny Crosby (with music by Phoebe Palmer Knapp) in 1873. It's in both *The Broadman Hymnal* (no. 120) and *Melodies of Praise* (no. 155).

Tell It Again
(The Gypsy Boy)

Into the tent where the gypsy boy lay
Dying alone at the close of the day
News of salvation was carried, said he,
"Nobody ever has told it to me."

CHORUS

Tell it again, tell it again
Salvation's story, repeat it o'er and o'er
Till none can say of the children of man,
"Nobody ever has told it before."

"Did he so love me, a poor little boy
Send unto me the good tidings of joy?
Need I not perish, my hand will he hold
Nobody ever this story has told."

Bending we caught the last words of his breath
Just as he entered the Valley of Death
"God sent His son, Who-so-ever," said He,
"Then I am sure that He sent Him for me."

Smiling, he said, as his last sigh he spent,
"I am so glad that for me He was sent,"
Whispered while low sank the sun in the west,
"Lord I believe, tell it now to the rest."

Chorus repeated after each verse.

Copied from *Broadman Hymnal,* words by Mrs. M. B. C. Slade, music by R. M. McIntosh. No date of copyright, but mother sang it to us at least 65 years ago. H. F.

This one was one of Mother's. And I didn't find it for a long time. And . . . I found it in this hymnal. I think I still have a copy of it. [P. H., taped interview conducted by Elizabeth Foster, Fayetteville, Arkansas, May 15, 1992]

[This is no. 378 in *The Broadman Hymnal.*]

Jesus Loves Me

Not in the songbook. This widely known favorite is included in both *Melodies of Praise* (no. 298) and *The Broadman Hymnal* (no. 307); *Melodies of Praise* gives composer credit to Anna Bartlett Warner; both credit the music to William B. Bradbury. *The Broadman Hymnal* notes it as "The favorite Hymn of China."

If I Could Hear My Mother Pray Again

Not in the songbook. This piece entered the country music repertoire early on; the Jenkins Family recorded it in their first session in 1924. It's missing from the regional folksong collections, but there is a version (titled "If I Could Only Hear My Mother Pray Again") in Thomas G. Burton and Ambrose N. Manning, *East Tennessee State University Collection of Folklore: Folksongs* (89).

I'm Gonna Walk and Talk with My Lord

Oh I heard a voice from Heaven
Saying come unto me
And I will make you happy
If you'll just abide with me

CHORUS

I'm gonna walk, walk, and talk with my Lord
I'm gonna walk, walk, and talk with my Lord
He rolled away my burden, put in my heart a song
I'm gonna walk, walk, and talk with my Lord.

I had an introduction
To the Father and the Son
And if I stand upon his promise
I know I'll hear him say, well done.

I may meet with tribulations
Heavy burden with distress
But when my earthly race is over
I know he'll give me peace and rest

Repeat CHORUS and sing second CHORUS
I'm gonna walk, walk, and talk with my Lord
I'm gonna walk, walk, and talk with my Lord
He's the Lily of the Valley, he's the bright and the morning star
And I'm gonna walk, walk, and talk with my Lord.

Martha Carson sings it. We sing it at church *now*. H. F.

[Martha Carson not only sang it, she wrote it. It's not found in the regional folk-song collections, but Carson's turbulent career is discussed in Richard Carlin's *The Big Book of Country Music* (68–69) and in Mary A. Bufwack and Robert K. Oermann's *Finding Her Voice: The Saga of Women in Country Music* (208–9).]

The Great Speckled Bird

Not in the songbook. Though the authorship of this piece has been a matter of some dispute, it has been a great favorite ever since it was a hit for Roy Acuff in 1936. Randolph prints two versions (*Ozark Folksongs*, 4: 59–60) from the late 1930s.

I'll Fly Away

Not in the songbook. Widely known and often recorded, this is the prolific composer Albert E. Brumley's best-known song. First published in 1932.

Dust on the Bible

Not in the songbook. This number has been much recorded ever since the Bailes Brothers had a hit with it in 1945 (Johnny and Walter Bailes wrote it). The Blue Sky Boys also recorded a popular version, as did Kitty Wells.

Peace in the Valley

Not in the songbook. Written by the great gospel composer Thomas A. Dorsey, this number was a huge hit (often cited as the first gospel million-seller) for Red Foley in 1951.

I Saw the Light

Not in the songbook. Hank Williams wrote this country gospel classic, and first recorded it in 1948.

The Great Judgment Day

I dreamed that the great judg - ment mor - ning had
dawned and the trum - pet had blown.   I dreamed that all
na - tions had ga - thered to - ge - ther be - fore the white
throne   From the throne came a great shi - ning an -
gel   and stood on the land and the sea
and cried with his hands raised toward hea - ven,
that time was no lon - ger to be.

I dreamed that the great judgment morning
Had dawned and the trumpet had blown
I dreamed that all nations had gathered
Together around the White throne

CHORUS #1

From the throne came a great shining angel
Who stood on the land and the sea
And cried with his hands raised to heaven
That time no longer would be.

The rich man was there but his money
Had faded and vanished away

A pauper he stood at the judgment
His debts were too heavy to pay.

CHORUS #2

And oh what a weeping and wailing
When the lost ones were told of their fate
They cried for the rocks and the mountains
They prayed but their prayers were too late.

The widow was there, and the orphan
God heard and remembered their cries
No sorrow in heaven forever
He wiped all the tears from their eyes.

Repeat #2 chorus

Mother really could sing this and so could Dad.

This is one Dad sang—he really sang that one out. He usually sang bass
when we sang together. When he sang it alone he could really make
that one sound great. And I loved it. And then Mother, when she'd sing,
"And Oh, what a weeping and wailing / When the lost ones were told
of their fate / They cried for the rocks and the mountains / They prayed
but their prayers were too late." I'd just get shivers! [P. H., taped interview conducted by Elizabeth Foster, Fayetteville, Arkansas, May 15,
1992]

[Randolph has this as "The Great Judgment" (*Ozark Folksongs,* 4: 53–55). Stilley's
"The Great Judgment Day" ("The Stilley Collection: Part One," 35–36) is a different
song, as is the "Great Judgment Day" in Odum and Johnson's *The Negro and His Songs*
(99).]

Why Will You in Bondage Stay

Why will you in bondage stay
Sin and death no hope can offer
Of a better, brighter day
Why to evil bow?
Prison doors are opened wide
By the Saviour, crucified
Richly he will you endow
Seek salvation now.

CHORUS (Bass lead)

Come, come, come, come, come
why will you linger
here in bondage, sin rules in the darkness
Jesus will redeem you, Come into the light while it is
day . . . Why will you linger, here in bondage . . . let Him
loose your fetters
He now opens the prison wide, so come unto the light while you
    may.

All we can remember of this old hymn learned at War Eagle about 1921.
There were two more verses.

This is another one my older sisters sang more. Like they say they
learned it at War Eagle too. [P. H., taped interview conducted by
Elizabeth Foster, Fayetteville, Arkansas, May 15, 1992]

[The regional folksong collections lack this piece, and I have not yet found it in
any hymnal.]

Come Unto Me

Hear the blessed Savior calling the oppressed
Oh ye heavy laden, come to Me and rest
Come no longer tarry, I your load will bear
Bring me every burden, bring me every care.

CHORUS

Come unto me, I will give you rest
Take my yoke upon you
Hear me and be blest
I am meek and lowly
Come and trust my might
Come my yoke is easy
And my burden light.

Are you disappointed wandering here and there
Dragging chains of doubt and loaded down with care
Do unholy feelings struggle in your breast
Bring your cares to Jesus He will give you rest.

Have you by temptation often conquered been
Has a sense of weakness brought distress within
Christ will sanctify you if you'll claim His best
In the holy spirit He will give you rest.

Another family favorite. Needs at least two voices for harmony. It never
lacked a second one at home and usually had three or four. P.H.

[This is no. 275 in *Melodies of Praise*, where words and music are credited to
Charles P. Jones.]

Drifting Away

On the surging billows mid the raging waves
Cries the dying sailor, Save, oh save
Dashing o'er the white-caps drifting from the goal
Drifting onward, pleading for the rescue of the soul.

CHORUS

They're drifting away, yes drifting today
They cry, Jesus save, Oh Master, stay the waves
They sink beneath the foam
Too late, they are gone
Too late, will be the cry
Be saved, why will ye die?

Can you not do something in this trying hour
Beg them look to Jesus, look just now
See the surging billows, hear the raging storm
They are drifting, drifting, soon they're gone, forever gone.

That's another one the girls learned, and Mother probably too, in the Church of Christ. But we used to sing that quite a bit. [P. H., taped interview conducted by Elizabeth Foster, Fayetteville, Arkansas, May 15, 1992]

Seems like Thelma and Billie sang this at Habberton, but maybe it was even earlier. [P. H., note added in her draft copy of songbook, August 28, 1994]

[This is absent from the regional folksong collections, and I have not been able to locate it in any hymnal.]

No Hiding Place

Not in the songbook. This is often found in the African American sacred music repertoire. Owens has it in *Tell Me a Story* (276–77), and Work's *American Negro Songs* also has it (149). Dorothy Love Coates and the Gospel Harmonettes recorded it in the 1950s.

Bring Down the Latter Rain

Not in the songbook. Kentucky gospel shouter Brother Claude Ely recorded this fiery number as "Send Down That Rain" in 1953.

He Will Set Your Fields on Fire

Not in the songbook. Credited to L. L. Brackett and H. L. Ballen, this number was recorded in 1996 by the Browns.

Day of Wrath

Not in the songbook.

Onward Christian Soldiers

Not in the songbook. This favorite is no. 46 in *The Broadman Hymnal* and no. 209 in *Melodies of Praise*, with composer credits to Sabine Baring-Gould for text and Arthur Sullivan for music in both cases.

Faith of Our Fathers

Not in the songbook. This is no. 201 in *The Broadman Hymnal* and no. 60 in *Melodies of Praise*, where it's titled "Faith of Our Father's! Living Still." The words are credited to Frederick W. Faber and the music to H. F. Hemy.

The Evergreen Mountains of Life

There's a land far away, mid the stars, we are told,
Where they know not the sorrow of time
Where the pure waters flow, through the valleys of gold
And where life is a treasure sublime.

CHORUS

Tis the land of our God, tis the home of the Soul
Where the ages of splendor eternally roll
Where the tired weary traveler reaches his goal
On the evergreen mountain of life.

Here our gaze cannot soar to that beautiful home
But our visions have told of its bliss
Where the stars ever trod the blue Heavens at night,
We'd fain be in a desert of this.

Thelma and Alma sang this, and I believe it was at the Church of Christ where they sang it. We had a little Church of Christ [at Habberton]— Mother belonged to the Church of Christ. The rest of the family I think all belonged to the Methodist church, in later years anyway. And Dad was a Methodist. But this one had such beautiful harmony to it, and Thelma used to play it on the harp. . . . I always thought, Oh beautiful! I could just see the scenes passing in front of me when they'd sing it that way. And the "evergreen mountain of life"—I could relate to mountains. I really liked it. Billie and Thelma really sang it pretty. I don't remember Carl singing that one with them, but I'm sure he did. And Buck didn't do much singing; he just played. . . . Helen and I sang it, but I don't think we ever quite did it the justice they did. [P. H., taped interview conducted by Elizabeth Foster, Fayetteville, Arkansas, May 15, 1992]

We loved this one. Don't remember where we learned it except I remember the older kids singing it when I was very small. [P. H., note added in her draft copy of songbook, August 28, 1994]

[This is not found in the regional folksong collections, and I have not been able to locate it in any hymnal.]

Home of the Soul

If for the prize we have striven
After our labors are o'er
Rest to our souls (?) shall be given
On that eternal shore.

CHORUS

Alto Lead: Home of the soul, Blessed Kingdom of light
Soprano: Home of the soul, beautiful home, there we shall
    rest, never to roam

Free from all care, and where cometh no night
Free from all care, happy and bright
Jesus is there, He is the light

Oft in the storm we are crying for Thee
Oft in the storm, lonely are we
Crying for home, longing for Thee

Together: Beautiful home of the ransomed beside the crystal sea.

Soon the bright homeland adorning
We shall behold the glad dawn
Lean on the Lord till the morning
Trust till the night has gone.

Yes a sweet rest is remaining
For the true children of God
Where there will be no complaining
Never a chastening rod.

Favorite hymn sung as usual, every time we found or made a chance.
Especially good when accompanied by the harp.

Mother sang this but I don't know where we got it. [P. H., note added
in her draft copy of songbook, August 1994]

[This is not found in the regional folksong collections, and I have failed to locate
it in hymnals. There is a "Home of the Soul" in the 1933 Stamps-Baxter songbook,
Song Service and Revival (no. 125), but this is a different song.]

Where the Soul Never Dies

I'm sure we sang this at Zion but am not sure if we learned it from a
radio program or if it was in a church hymnal. I believe, though, it was
a song from some quartet—maybe Stamps-Baxter? [P. H., note added
in her draft copy of songbook, August 1994]

[A four-stanza version of this song appears in the Gilbert songbook, but copyright
restrictions do not allow for its printing here.]

[The usual title of this is "Where the Soul of Man Never Dies." It was composed
by former Oak Ridge Boys member William M. Golden and was a hit for that group
in 1976. This may be the most recent composition to be included in the songbook.]

As the Life of a Flower

As the life of a flower be our lives pure and sweet
May we brighten the way for the friends that we greet
And sweet incense arise from our hearts as we live
Close to him who doth teach us to love and forgive.

CHORUS

As the life of a flower,
As the breath or a sigh
So the years glide away
And alas we must die.

As we tarry below let us trust and adore
Him who leads us each day toward the radiant shore
Where the sun never sets and the stars never fade
Where no sorrow or death may its borders invade.

As the life of a flower as a breath or a sigh
So the years glide away and alas we must die
True today we are here, but tomorrow may see
Just a grave in a vale and a memory of me.

We sang this first at War Eagle Mills, Arkansas. With the "harp," banjo or guitar and at least four of us singing, the old pine trees on the hillside seemed to lean forward just to listen.

War Eagle Mills I wouldn't remember, so Billie is the one that did that. But it was beautiful, and we sang it a lot. . . . But it was really pretty done on the harp especially. . . . Mother liked this one. [P. H., taped interview conducted by Elizabeth Foster, Fayetteville, Arkansas, May 15, 1992]

The first comment above was from Billie Allen. I was too little to remember where we learned it and Helen wasn't even born yet. But we both sang it, especially for our church "specials." [P. H., note added in her draft copy of songbook, August 28, 1994]

[I learn from W. K. McNeil that this was written by Will M. Ramsey, a gospel music publisher from Little Rock, with recordings by the Herrington Sisters in 1944 and the Chuck Wagon Gang in the 1950s. It's not found in the regional folksong collections.]

How Great Thou Art

When I look down from lofty mountain grandeur
And hear the birds sing sweetly in the trees
Then I look up in humble adoration
And hear the brook and feel the gentle breeze.

Then sings my soul, my Saviour God, to Thee
How great Thou art, how great Thou art
Then sings my soul, my Saviour God, to Thee
How great Thou art, how great Thou art.

Oh, Lord, my God, when I in awesome wonder
Consider all the worlds Thy hands have made
I see the flash, I hear the rolling thunder
Thy power throughout the universe displayed.

I don't know where we learned this but I'm sure it's still in songbooks. [P. H., note added in her draft copy of songbook, August 28, 1994]

[This is no. 34 in *Favorite Hymns of Praise,* a hymnbook owned by Martha Hogan Estes as a gift from Phydella Hogan. The text is credited to Carl Boberg, as translated by Stuart K. Hine; the tune is listed as a Swedish folk melody. It's missing from the regional folksong collections.]

Jerusalem the Golden

Not in the songbook. This is no. 219 in *The Broadman Hymnal,* were the tune is credited to Alexander Ewing and the text to "Bernard of Cluny."

When We All Get to Heaven

Not in the songbook. This is no. 281 in *The Broadman Hymnal* and no. 173 in *Melodies of Praise*. Text by E. E. Hewitt and tune by Mrs. J. G. Wilson.

I Will Sing You a Song

Not in the songbook. *The Broadman Hymnal* includes this (no. 42), crediting the text to Ellen H. Gates and the tune to Philip Phillips.

No, Never Alone

I saw the lightning flashing
I heard the thunder roll
I felt sin's breakers dashing
Trying to conquer my soul
I heard the voice of my Saviour
Telling me still to fight on
He promised never to leave me
Never to leave me alone.

CHORUS

No never alone! No, no never alone.
He promised never to leave me
Never to leave me alone.

Sure wish someone knew the rest of this. It's such an old one and I can hear Mother's voice as she busied herself about the kitchen, walking to and fro from stove to cook-table with a spoon in her hand, stirring, mixing, and singing. One of the best memories of Mama is the way she sang about her morning work.

Also Billie's comments. [P. H., note added in her draft copy of songbook, August 1994]

[Both *The Broadman Hymnal* (no. 400) and *Melodies of Praise* (no. 197) include this number; the former lists it as "Anonymous" and names B. B. McKinney as arranger, while the latter offers no credits at all. Owens includes a text in his *Tell Me a Story,* remembering it as sung by "women in my family working in the fields" (239).]

Farther Along

Not in the songbook. This is a Stamps-Baxter publication from the 1930s, with words and music by Rev. W. B. Stevens, arranged by J. R. Baxter Jr. *Melodies of Praise* prints it as no. 36.

Precious Memories

Not in the songbook. This has been much recorded by both black and white country and gospel artists.

The Wayfaring Stranger

Not in the songbook. This is no. 74 in *The Broadman Hymnal,* but no composer credit is given.

The Family Who Prays

Not in the songbook. Charlie and Ira Louvin wrote this and first recorded it in 1951.

My Mother's Prayer

Not in the songbook. This is no. 95 in *The Broadman Hymnal,* with words credited to J. W. Van DeVenter and music to W. S. Weeden.

The Wandering Cowboy

See "Home Sweet Home."

Holy Boly

There was an old woman
In London she did dwell
She loved her old man dearly
And another one twice as well.

She went to the doctor
To see if she could find
Some kind of medicine
To run her old man blind.

She got some Holy-boly
And she made him eat it all
And then he said, my dear old wife
I cannot see you at all.

She began to kick and squall around
Because he was blind
He said I'll go and drown myself
If the river I can find.

She said, oh no, my dear old man
For fear you go astray
I'll take you by your dear old hand
And lead you all the way.

She led him to the river
And then up to the shore
Then she stepped back a little
To run and push him o'er.

When she stepped back a little
To run and push him in
The old man stepped aside a little
The old lady, she went in.

She began to kick and scramble
And then began to bawl
But the old man said, my dear old wife
I cannot see you at all.

She kicked and scrambled around awhile
And then began to swim
The old man cut a great long pole
And pushed her farther in.

And now my song is ended
I can't sing any more
But don't you know that silly old fool
Came a-swimmin' to the shore.

I'm pretty sure this was one of Dad's songs. P. H.

[This is found everywhere in the regional folksong collections, though never under this title. Randolph (*Ozark Folksongs*, 4: 246–49), Belden (*Ballads and Songs*, 237–39), and Moore and Moore (*Ballads and Folk Songs of the Southwest*, 218–20) have it as "Johnny Sands," while Owens calls it "The Old Woman From Ireland" (*Texas Folksongs*, 207–9). In Garrison's 1944 University of Arkansas M.A. thesis, it's "The Old Woman in Ireland" ("Forty-Five Folk Songs," 86–88), while Rainey has it as "Old Woman in Ireland" (*Songs of the Ozark Folk*, 11). Max Hunter's Ozark collection includes a version by Helen Fultz, recorded in 1960 in Fayetteville (folksong collection, no. 257). Brown's North Carolina collection calls it "The Old Woman's Blind Husband" (2: 450–52).]

Johnny Sands

See "Holy Boly."

The Old Woman in Ireland

See "Holy Boly."

Rich Old Lady

See "Holy Boly."

The Sweet Trinity

See "The Green Willow Tree."

The Lowlands Low

See "The Green Willow Tree."

The Golden Vanity

See "The Green Willow Tree."

The Merry Golden Tree

See "The Green Willow Tree."

Chingaling Chan

In China there lived a little man
His name was Ching-a-ling Ching-a-ling Chan
His legs were fat and his feet were small
And this little man couldn't walk at all.

CHORUS

Chingaling, Chingaling, Chingaling Chan
Rye-go dago a happy man
Karo-disco-cordy-o
Gallopy-wallopy China use'd go.

Mis Ki Ki was short and fat
She had money and he had not
Under her window he would go
Playing a tune on his little banjo.

CHORUS

Miss Ki Ki heard his notes of love
Held her washboard high above
Let it fall on Ching-a-ling Chan
And that was the end of the China man.

CHORUS

Learned at Zion. At school, from a teacher.

Phydella and her mother and father knew that song. She's known it for years. I remember Phydella singing it, and I remember my mother teaching it to me after that. [Oliva Vaughan, taped interview conducted by Elizabeth Foster, Fayetteville, Arkansas, October 3, 1992]

[This piece shows up only in Burdine and McCarthy ("Sister Singers," 409, 411–12) and in a 1959 version in the University of Arkansas folksong archive (289/9).]

China Man

See "Chingaling Chan."

Bill Vanero

Bill Vanero heard them say in an Arizona town one day
That a band of Apache Indians were on the trail that way.
Bill had heard of murder done, two men killed on Rocky Run
But his thoughts were of a cow ranch not many miles away.

Bill stood gazing all around, picked his lasso from the ground
And called to his little brown pony not many steps away.
Bill you'd better save your breath you are riding straight to death
If I never reach that cow ranch, I'll do the best I can.

Cow ranch forty miles away
Was a little place that lay

In a deep and shady valley of the mighty wilderness
Half a score of homes were there
And in one a maiden fair
Held the heart of Bill Vanero
Bill Vanero's little Bess
So no wonder he grew pale
When he heard the cowboy's tale
Of the men that he's seen murdered
The day before at Rocky Run

The cowboy saw his hurry, heard the jingle of his spurs
As little Chappo bore him away from home and friends.
Across the alkali flats he sped but his thoughts were on ahead
Of Little Bessie at the cow ranch and the boys on Rocky Run.

Just then a rifle shot broke the echo of the spot
I'm wounded, cried Vanero, as he swayed from side to side.
But as long as there's life, there's hope, slowly onward I will lope
And he halted his little brown pony in the shadow of a hill.

Then with trembling hands he took from his chaps a little book
And tore a blank leaf from it, saying this shall be my will.
From a tree a twig he broke, slowly dipped his pen of oak
In the life-blood flowing from the wound above his heart.

This message he wrote fast, his first love-letter and his last
Tied it firmly to his saddle, then gave his horse the reins ["tied him-
    self to his saddle" written in the margin by this line] .
To Little Bessie, Chappo, said he, take this message if not me
If I never reach that cow-ranch Little Bessie will know I tried

This little horse of a dusky brown covered in sweat came panting
    down
Alone to the cow-ranch, stopped in front of Bessie's door.
This poor cowboy was asleep though his slumbers were so deep
Little Bessie could not wake him, though she tried forever more.

Many years have passed away, Little Bessie's hair turned grey
Still she places a wreath of flowers on Bill Vanero's grave.
Now you've heard the story told, of the young and by the old
How the Indians killed Vanero on the ride of Rocky Run.

I remember we always sang this when we sang "Utah Carrol." It just seemed to fall next in line but I can't remember *not* knowing it. [H. F., note added in her draft copy of songbook, December 1993]

I may be wrong, but I think maybe Blanche Garriott gave us this one. She had lots of cowboy songs. I'm sure we got "My Lover Is a Cowboy" from her. [P. H., note added in her draft copy of songbook, August 1994]

[This cowboy ballad (Laws B6) is in Randolph (*Ozark Folksongs*, 2: 222–27). There are also two versions in Max Hunter's Ozark folksong collection (no. 69). The lyrics originate in a poem by Eben E. Rexford, published in 1881. John Lomax included it in *Cowboy Songs and Other Frontier Ballads* (299–302).]

Lord Lovel

Not in the songbook. This Child ballad (75) is in Randolph (*Ozark Folksongs*, 1: 112–15), Belden (*Ballads and Songs*, 52–54), and Moore and Moore (*Ballads and Folk Songs of the Southwest*, 56–58).

Geisha Girl

Not in the songbook. Lawton Williams wrote it; Hank Locklin had a hit recording in 1957.

Put My Little Shoes Away

Mother dear come bathe my forehead
For I'm growing very weak
Let one drop of water, mother
Fall upon my burning cheek.
Mother I am growing weaker
Please forgive me what I say
You were angry when you told me
I was always in the way.

Mother I will be an angel
By perhaps another day
So remember what I tell you
Put my little shoes away.
Santa Claus he brought them to me
With so many other things
And I think he sent an angel
With a pair of golden wings.

Soon the baby will be older
Then they'll fit his little feet
Won't he look so sweet and cunning
As he walks along the street.
Go tell all my little playmates
That no more with them I'll play
Give them all my toys but mother
Put my little shoes away.

This was one of Mother's songs. I think the aunts and Grandma [Scott] sang it too. Anyway I can't remember not knowing it. [P. H., note added in her draft copy of songbook, August 1994]

[This was composed in 1873 by Samuel Mitchell and Charles E. Pratt. It's rare in the regional folksong collections, but Randolph prints three versions (*Ozark Folksongs,* 4: 178–80). Arkansas singer Noble Cowden recorded it in 1984—see her album *Songs My Family Loves* (Arkansas Traditions).]

The Four Marys

Not in the songbook. This Child ballad (173) is in Randolph (*Ozark Folksongs,* 1: 151) and Moore and Moore as "Mary Hamilton" (*Ballads and Folk Songs of the Southwest,* 93–94).

The House of the Rising Sun
by Al Price
as sung by The Animals

[A six-stanza version of this song appears in the Gilbert songbook, but copyright restrictions do not allow for its printing here.]

[Al Price played with the Animals, but he didn't write "House of the Rising Sun." Bob Dylan did it on his first album, but the Animals evidently got it from Josh White (and Dylan evidently got it from fellow folkie Dave Van Ronk). It was a number-one hit for the Animals in 1964.]

Looking out My Back Door

Not in the songbook. John Fogerty wrote it, and Creedence Clearwater had a hit with it in 1970.

The Malibu Trail

Sung to tune of The Dying Cowboy

Out in the west where the riders are ready
They sing an old song and they tell an old tale
And the moral is plain, take it easy, go steady
While riding a horse on the Malibu Trail.

It's a high rocky trail full of switchbacks and doubles
It has no beginning and never an end
It's risky and rough and it's plumb full of trouble
From Shifty—that's shale—up to Powdercut Bend.

Old timers will tell you the rangers that made it
Sang, "Roll a rock down" with a stiff upper lip.
And cussed all creation but managed to grade it
With a thousand foot drop if a pony should slip.

The day it was wet and the sky it was cloudy
And the trail was as slick as an oil rigger's pants
When Ranger McCabe on his pony, Old Rowdy,
Came ridin' where walkin' was takin' a chance.

Oh, "Roll a rock down" picks and shovels was clangin'
And Rowdy was steppin' that easy and light
When the edge it gave way and McCabe was left hangin'
Clean over the rim with no bottom in sight.

I shook out a noose, bein' crowded for throwin'
I flipped a fair noose for a rope that was wet
It caught just as Mac lost his hold and was goin'
It burned through my fingers, it's burnin' them yet.

So roll a rock down where a Ranger is sleepin'
By the side of his pony in Powdercut Bend
I ride and I look where the shadows are creepin'
And roll a rock down for McCabe was my friend.

I've sung you my song and I've told you my story
And all that I ask when I'm done with the show
Is to roll a rock down when I slide into Glory
And say that I went like a Ranger should go.

Copied from *Western Story Magazine* about 1930 by Phydella Gilbert (Hogan)

It was just a poem, but when I read it it just seemed to fit as a song. I set it to the tune of "The Dying Cowboy"—that's usually called "Streets of Laredo" now—but our tune is different than the one that's used now. Everybody liked it. That was one of the ones I taught Bill Hogan, and he sung it all the time. My son Bill still sings it. We liked it because it showed the dangers that were in the making of that trail, and the emotions the man felt when the rope burned through his hands and his partner fell. It's a complete story. You can just see the whole thing. We drove over that when I lived out there—I was surprised they *ever* got it built. [P. H., Fayetteville, Arkansas, April 14, 1994]

Wishing Rug

I wish I had a wishing rug.
I'd wrap myself up in it warm and snug.
I'd close my eyes and make a wish,
And away I'd go like a flying fish.

It would be lonely by myself.
Perhaps the clock on the kitchen shelf
With its tick-tock-tick would sound like home
No matter how far away I'd roam.

I'd take the clock and kitty and lunch,
Something for kitty and me to munch,
Say sugar or mince or a chocolate cake,
Something like that we'd probably take.

Perhaps I'd better take Maisie, too,
For you never can tell what a doll will do.

If you leave her behind why she might cry,
And ruin the shine of her best blue eye.

I'd take all this and travel far
Beyond the first small shining star
Where all sky children come and go
To see the round moon's puppet show.

Perhaps we'd sail across the park
And see the lions before it got dark,
And watch the tigers yawn and blink
As if they never had slept a wink.

And then the very next place we'd stop
We'd find a wonderful toy shop,
And there we'd choose all kinds of toys
To bring to all the girls and boys
In school and those who live right here
We'd bring enough toys to last for a year.

I'd bring my daddy a nice new moon,
And I'd bring my mother a silver spoon,
And a collar for kitty of a star or two,
And a dress for Maisie of blue sky blue.

I'd sail back home and eat my bread,
And drink my milk and go to bed,
But first I'd fold my rug away,
And save it for another day.

This was a poem published in the *Kansas City Star*. Phydella put a tune to it and we all three sang it to our kids. I still sing it to my youngest granddaughter Andrea. H. F.

Blue Suede Shoes

Not in the songbook. A hit in 1956 for Carl Perkins, this rocka-billy classic was also recorded early on by Elvis Presley.

Sweet Evelina

Way down in the meadow where the lily first blows
Where the wind from the mountains never ruffled the rose
Lives fond Evelina the sweet little dove
The pride of the valley, the girl that I love.

CHORUS

Dear Evelina, sweet Evelina, my love for you shall never, never die.
Dear Evelina, sweet Evelina, my love for you shall never, never die.

She's fair like a rose, like a lamb she is meek
And she never was known to put paint on her cheek
In the most graceful curls hangs her raven black hair
And she never requires perfumery there.

Evelina and I one fine evening in June
Took a walk all alone by the light of the moon
The planets all shone, for the heavens were clear
And I felt round the heart tremendously queer.

Three years have gone by and I've not got a dollar
Evelina still lives in that green grassy holler
Although I am fated to marry her never
I've sworn that I'll love her forever and ever.

Heart Songs, p. 417

Now this was one Mother sang all her life. This is a copy from *Heart Songs* because we didn't have all of it, and so I copied it all down. That was one of her favorites. . . . That's why I got the book was that so many of the songs—I got it out of the library up there in Lincoln [Nebraska] I'd go through these songs and I'd think, 'Gee, there's got to be more to 'em than this, and this is all we remember.' So I got this *Heart Songs* book, and started looking them up. [P. H., taped interview, Fayetteville, Arkansas, August 3, 1990]

I remember Dad would say, "He didn't want to marry her very bad or he'd have a dollar in three years!" [H. F., note added in her draft copy of songbook, January 1994]

This was also one of Mother's songs. [P. H., note added in her draft copy of songbook, August 28, 1994]

[*Heart Songs* lists no composer, and calls this "Dear Evalina, Sweet Evalina." Randolph includes it (*Ozark Folksongs,* 4: 344). Pound prints version close to the Gilbert text in *American Ballads and Songs* (101), and Max Hunter's Ozark collection also has it (folksong collection, no. 602). Sigmund Spaeth's *A History of Popular Music* lists a "Sweet Evalina" dating from 1863 (160).]

The Shadow of the Pines

We wan - dered 'neath the sha - dow of the

pines my love and I while the wind was blow - ing fresh - ly from the

sea, and the sud - den fit of dark -ness stole a - cross the sum -mer sky and the

sha - dow came be -tween my love and I. Some has - ty words were spo - ken and

al - most un - a - ware the an -swers to un - think - ing an - ger led. All our

heart - sick bit - ter long - ing, all our wee - ping and our pride, ne'er can

make those harsh and cru - el words un - said.

Come back to me sweet - heart and love me as be - fore. Come

back to me dar - ling and leave me ne - ver more. Through

life's dark path - way the sun no lon - ger shines. Come,

love, and meet me in the sha - dow of the pines.

We wandered neath the shadow of the pines, my love and I
And the wind was blowing freshly from the sea,
When a sudden fit of darkness stole across the summer sky
And a shadow came between my love and me
Some hasty words were spoken and almost unaware
Hasty answers to unthinking anger led
All our heartsick bitter longing, all our weeping and our pride
Ne'er can make those harsh and cruel words unsaid.

CHORUS

Come back to me sweetheart and love me as before
Come back to me darling and leave me nevermore
Through life's dark pathway the sun no longer shines
Come love and meet me in the shadows of the pines.

You took the ring I gave you and ne'er cast one glance at me.
As you held the jeweled trinket in your hand
And then you turned and tossed it in the waters of the sea
While the waves were splashing idly on the sand
You went your way unheeding the tears I could not hide
You went your way and not a word was said
But my stubborn heart was breaking underneath the mask of pride
And the pine trees sobbed in pity overhead.

CHORUS

I wake from bitter dreaming but to shout aloud your name
I sleep again to dream of you once more
But my stubborn pride has left me, I'll admit I was to blame
Forgive me dear and love me as before.
The future is o'ershadowed by the darkness of despair
Through the sky of life the sun no longer shines
I would give this whole world gladly once again to meet you there
Reunited in the shadow of the pines.

CHORUS

We have sung this song for as long as I can remember and it was always
a favorite number. Copied in 1960 by Phydella Hogan

I think this is a very beautiful love song. [H. F., note added in her draft copy of songbook, December 1993]

This is a little unusual in that the singer was a man. Most of those broken-hearted love songs—least nobody dies—have women as the speaker. It's got a real tricky tune, too. The chorus is in 3/4 time while the verses are in 4/4. I've never heard anybody outside the family sing it. Ward Simmons, Carl's second wife Cora's second husband, told us he remembered hearing it sung in his family. [P. H., Fayetteville, Arkansas, May 3, 1994]

[This is rare in folksong collections. McNeil gives a 1967 version from Georgia (*Southern Folk Ballads,* 1: 135–36, 203). His notes give an 1895 publication date and attribute authorship to Hattie Lummis and G. O. Lang. There were popular early country music recordings by Gene Autry, Bradley Kincaid, and Kelly Harrell.]

The Days Are a Burden

My old pappy he's mighty cross
He'll neither give me a cow nor a horse
He's none the better and I'm none the worse
The days are a burden and a slang-o.

CHORUS

Shirl, shirl, shirl go round
Shirl-i-shickle and a shinny pop a tune
Toad cut the waddin' and a hot-tot-toddin'
The days are a burden and a slang-o.

My old mammy she's mean as a sin
She won't give me a needle or a pin
She's none the better and I'm none the worse
The days are a burden and slang-o.

Repeat nonsense chorus

My old lady she's mighty mean
She won't wash my britches clean

She's none the better and I'm none the worse
The days are a burden and a slang-o.

Repeat chorus

My sister Marian she went to France
For her fortune to advance
She's none the better and I'm none the worse
The days are a burden and a slang-o

I'm not sure these are exactly like Mother sang them but it probably didn't matter. I think it was another old "Play-party" song where you simply added whatever came into your head so the couples could keep dancing.

Some more nonsense we learned at our mother's knee. Lots of fun, our mother, and very wise to mix the nonsense up along with the lovely old church songs and ballads, stories from the Bible, from Grimm's fairy tales, ghost stories, and samples of all the good literature, given in small doses while we were young enough to develop a taste for the best in everything. [P. H., note added in her draft copy of songbook, August 26, 1994]

[Randolph has this as "Shule, Shule" (*Ozark Folksongs*, 1: 400–402), though only his C version resembles the Gilbert text. But see also the "Putman's Hill" (especially the D version) in Mary O. Eddy's *Ballads and Songs from Ohio* (128).]

Barbara Allen

'Twas in the merry month of May
When green buds they were swellin',
Sweet William on his death-bed lay
For the love of Barbara Allen.

Slowly, slowly she got up
And slowly she drew nigh him,
And all she said when she got there,
"Young man I think you're dying."

"O yes I'm sick and very low,
And death is on me dwellin',
No better shall I ever be
If I don't get Barbara Allen."

"Don't you remember the other day
When you were in the tavern,
You toasted all the ladies there
And slighted Barbara Allen."

"O yes, I remember the other day
When we were in the tavern,
I toasted all the ladies there,
Gave my love to Barbara Allen."

He turned his pale face to the wall,
And death was on him dwellin',
"Adieu, adieu, my kind friends all,
Be kind to Barbara Allen."

As she was walkin' through the fields,
She heard the death bells knellin',
And every toll they seemed to say
Hardhearted Barbara Allen.

She looked east, and she looked west
She saw his corpse a-comin',
"Lay down, lay down the corpse," she said
"And let me gaze upon him."

"O mother, mother make my bed,
O make it long and narrow,
Sweet William died for me today,
I'll die for him tomorrow."

They buried her in the old churchyard
With Willie close beside her
On Willie's grave grew a red, red rose
On Barbara's grew a briar.

They grew and grew in the old churchyard
Till they could grow no higher
They lapped and tied in a true lover's knot
The red rose and the briar.

I can't remember singing this—maybe Alma did? [H. F., note added in her draft copy of songbook, January 1994]

Mother sang parts of this, but I don't think we did very much. She didn't know all the verses but I later copied some from *Heart Songs*, a book from the city library at Lincoln, NE. [P. H., note added in her draft copy of songbook, August 1994]

[This famous Child ballad (84) is included in Randolph (*Ozark Folksongs*, 1: 126–39), Belden (*Ballads and Songs*, 60–65), and Moore and Moore (*Ballads and Folk Songs of the Southwest*, 68–70). It's also in the Carlisle University of Arkansas M.A. thesis ("Fifty Ballads and Songs," 27–29), McNeil (*Southern Folk Ballads*, 1: 102–5), and Riddle (*A Singer and Her Songs*, 87–89, 177). Rainey prints a version from Noble Cowden (*Songs of the Ozark Folk*, 27), and the Max Hunter Ozark folksong collection has eight versions (no. 38).]

The Farmer's Curst Wife

See "Ty-Oh-Rattle-Ding-Day."

The Old Man under the Hill

See "Ty-Oh-Rattle-Ding-Day."

Ty-Oh-Rattle-Ding-Day

There was an old man and his name was Bill
(whistle the tune of above) or hum de-oodle-de-oodle-de oodle ?
He lived all alone on top of a hill
Sing ty-oh-rattle-ding-day.

He hitched up his hogs one morning to plow
(whistle)
And plowed out a furrow the devil knows how
Sing ty-oh-rattle-ding-day.

He hitched up his horses next morning to plow
(whistle)
And then the old devil rose up right now
Sing etc.

Said he, me old devil ye must be in fun
(whistle)
Ye cannot have my eldest son
Sing etc.

'Tis not your oldest son that I crave
(whistle)
But your cranky old wife and her I will have
Sing etc.

Well take her along with all of my heart
(whistle)
Here's hopin' to God that you never do part
Sing etc.

He took her right upon his back
(whistle)
And you never saw a peddler more proud of his pack
Sing etc.

He took her down to the gates of sin
(whistle)
And there by God he did tumble her in
Sing etc.

Now ten little devils were hangin' up chains
(whistle)
She picked one up and warped(?) out his brains
Sing etc.
There was one little devil who wore a blue hat
(whistle)
She picked up the ax and by God she killed that
Sing etc.

But eight little devils took up over the wall
(whistle)
Saying, take her back daddy she's killin' us all
Sing etc.

He picked up the ax and he gave her a whack
(whistle)
Saying if you don't quit you will have to go back
Sing etc.

She grabbed up the hammer and gave him a whack
(whistle)
Said, you trotted me here but you'll gallop me back
Sing etc.

He took her right upon his back
(whistle)
And like an old hound dog he took a back track
Sing etc.

When the old man saw 'em he took up over the hill
(whistle)
Said, if the devil won't have you I don't know who will
Sing etc.

One day she caught him asleep in bed
(whistle)
With her old pewter pipe she knocked him stone dead
Sing etc.

And now you see what a woman can do
(whistle)
She can conquer all Hell and her husband too
Sing ty-oh-rattle-ding-day.

One of Dad's songs. If you can't whistle, try the oodle de oodle de bit
and rhyme it with the line above it—"wall," "back," "do," etc.

I dearly loved to hear Dad sing this. [H. F., note added in her draft copy
of songbook, January 1994]

[This Child ballad (278) has been much collected in the region. Randolph has it
as "The Old Man Under the Hill" (*Ozark Folksongs*, 1: 189–93), Belden calls it "The
Farmer's Curst Wife" (*Ballads and Songs*, 94–97), and Moore and Moore also use that
title (*Ballads and Folk Songs of the Southwest*, 127–28). In Owens it's titled "The Devil's
Song" (*Texas Folksongs*, 55–56), while Garrison's 1944 University of Arkansas M.A.
thesis has a version titled "The Old Devil Came to My Plow" ("Forty-Five Folk
Songs," 13–15). Max Hunter's Ozark folksong collection calls it "Devil Doings" (no.
149).]

Jinny Fer Jinny

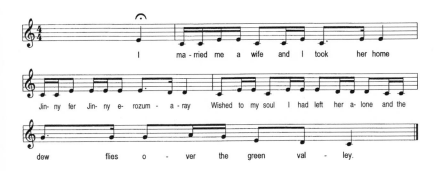

I married a wife and took her home
Jinny-fer-jinny-e-roz-um-a-ray
And I wished to my soul I had left her alone
As the dew flies over the green valley.

To go in the kitchen she did not choose
Jinny-fer-jinny-e-roz-um-a-ray
For fear she would spoil her new cloth shoes
As the dew flies over the green valley.

The very first day I come in from my plow
Jinny-fer-jinny-e-roz-um-a-ray
Said oh, my dear wife is my dinner done now?
As the dew flies over the green valley.

No, you lazy and dirty whelp!
Jinny-fer-jinny-e-roz-um-a-ray
If you want any dinner go cook it yourself
As the dew flies over the green valley.

I gets mad and I goes to the barn
Jinny-fer-jinny-e-roz-um-a-ray
And I cuts me a switch as long as my arm
As the dew flies over the green valley.

I picks it up and I walks straight back
Jinny-fer-jinny-e-roz-um-a-ray
And over her back it goes clickety clack
As the dew flies over the green valley.

The very next day I come in from my plow
Jinny-fer-jinny-e-roz-um-a-ray
Said oh, my dear wife is my dinner done now
As the dew flies over the green valley.

Up she jumps and spreads the board
Jinny-fer-jinny-e-roz-um-a-ray
Yes-sir and No-sir to every word said
As the dew flies over the green valley.

We live in peace and for wealth we strive
Jinny-fer-jinny-e-roz-um-a-ray
I hope she will live to the end of her life
As the dew flies over the green valley.

Our mother sung this old song or whatever it is as far back as I can remember, and we loved it for its nonsense just as we loved "Old Graybeard and His Leggin's," "Where Are You Going My Good Old Man," and "Nickety Nackety Now Now Now."

Phydella later found the words in a song book and our "Jinny-fer-jinny-e-roz-um-a-ray" was actually "Jennifer-Jenny-sweet Rosamarie!" [H. F., note added in her draft copy of songbook, January 1994]

[This Child ballad (277) has been much collected in the region, though usually under other titles. Randolph has it as "Dan-Doo" (*Ozark Folksongs*, 1: 187–88), and Belden as "The Wife Wrapt In Wether's Skin" (*Ballads and Songs*, 92–94), the same title used by Moore and Moore (*Ballads and Folk Songs of the Southwest*, 124–26). Max Hunter's Ozark collection has two versions, including one titled "Jenny Fair Jen" (no. 131). McNeil (*Southern Folk Ballads*, 2: 58–63, 192–93) provides two versions and good notes.]

The Wife Wrapt in Wether's Skin

See "Jinny Fer Jinny."

Dandoo

See "Jinny Fer Jinny."

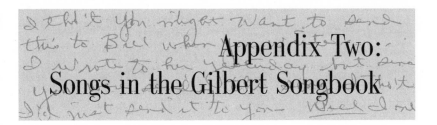

Appendix Two:
Songs in the Gilbert Songbook

[Titles Only]

After the Ball
Ain't We Crazy
All Around the Water Tank
Amazing Grace
Anything
Arkansas Traveler
As the Life of a Flower

Bad Companions
Baggage Coach Ahead, The
Barbara Allen
Battleship Maine, The
Bill Vanero
Blessed Rock of Ages
Blind Child, The
Blue Ridge Mountain Blues
Boy in Blue, The
Bring Back to Me My Wandering
   Boy
Buffalo Gals
Bury Me Beneath the Willow

Camptown Races
Carry Me Back To Old Virginny
Chingaling Chan
Church in the Wildwood
Cindy
Come Unto Me

Cottoneyed Joe
Count Your Blessings
Courtin'
Cowboy's Judgment
Cradle Song
Cripple Creek

Daddy and Home
Days Are A Burden, The
Dear Charlie
Derby Ram, The
Dirty Faced Brat
Dixie
Don't Take Me Back to the Chain
   Gang
Drifting Away
Driftwood on the River
Drunkard's Dream, The

Echoes From the Hills
Empty Cot in the Bunkhouse
Evergreen Mountains of Life, The

Fair Lady of the Plains, A
Fair Nottingham Town
Five Foot Two
Floyd Collins
Foggy Mountain Top

Four in the Middle
Frankie and Johnny
Frozen Girl, The

Girl I Left Behind Me, The
Girl I Loved in Sunny Tennessee,
   The
Git Along Little Dogies
Go Tell Aunt Rhodie
Going Back to Where I Come From
Going from the Cottonfields
Golden Slippers
Good Old Mountain Dew
Grandfather's Clock
Great Judgment Day, The
Green Corn
Green Grass Grew All Around, The
Green Willow Tree, The
Ground Hog

Hang Out the Front Door Key
Holy Boly
Home of the Soul
Home Sweet Home
Homestead on the Farm, The
Hot Winds
House of the Rising Sun, The
How Great Thou Art
Hush My Babe

I Could Not Call Her Mother
I Don't Want to Play in Your Yard
I Sat Alone
I Walked Back From the Buggy Ride
I Was Born About Four Thousand
   Years Ago
I Wish I Was Single Again
Ida Red
If You Want Your Girl To Love
   You, Boys

I'll Be All Smiles Tonight
I'm Alone, All Alone
I'm Gonna Walk and Talk with
   My Lord
I'm In the Army
I'm Thinking Tonight of My
   Blue Eyes

Jealous Lover
Jerry, Go and Ile That Car
Jesse James
Jesus at the Well
Jinny Fer Jinny
Juanita
Just Before the Battle, Mother

Kitty Wells

Lamplighting Time in the Valley
Let the Lower Lights Be Burning
Let the Rest of the World Go By
Letter Edged in Black, The
Listen to the Mockingbird
Little Black Mustache
Little Green Valley
Little Home in Tennessee
Little Mohee
Little Old Nigger Baby
Little Omie
Little Rosewood Casket, A
Little White Washed Chimney
Lolly Truedom

Making Little Ones Out of Big Ones
Malibu Trail, The
Maple on the Hill
Marching Through Georgia
Marian Parker
Massa's in De Cold Ground

May I Sleep in Your Barn Tonight
   Mister
Midnight Express, The
Mississippi Flood, The
Missouri Waltz
Model Church, The
Moonlight and Skies
Mountain Top, The
My Blue-Eyed Boy
My Clinch Mountain Home
My Horses Ain't Hungry
My Lover Is a Cowboy
My Mother Was a Lady
My Old Kentucky Home

Nellie Gray
New River Train, The
Nickety Nackety Now Now Now
Nightingale Song, The
No, Never Alone
Nobody's Darling

Oh Bury Me Not on the Lone
   Prairie
Oh Susanna
Old Blue
Old Chisholm Trail, The
Old Cornet, The
Old Dan Tucker
Old Grass Widow, The
Old Grey Beard and His Leggins
Old Jerusalem Wall, The
Old Joe Clark
Old John Bull
Old Number Nine
Old Number Three
Old Pal
Old Pal of Yesterday
Old Wooden Rocker, The

Only a Bird in a Gilded Cage
Orphan Girl, The
Ottie Brooks

Papa Stole the Parson's Sheep
Parlor is a Pleasant Place to Sit in
   Sunday Night, The
Peter Gray
Picture from Life's Other Side, A
Poor Bennie
Poor Dianah
Poor Little Children in the State
   Orphan's Home
Poor Old Bumble Bee
Poor Old Christmas Dolls
Preacher and the Bear, The
Put My Little Shoes Away

Quilting Party, The

Red Wing
Remember Me
Rovin' Gambler
Rye Cove
Rye Whiskey

Sally Anne
Save My Mother's Picture From
   the Sale
Seven Years with the Wrong Man
Seven Years with the Wrong
   Woman
Shadow of the Pines, The
Shady Grove
She'll Be Comin' Around the
   Mountain
Silver Colorado, The
Silver Haired Daddy
Soldier's Joy

Spanish Cavalier, A
State of Arkansas, The
Stay in Your Own Back Yard
Stern Old Bachelor, A
Streets of Laredo, The
Sugar Foot Rag
Summer Land of Love
Surrender
Sweet Bunch of Daisies
Sweet Evelina
Sweet Lorraine
Sweet Violets

Tell It Again
Tornado of Sherman Texas, The
True Young Maid, The
There Ain't No Pockets in a Shroud
They Cut Down the Old Pine Tree
They Were Standing By the
    Window
Those Two Blue Eyes
Three Nights Drunk
Twenty-One Years
Ty-Oh-Rattle-Ding-Day

Utah Carrol

Very Fine Gander, A

Washed My Hands in Muddy Water
Way Over in the Promised Land
When I Was a Little Boy
When the Bees Are in the Hive
When the Roses Bloom Again
When the Work's All Done This
    Fall
Where Are You Going My Good
    Old Man?
Where the River Shannon Flows

Where the Soul Never Dies
Whistlin' Rufus
White Pilgrim, The
White River Flows
Why Will You in Bondage Stay
Widow's Daughter, The
Wishing Rug
Wreck of Old Ninety-Seven, The

Young Man Who Wouldn't Hoe
    His Corn
Your Love Is Like a Flower

Notes

1. Phydella Hogan, note to "I Could Not Call Her Mother" in original songbook manuscript. Texts of songs, in order of their mention in the text and with music where available, may be found in appendix 1.

2. Alma Allen, quoted by Phydella Hogan in her note to "Kitty Wells" in original songbook manuscript.

3. Helen Fultz, comment on audiotape made in 1974, copied for the author by Jeanie Fultz Miller in 1991. All audiotapes, letters, and interviews are in possession of the author unless otherwise noted.

4. Joe Hogan, letter to the author, August 6, 1994.

5. Phydella Hogan, note to "My Horses Ain't Hungry" in original songbook manuscript.

6. Helen Fultz, written reminiscence, Mayfield, Arkansas, November 20, 1990, 1.

7. Four substantial folksong collections have been published for regions near the Gilbert home territory in northwest Arkansas. H. M. Belden's pioneering work, *Ballads and Songs Collected by the Missouri Folklore Society* (reprint, Columbia: University of Missouri Studies, 1955), appeared in 1940, followed first by Vance Randolph's enormous *Ozark Folksongs* (reprint, Columbia: University of Missouri Press, 1980), a four-volume work issued from 1946 to 1950, and then by William A. Owens's *Texas Folk Songs* (Dallas: Southern Methodist University Press, 1950), and by Ethel and Chauncey Moore's *Ballads and Folk Songs of the Southwest,* (Norman: University of Oklahoma Press, 1964), an Oklahoma collection centered on the Tulsa area. The ground-breaking study focused on an individual singer was Roger Abrahams's edition of the musical autobiography of Almeda Riddle, *A Singer and Her Songs* (Baton Rouge: Louisiana State University Press, 1970). For a thorough survey of the history of folksong collecting in the Ozark region, see W. K. McNeil's introduction to the 1980 reprint of Randolph's *Ozark Folksongs*.

8. Gregory Nagy translates Demodokhos as "received by the *deme*" in *The Best of the Achaeans: Concepts of the Hero in Archaic Greek Poetry* (Baltimore: Johns Hopkins University Press, 1979), 17. My thinking on these matters was stimulated and clarified by conversations with Gregory Nagy and John Miles Foley at the 1994 NEH Institute on "Homer and Oral Traditions" at the University of Arizona. My appreciation of the whole world of oral tradition, this study's largest conceptual frame, owes a great debt to both. I also learned from conversations with institute director Norman Austin and from fellow participants Lillian Corti, Mark Nowak, Emmanuel Obeichina, John Paine, John Thorndike, and Terri Whitney.

9. John Miles Foley, *Immanent Art* (Bloomington: Indiana University Press, 1991), 10. Foley's study, focusing as it does on Serbo-Croatian, Homeric, and Anglo-Saxon "heroic" poetry, has nevertheless been a crucial theoretical inspiration for my own work. His claims for "oral tradition," so bold they can only be made explicit in terms

of paradox, are to my mind and experience both valid and eloquently stated. They have guided my understanding of northwest Arkansas local and family music traditions as I encountered them in the Gilberts.

10. Ibid., 10, 7, 10.

11. Ibid., 60.

12. Roger Abrahams, "Bakhtin, the Critics, and Folklore," *Journal of American Folklore* 102 (1989): 204.

13. James Clifford, "On Ethnographic Allegory," in *Writing Culture: The Poetics and Politics of Ethnography,* ed. James Clifford and George Marcus (Berkeley: University of California Press, 1986), 104.

14. Ibid., 105. It might also be emphasized that this investigation of oral tradition centers on motives rather than mechanism, on situational and contextual matters as opposed to mnemonic and formal ones. For an impressive approach to the latter from the perspective of cognitive psychology, see David C. Rubin's *Memory in Oral Traditions* (New York: Oxford University Press, 1995), esp. chap. 11, "North Carolina Ballads," which is of particular interest to students of traditional music.

15. Samuel Beckett, *Molloy,* in *Three Novels* (New York: Grove Press, 1965), 169.

16. Martha Gellhorn, "The Carpathian Lancers," in *The Face of War* (New York: Atlantic Monthly Press, 1988), 125–26.

17. Renato Rosaldo, "From the Door of His Tent," in *Writing Culture,* ed. Clifford and Marcus, 97; Clifford, "On Ethnographic Allegory," 110, 113.

18. Jerry Hogan, letter to the author, September 15, 1994.

19. Greg Sarris, *Keeping Slug Woman Alive* (Berkeley: University of California Press, 1993), 84–85. Sarris employs and cites David Brumble, *American Indian Autobiography* (Berkeley: University of California Press, 1988), which specifically addresses American Indian autobiography, in his discussion.

20. Sarris, *Keeping Slug Woman Alive,* 33.

21. Billie [Alma] Allen, *A Way of Life* (a personal memoir, bound and printed by the author's daughters in 1978 as a fifty-first wedding anniversary present), 3. Subsequent references to this work are cited as *A Way of Life* followed by a page number.

22. Phydella Hogan, note to "Fair Nottingham Town" in original songbook manuscript.

23. Phydella Hogan, taped interview, Fayetteville, Arkansas, October 3, 1989.

24. Ibid.

25. Phydella Hogan, taped interview conducted by Elizabeth Foster, Fayetteville, Arkansas, October 15, 1991.

26. Ibid.

27. Phydella Hogan interview, October 3, 1989.

28. Martha Hogan Estes, taped interview conducted by Amy Kreitlein, Fayetteville, Arkansas, November 21, 1993.

29. Billie [Alma] Allen, "Music, Song, Music," unpublished typescript written as a supplement to *A Way of Life,* 1–3.

30. Allen, "Music, Song, Music," 3.

31. Phydella Hogan interview, October 3, 1989. I would not call the instrument in question a zither. Mandolin-guitar-harp is as good a name as any. Many such instruments were produced for mail-order sale in the first half of the twentieth century.

32. Ibid.

33. Clarence St. Clair "Buck" Gilbert, unpublished, untitled handwritten memoir of seventy-two numbered pages dated August 25, 1978, on the first page and July 14, 1980, on page fifty-two. The passage cited is from p. 25B (one of four pages numbered 25).

34. Allen, "Music, Song, Music," 4. Elaborate narratives centered on the acquisition of instruments, especially first instruments and instruments received from older musicians, are traditional features of autobiographical narratives of musicians. For several vivid examples from African American blues musicians, see Barry Lee Pearson, *Sounds So Good to Me: The Bluesman's Story* (Philadelphia: University of Pennsylvania Press, 1984). See esp. chap. 4, "I'm Gonna Get Me a Guitar If It's the Last Thing I Do," 46–59.

35. Allen, "Music, Song, Music," 4.

36. Jeanie Fultz Miller, taped interview, Mayfield, Arkansas, February 17, 1994. For more about *Ozark Jubilee* see Reta Spears-Stewart, *Remembering the Ozark Jubilee* (Springfield, Mo.: Stewart, Dilbeck & White Productions, 1993). The Promenaders are discussed on 52–54 and pictured on 50, 59.

37. Phydella Hogan interview, October 3, 1989.

38. Jeanie Fultz Miller interview, February 17, 1994.

39. Phydella Hogan interview, October 3, 1989.

40. Phydella Hogan, taped interview, Fayetteville, Arkansas, October 5, 1989.

41. Eduardo Galeano, *Century of the Wind* (New York: Pantheon, 1988), 129.

42. Mrs. Julianne Stewart, taped interview, Elkins, Arkansas, March 15, 1994.

43. Mrs. Mildred [Ragsdale] Bailey, taped interview, Farmington, Arkansas, January 27, 1994.

44. Mrs. Georgia Guilliams Lamb, handwritten notes, Fayetteville, Arkansas, February 14, 1994.

45. Helen Fultz and Phydella Hogan, taped interview, Mayfield, Arkansas, January 18, 1990.

46. Phydella Hogan, taped interview, Fayetteville, Arkansas, August 16, 1994.

47. Oliva [Davis] Vaughan, taped interview conducted by Elizabeth Foster, Fayetteville, Arkansas, October 3, 1992. Elizabeth Foster, my student at the time, conducted several wonderful interviews with Mrs. Vaughan, including one with Phydella Hogan present. Mrs. Lula Davis contributed eleven songs to Eleanor Henderson's "An Ozark Song Book: A Collection of Songs and Ballads from the Fayetteville Area," a 1950 University of Arkansas M.A. thesis. Henderson also recorded the singing of Mary Jo Davis and Oliva Davis Houser. Both Mr. and Mrs. Davis contributed to Irene Carlisle's 1952 University of Arkansas M.A. thesis, "Fifty Ballads and Songs from Northwest Arkansas," Mr. Davis contributing one song and Mrs. Davis three. The television program was called "The Search." It aired on November 14, 1954, and featured several northwest Arkansas singers as recorded by University of Arkansas professor Mary Celestia Parler.

48. Phydella Hogan, taped interview, Fayetteville, Arkansas, March 3, 1994. It should be noted that Oliva Vaughan's memories are quite different with regard to the two families learning songs from each other: "My mother and father would collect songs from the Gilberts. And the Gilberts liked to come over there and collect songs from us. So we just kind of exchanged songs" (Oliva Vaughan interview, October 3,

1992.) Even the generalization about the Davis family not singing in the community may be overstated, and in fact applicable only to Zion. They may, for example, have been much appreciated in Fayetteville.

49. Abrahams, *A Singer and Her Songs,* 150, 151.

50. Communities like Zion and Habberton were much too small, of course, to support professional musicians. Both Fayetteville and Springdale are large enough to boast local music scenes—clubs and dance halls where area musicians can be heard and paid—but the Gilberts were never a part of this milieu in either town. Phydella Hogan performed professionally in Lincoln, Nebraska, from about 1965 to 1971 with several bands headed by her son Bill, but the missed opportunity to sing on the radio in Fayetteville in the late 1920s was the sisters' closest brush with the local semiprofessional music industry. For a discussion of music as it correlates with town size and function, see Mark Slobin, "Music and the Structure of Town Life in Northern Afghanistan," *Ethnomusicology* 14 (1970): 450–57. See also George O. Carney, ed., *The Sounds of People and Places: Readings in the Geography of Music* (Washington, D.C.: University Press of America, 1978).

51. Phydella Hogan interview, October 15, 1991.

52. Abrahams, *A Singer and Her Songs,* 104–5.

53. Helen Fultz and Phydella Hogan interview, January 18, 1990.

54. Helen Fultz, note to "Empty Cot in the Bunkhouse" in original songbook manuscript.

55. Phydella Hogan, taped interview, Fayetteville, Arkansas, November 2, 1993.

56. Helen Fultz, written reminiscence, November 20, 1990, 2.

57. John Minton, "The Reverend Lamar Roberts and the Mediation of Oral Tradition," *Journal of American Folklore* 108 (1995): 5, 6. Such "mediation" of course occurred (and occurs) in other regions as well.

58. For a history of KFMQ and early radio in Fayetteville, see Ray Poindexter, *Arkansas Airwaves* (n.p., n.d.), 47–79. For a more detailed description of the old-time fiddlers' contests, see "Annual Fiddlers' Contest To Be Broadcast on Feb. 23," *Arkansas Alumnus,* February 1927, 5–6.

59. Phydella Hogan, telephone interview, Fayetteville, Arkansas, September 29, 1994.

60. Information about KWTO is from Spears-Stewart, *Remembering the Ozark Jubilee.* KVOO, the Grand Ole Opry, and the *Louisiana Hayride* are discussed in Bill C. Malone, *Country Music U.S.A.* (Austin: University of Texas Press, 1985). For general treatments of the early years of radio in the southwest, see Poindexter, *Arkansas Airwaves,* and William W. Savage Jr., *Singing Cowboys and All That Jazz: A Short History of Popular Music in Oklahoma* (Norman: University of Oklahoma Press, 1983).

61. Phydella Hogan, telephone interview, Fayetteville, Arkansas, September 27, 1994.

62. Phydella Hogan interview conducted by Elizabeth Foster, Fayetteville, Arkansas, May 15, 1992.

63. Abrahams, *A Singer and Her Songs,* 80. There are detailed studies of both cowboy and railroad songs. For the latter, see especially Norm Cohen, *Long Steel Rail: The Railroad in American Folksong* (Urbana: University of Illinois Press, 1981). For cowboy songs, see, among other works, Glenn Ohrlin, *The Hell-Bound Train: A Cowboy Songbook* (Urbana: University of Illinois Press, 1973). The dates Riddle gives for the

wide popularity of cowboy songs are strikingly early—William W. Savage Jr., in *Singing Cowboys*, identifies Otto Gray, whose Oklahoma Cowboys began performing on radio in 1924, as the "first singing cowboy" in American popular music (34).

64. Phydella Hogan and Alma Allen, note to "Way Over in the Promised Land" in original songbook manuscript.

65. Jean Ritchie, *Singing Family of the Cumberlands* (New York: Oxford University Press, 1955), 231.

66. Martha Hogan Estes interview, November 21, 1993.

67. Abrahams, *A Singer and Her Songs*, 112.

68. John Minton makes a similar observation concerning the songs selected for performance during a particular recording session by Texas singer Reverend Lamar Roberts: "While the songs Roberts summoned during our visit obviously do not represent his total lifetime repertoire, they are neither a random residue; rather they represent a coherent aesthetic informing both general currents in southern song and his own conversance with these traditions, modified by personal selection and rejection" (Minton, "Reverend Lamar Roberts," 22).

69. Phydella Hogan, written reminiscence, November 3, 1993.

70. "Buck" Gilbert, untitled memoir, 42.

71. Jeanie Fultz Miller interview, February 17, 1994.

72. Foley, *Immanent Art*, 51.

73. Debora K. Shuger, *Habits of Thought in the English Renaissance* (Berkeley: University of California Press, 1990), 6.

74. Ritchie, *Singing Family of the Cumberlands*, 210, 212.

75. Helen Fultz and Phydella Hogan interview, January 18, 1990. The epigraph above is from "All Along the Watchtower," on U2's album *Rattle and Hum* (Island, 1988).

76. The utilization of traditional means to conduct discussions of contemporary issues has been examined in several contexts. For a good survey of various forms of verbal contest in the Ozarks, see Robert K. Gilmore, *Ozark Baptizings, Hangings, and Other Diversions* (Norman: University of Oklahoma Press, 1984), especially chapter 2, "Literaries," which treats debates, kangaroo courts, spelling bees, and ciphering matches. Another superb study, this one centered on competitive storytelling among the Mande of Sierra Leone, is Donald Cosentino, *Defiant Maids and Stubborn Farmers* (Cambridge: Cambridge University Press, 1982). Here the most pertinent section is chapter 5, "Defiant Maids."

77. William B. McCarthy, *The Ballad Matrix* (Bloomington: Indiana University Press, 1990), 144, 33, 13.

78. Ibid., 132.

79. Abrahams, *A Singer and Her Songs*, 158.

80. Lucille Burdine and William B. McCarthy, "Sister Singers," *Western Folklore* 49 (1990): 416.

81. Ibid., 406, 407.

82. Phydella Hogan, taped interview, Fayetteville, Arkansas, May 3, 1994.

83. Ibid.

84. Ibid.

85. Helen Fultz, written reminiscence, November 20, 1990.

254 ℬ Notes to Pages 58–75

86. Phydella Hogan, taped interview, Fayetteville, Arkansas, May 19, 1994.

87. Vance Randolph, "Introduction," *Ozark Folksongs* (Columbia: University of Missouri Press, 1980), 1: 34–35.

88. Helen Fultz, taped interview, Mayfield, Arkansas, April 22, 1993.

89. Phydella Hogan, taped interview, Fayetteville, Arkansas, October 12, 1989.

90. Phydella Hogan, taped interview, Mayfield, Arkansas, August 15, 1990.

91. Phydella Hogan interview, November 2, 1993.

92. Ibid.

93. Martha Hogan Estes interview, November 21, 1993.

94. Phydella Hogan, taped interview, Fayetteville, Arkansas, August 3, 1990.

95. Phydella Hogan interview, November 2, 1993.

96. Phydella Hogan interview, August 3, 1990.

97. Phydella Hogan interview, November 2, 1993. My years in Arkansas have taught me that caution must be exercised in using attitudes toward Mr. Faubus as indicators of views on race. I'm no longer surprised to encounter Arkansans who decry Faubus's actions in the Little Rock school crisis, but insist at the same time that he was no ideological segregationist. See, for example, the view articulated by musician and actor Levon Helm: "In September 1957 Governor Orval Faubus tried to stop the integration of Central High in Little Rock. This caused a big scene, as President Dwight Eisenhower sent in federal troops and Faubus was branded an arch-segregationist. We knew it wasn't true. He'd been a progressive governor, but it would have destroyed his career in Arkansas politics if he'd been branded pro-integration. The way it happened, the Arkansas schools integrated pretty quietly after my senior year in high school, and Governor Faubus won four more terms, which was just fine with us. Orval dragged Arkansas into the twentieth century by the scruff of its rough red neck" (Levon Helm with Stephen Davis, *This Wheel's On Fire: Levon Helm and the Story of the Band* [New York: William Morrow, 1993], 45). My own view is still much closer to Phydella Hogan's, but I guess I agree that an otherwise progressive Machiavellian willing to pander to yahoos in the name of his own reelection is one notch better than a firebrand bigot righteously committed to American apartheid.

98. Helen Fultz, note to "Oh Susanna" in draft copy of edited songbook manuscript. The omission of the author's name from the *Heart Songs* anthology was of course not motivated by sensitivity to racial feelings. *Heart Songs* was originally issued in 1909; different standards prevailed.

99. Phydella Hogan interview, May 3, 1994.

100. Phydella Hogan interview, October 3, 1989. The epigraph above is from Michael W. Harris, *The Rise of Gospel Blues: The Music of Thomas Andrew Dorsey in the Urban Church* (New York: Oxford University Press, 1992), 97–98.

101. Phydella Hogan interview, October 3, 1989.

102. Ibid.

103. Phydella Hogan interview, May 19, 1994.

104. Helen Fultz, written reminiscence, November 20, 1990.

105. Helen Fultz, note to "I'm Gonna Walk and Talk With My Lord" in original songbook manuscript.

106. Phydella Hogan, telephone interview, Fayetteville, Arkansas, September 29, 1994.

107. Malone, *Country Music, U.S.A.*, 214.

108. The phrase "one of ours" comes from no particular interview. It is recurrent in our talks both for inclusion ("one of ours") and exclusion ("not one of ours"). Helen Fultz does sing "Each Ring of the Hammer," a number vivid in its depiction of hellish travail. It's not in the family collection, but like the very different "Nighttime in Nevada" it is an individual favorite.

109. Phydella Hogan interview, May 3, 1994.

110. Phydella Hogan interview, May 15, 1992.

111. Malone, *Country Music, U.S.A.*, 12, 13.

112. Helen Fultz, taped interview, Mayfield, Arkansas, January 18, 1990.

113. Randolph, *Ozark Folksongs*, 2: 207.

114. See Phydella Hogan, note to "The True Young Maid."

115. Theodore Garrison, "Forty-Five Folk Songs From Searcy County, Arkansas" (M.A. thesis, University of Arkansas, 1944), 87–88.

116. Rorie's performance is included in *Not Far from Here: Traditional Tales and Songs Recorded in the Arkansas Ozarks,* a two-record album on the Arkansas Traditions label, issued by the Ozark Folk Center in Mountain View, Arkansas, in 1981.

117. Burdine and McCarthy, "Sister Singers," 411. Burdine and McCarthy describe "China Man" as a "children's game song" and note that they "have not found any earlier recording"(411). I have a taped performance by Helen Fultz from 1974. Another version, sung by Sue Holley in Fayetteville, Arkansas, for Mary Celestia Parler in 1959 and titled "Ching Ling Chan," is in the folksong archive at the University of Arkansas (Reel 289, No. 9).

118. Helen Fultz and Phydella Hogan, taped interview, Mayfield, Arkansas, June 15, 1990.

119. Phydella Hogan, telephone interview, Fayetteville, Arkansas, July 16, 1995.

120. Helen Fultz interview, April 22, 1993.

121. Abrahams, *A Singer and Her Songs,* 137.

122. Phydella Hogan interview, November 2, 1993.

123. Helen Fultz, comment on audiotape, 1974.

124. Phydella Hogan interview, August 3, 1990. The epigraph above is from Don DeLillo, *Underworld* (New York: Scribners, 1997), 492.

125. Phydella Hogan interview, October 12, 1989.

126. Phydella Hogan interview, August 15, 1990.

127. Helen Fultz, taped interview, Mayfield, Arkansas, October 17, 1992.

128. Academic researchers specifically concerned with the influence of electronic media upon traditional cultures have been much more interested in singers like the Gilberts in recent years. See, for example, the article by John Minton cited in notes 57 and 68 above (and the references cited there).

129. Phydella Hogan, taped interview, Fayetteville, Arkansas, April 21, 1994. Helen Fultz's recollections are quite similar: "I can't remember that we ever wrote down a song for ourselves. We heard them twice and knew them. But when Phydella and Bill decided we should copy them while we could remember them, I was all for it. They knew so many that I couldn't remember, but I helped with a line or two once in a while" (Helen Fultz, written reminiscence, November 20, 1990).

130. Phydella Hogan, written reminiscence, September 22, 1993.

131. Ibid.

132. Martha Hogan Estes, letter to the author, July 2, 1991.

133. Bill Hogan, telephone interview, September 1, 1994.

134. Jerry Hogan, letter to the author, September 15, 1994.

135. This scene was not recorded. I later verified New Mexico as the place Bob Fultz worked, and Aunt Magna and Uncle George as the people he stayed with. I have a tape of Helen Fultz singing "Nighttime in Nevada." But this scene is built upon memory, though Phydella's comments are recorded and interpolated here from another time. I cannot vouch for the verbatim accuracy of Helen Fultz's reminder to her husband, or for my own final, enthusiastic query. But I'm as certain as I can be that I have her answer correctly. I knew when I heard it that it would be my study's final word.

136. Andrei Codrescu, *The Hole in the Flag* (New York: William Morrow, 1991), 75–76.

137. Phydella Hogan interview, November 2, 1993.

138. Paul G. Zolbrod, *Diné bahane': The Navajo Creation Story* (Albuquerque: University of New Mexico Press, 1984), 173.

139. Phydella Hogan interview, November 2, 1993.

140. Martha Hogan Estes, letter to the author, July 2, 1991.

References for
Song Annotations

Abrahams, Roger, ed. *A Singer and Her Songs: Almeda Riddle's Book of Ballads*. Baton Rouge: Louisiana State University Press, 1970.

Arnold, Byron. *Folksongs of Alabama*. University: University of Alabama Press, 1950.

Belden, Henry M. *Ballads and Songs Collected By the Missouri Folk-Lore Society*. Reprint, Columbia: University of Missouri Studies, 1955.

The Broadman Hymnal. Nashville: The Broadman Press, 1940.

Brown, Frank C. *The Frank C. Brown Collection of North Carolina Folklore*. Vol. 2: *Folk Ballads*. Durham: Duke University Press, 1952.

Brown, Frank C. *The Frank C. Brown Collection of North Carolina Folklore*. Vol. 3: *Folk Songs*. Durham: Duke University Press, 1952.

Bufwack, Mary A., and Robert K. Oermann. *Finding Her Voice: The Saga of Women in Country Music*. New York: Crown, 1993.

Burdine, Lucille, and William B. McCarthy. "Sister Singers," *Western Folklore* 49 (1990): 406–17.

Burton, Thomas G., and Ambrose N. Manning. *East Tennessee State University Collection of Folklore: Folksongs*. Johnson City: East Tennessee State University Press, 1967.

Carlin, Richard. *The Big Book of Country Music*. New York: Penguin, 1995.

Carlisle, Irene Jones. "Fifty Ballads and Songs from Northwest Arkansas." M.A. thesis, University of Arkansas, 1952.

Chapple, Joe Mitchell. *Heart Songs*. Reprint, Baltimore: Clearfield, 1997.

Child, Francis James. *The English and Scottish Popular Ballads*. Boston and New York: Houghton, Mifflin and Company, 1882–98.

Cohen, Norm. *Long Steel Rail: The Railroad in American Folksong*. Urbana: University of Illinois Press, 1981.

Devotional Hymns. Chicago: Hope Publishing Co., 1935.

Dugaw, Dianne. "Dreams of the Past: A Collection of Ozark Songs and Tunes." *Mid-America Folklore* 11 (1983): 1–79.

Eddy, Mary O. *Ballads and Songs from Ohio*. New York: J. Augustin, 1939.

Emerson, Ken. *Doo-Dah!: Stephen Foster and the Rise of American Popular Culture*. New York: Simon and Schuster, 1997.

Ewen, David. *American Popular Music*. New York: Random House, 1966.

Favorite Hymns of Praise. Chicago: Tabernacle Publishing Company, 1970.

Garrison, Theodore. "Forty-Five Folk Songs Collected from Searcy County, Arkansas." M.A. thesis, University of Arkansas, 1944.

Green, Archie. *Only a Miner.* Urbana: University of Illinois Press, 1972.

Hamm, Charles. *Yesterdays: Popular Song in America.* New York: W. W. Norton, 1983.

Henderson, Eleanor. "An Ozark Song Book: A Collection of Songs and Ballads from the Fayetteville Area." M.A. thesis, University of Arkansas, 1950.

High, Fred. *Old, Old Folk Songs.* No publisher or date of publication given.

Hunter Max. Taped folksong collection housed in the Springfield/Greene County Library, Springfield, Mo.

Joy To the World [hymnal]. Chicago: Hope Publishing Co., 1915.

Jones, Loyal. *Radio's "Kentucky Mountain Boy" Bradley Kincaid.* Berea: Appalachian Center/Berea College, 1980.

Laws, G. Malcolm. *Native American Balladry.* Philadelphia: American Folklore Society, 1964.

Lomax, John A. *Cowboy Songs and Other Frontier Ballads.* New York: Sturgis and Walton, 1910.

Luce, S. B. *Naval Songs: A Collection of Original, Selected, and Traditional Sea Songs.* Reprint, Portland, Maine: Longwood Press, 1976.

Malone, Bill C. *Country Music, U. S. A.* Austin: University of Texas Press, 1985.

Malone, Bill C., and Judith McCulloh. *The Stars of Country Music.* New York: Avon, 1976.

McNeil, W. K. *Not Far From Here: Traditional Tales and Songs Recorded in the Arkansas Ozarks* [record album]. Mountain View, Ark.: Arkansas Traditions, 1981.

———. *Southern Folk Ballads: Volume I.* Little Rock: August House, 1987.

———. *Southern Folk Ballads: Volume II.* Little Rock: August House, 1988.

———. *Southern Mountain Folksongs.* Little Rock: August House, 1993.

McNeil, W. K., and George West. *Songs My Family Loves* [record album]. Little Rock: Arkansas Traditions, 1984.

Melodies of Praise [hymnal]. Springfield, Mo.: Gospel Publishing House, 1957.

Moore, Ethel, and Chauncey O. Moore. *Ballads and Folk Songs of the Southwest.* Norman: University of Oklahoma Press, 1964.

Odum, Howard W., and Guy B. Johnson. *The Negro and His Songs.* Chapel Hill: University of North Carolina Press, 1925.

Ohrlin, Glenn. *The Hell-Bound Train: A Cowboy Songbook.* Urbana: University of Illinois Press, 1973.

Original Sacred Harp [hymnal]. Haleyville, Ala.: Sacred Harp Publishing Company, 1936.

Owens, William A. *Tell Me a Story, Sing Me a Song: A Texas Chronicle.* Austin: University of Texas Press, 1983.

———. *Texas Folk Songs.* Dallas: Southern Methodist University Press, 1950.

Popular Songs of the A. E. F. Paris: no publisher given, 1918.

Pound, Louise. *American Ballads and Songs.* New York: Scribner's, 1922.

Rainey, Leo. *Songs of the Ozark Folk*. Reprint, Branson, Mo.: Ozarks Mountaineer, 1976.

Randolph, Vance. *Ozark Folksongs*. Four volumes. Reprint, Columbia: University of Missouri Press, 1980.

———. *Roll Me in Your Arms: "Unprintable" Ozark Songs and Folklore*. Fayetteville: University of Arkansas Press, 1992.

Ritchie, Jean. *Singing Family of the Cumberlands*. Oxford: Oxford University Press, 1955.

Roberts, Leonard. *Sang Branch Settlers: Folksongs and Tales of a Kentucky Mountain Family*. Austin: University of Texas Press, 1974.

Shell, Lilith. "Folk Songs Furnished Most of Mountain Entertainment." *Arkansas Gazette*, March 11, 1928, sect. 2, 16.

Song Service and Revival [hymnal]. Dallas: Stamps-Baxter, 1933.

Spaeth, Sigmund. *A History of Popular Music in America*. New York: Random House, 1948.

Stilley, John. "The Stilley Collection of Ozark Folk Songs: Part One." *Mid-America Folklore* 20 (1992): 1–64.

———. "The Stilley Collection of Ozark Folk Songs: Part Two." *Mid-America Folklore* 20 (1992): 77–109.

Tinsley, Jim Bob. *He Was Singin' This Song*. Orlando: University Presses of Florida, 1981.

Wilgus, D. K. "'The White Pilgrim': Song, Legend, and Fact." *Southern Folklore Quarterly* 14 (1950): 177–84.

Work, John W. *American Negro Songs*. New York: Bonanza Books, 1940.

Index

"From the Door of His Tent," 250
"The Frozen Girl," 36, 124–26, 246
Fruit Jar Drinkers, 100
Fultz, Andrea, 14, 99, 103, 132, 230
Fultz, Bob, 14, 32, 43, 51, 68, 74, 84,
    92, 93, 96, 97, 98, 99, 100, 101,
    102, 103, 180
Fultz, Bobby, 14, 74, 93
Fultz, Bobby Lin, 14
Fultz, Gwendolyn, 14
Fultz, Helen (Gilbert), 2, 3, 5, 6, 9, 12,
    13, 14–15, 17, 23, 24, 25, 26,
    28, 29, 30, 31, 32, 37, 38, 42,
    43, 44, 45, 46, 47, 48, 49, 54,
    57, 58, 59, 63, 67, 68–69, 73,
    74, 75, 80, 81, 84, 85, 86, 88,
    89, 90, 91, 92, 93, 94, 95, 96,
    97, 98, 99, 100, 101, 102, 103,
    105, 109, 111, 112, 115, 116,
    118, 119, 121, 132, 133, 135,
    142, 144, 146, 150, 151, 152,
    153, 154, 162, 165, 167, 171,
    173, 174, 175, 176, 178, 180,
    181, 182, 185, 187, 189, 191,
    195, 197, 198, 200, 202, 215,
    220, 225, 230, 232, 235, 238,
    241, 243, 249, 251, 252, 253,
    254, 255, 256
Fultz, Larry [father], 14, 93, 99
Fultz, Larry [son], 14
Fultz, Lois, 74
Fultz, Mac, 14, 86, 93, 99, 103
Fultz, Pat (Clark), 95, 103
Fultz, Shannon, 14
Fultz, Vicki, 14

Galeano, Eduardo, 30, 251
"The Gambling Man," 148
Garriott, Blanche, 225
Garrison, Theodore, 81, 163, 220, 241,
    255, 258
Gates, Ellen H., 217
Gayer, Ruth, 95
Geddes, Will, 158
"Geisha Girl," 85, 225
Gellhorn, Martha, 7, 250
Geoffrey of Monmouth, 16

Gilbert, Addie, 14, 70, 71, 72
Gilbert, Betty, 14
Gilbert, Carl, 3, 14, 16, 21, 22, 37,
    44–49, 50, 52, 57, 67, 133, 147,
    148, 150, 211, 235
Gilbert, Clarence [Buck], 3, 17, 21, 22,
    23, 28, 42, 48, 57, 58, 67, 94,
    211, 251, 253
Gilbert, Cora, 46
Gilbert, Dennis, 14
Gilbert, Frances, 14
Gilbert, Jane, 14
Gilbert, Jesse [Jess], 14, 57
Gilbert, Jessie Jo, 14
Gilbert, Jessie Lee, 14, 16–17, 57
Gilbert, Joe, 9, 13, 14, 16, 17, 19, 20,
    23, 31, 37, 41, 42, 44, 48, 57,
    58, 61, 66, 67, 70, 71, 94, 96
Gilbert, Joyce, 14
Gilbert, Leslie, 15, 17, 32, 33, 67, 99
Gilbert, Lottie, 14
Gilbert, Melvin, 14
Gilbert, Ollie, 88
Gilbert, Ross, 14
Gilbert, Sophia (Scott), 13, 15, 16, 20,
    40, 42, 44, 46, 58, 67, 70, 71,
    89, 94
Gilbert, Wayne, 14, 46
Gilbert, William, 14, 16
Gilbert family: attitudes toward alco-
    hol, 60–65; attitudes toward
    marriage, 69–72; attitudes
    toward race, 65–69; family ver-
    sions of songs, 80–83; instru-
    ments, 21–23; musical talent,
    31–33, 92–93; reunions, 5–6,
    29, 65, 95; sacred songs, 72–80;
    songbook, 1, 2–4, 85, 90–92;
Gilmore, Robert K., 253
"The Girl I Left Behind Me," 246
"The Girl I Left in Sunny Tennessee,"
    153
"The Girl I Loved in Sunny
    Tennessee," 50, 152–53, 246
"The Girl With the Bandage On Her
    Eyes," 129
"Git Along Little Dogies," 246